Black Suburbanization
Access to Improved Quality of Life or Maintenance of the Status Quo?

Black Suburbanization

Access to Improved Quality of Life or Maintenance of the Status Quo?

Harold M. Rose

Ballinger Publishing Company ● **Cambridge, Massachusetts**
A Subsidiary of J.B. Lippincott Company

This book is printed on recycled paper.

International Standard Book Number: 0-88410-445-1

Library of Congress Catalog Card Number: 76-49004

Printed in the United States of America

Library of Congress Cataloging in Publication Data

Rose, Harold M
 Black suburbanization.

 Includes bibliographical references.
 1. Afro-Americans—Housing. 2. Suburbs—United States. 3. Residential mobility—United States.
 I. Title.
 E185.89.H6R58   301.36′2′0973   76-49004
 ISBN 0-88410-445-1

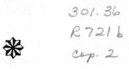

Contents

List of Tables

List of Figures

Preface

Ghettos, which serve as the modal place of residence of black Americans, have received extensive treatment by scholars representing a wide variety of disciplines during the previous ten years. But more recently a few scholars have turned their attention to the phenomenon of black suburbanization. This latter trend, however, has received more attention from representatives of the popular media than from the academic community. This book represents a single attempt to trace the development of emerging black residential zones beyond the margins of the central city. The perspective employed in this investigation is that of urban population geography.

Since the primary approach to the topic is geographic, the study format revolves around a set of places that have been nominally defined as suburban. Suburban in this instance refers simply to location within a set of metropolitan systems. Many persons will no doubt take exception to such a definition. Nevertheless, we have found this approach useful in attempting to evaluate the quality of life of that segment of the black population which lives outside central cities, but within large urban systems. We have attempted to evaluate just what residence outside the central city means in terms of improving the life chances of families who were most recently residents of central city ghettos.

The primary data upon which this study is based was secured in the summer of 1972, as an outgrowth of a field survey involving fifteen communities. The study was funded by the National Science Foundation and was titled the "Black Towns Project." We have combined the information collected during that period with secondary data in such a way as to permit us to transcend the narrow scope of the original project. As is true of most investigations of this type, we would like to have included a larger number of places in our field survey, but this was not possible. Thus one of the obvious weaknesses of this undertaking is our willingness to generalize from a small number of cases. Nevertheless, we have tried to integrate our findings in such a way as to permit us to evaluate that ephemeral concept, "quality of life." One of our basic concerns was related to the question of the extent to which suburbanization represented a distinct reversal of the ghettoization process or simply a continuation of that process. We have concluded that suburbanization, as we have observed it, is more akin to the latter than the former.

Many persons have been involved at various stages in the development of this project. For the inception of the idea for such a study I wish to thank Professor Donald R. Deskins of the University of Michigan. I also wish to extend my appreciation to those graduate students and faculty associates who gave up a summer to become involved in the data collecting process. I am especially indebted to the mayors of selected black communities who assisted us in many ways while we were present in their communities. Likewise, I wish to thank the staff at the Central Office of the Association of American Geographers for providing a variety of kinds of essential assistance. And to the following persons who were in some way involved in the production of the manuscript, I will be forever grateful: Ms. Linda Lutes, Mrs. Maribee Erikson, Ms. Licia Jennings, Ms. Rita Seitner, Mrs. Kerry Gardner and Mr. Don Temple. And finally I wish to extend thanks to a variety of persons at Washington University, St. Louis, Missouri, who made my 1973–74 Visiting Professorship there a delight, and which allowed me to complete the bulk of the manuscript during that interval.

Harold M. Rose
Milwaukee, 1976

✳ *Chapter One*

Black Movement to the Suburban Ring: The Beginning of a New Settlement Phase or Another Dead End?

During the period from 1910 to 1970, black Americans have evolved a pattern of national population distribution which cuts across all American regions and settlement types. Regional and settlement type emphasis has varied as the population has moved from one settlement stage to another. Much of the research on blacks prior to 1930 tended to emphasize aspects of black settlement in the rural South, while after World War Two emphasis had begun to shift to evolving patterns of black residential development in the urban North. To date much of the writing focusing on aspects of black life employs the modal environment of black residential occupance— the nation's principal central cities—irrespective of region of location. But there is mounting evidence that a secondary urban environment is emerging which is increasingly becoming the place of residence of an ever larger number of black residents. This emerging environment is found beyond the margins of the central city, but within what is sometimes identified as the metropolitan ring.

EMERGING BLACK POPULATION GROWTH ZONES

These new black population growth zones are often identified as zones of suburban residence, but one must be careful not to mislead the public, whose notion of what constitutes suburban residence is frequently related to what has been described as the myth of suburbia. Nevertheless, while such designations may be misleading, it is true that a new phase of black urban development is being ushered in by

1

the accelerated growth of the black population in metropolitan non-central city locations. To date, this more recent phase of black territorial development has received only scant attention in the social science literature. Farley was one of the first scholars to take note of this emerging trend.[1] However, the more recent works of Connolly and Pendelton[2] might represent increasing interest in this phenomenon. This book is designed to evaluate the impact of this emerging residential environment on selected aspects of economic and social development of a segment of the nation's black population.

No doubt, lack of interest in this topic revolves around its limited scale, its threatening possibilities of minimizing the buildup of black political power through central city population concentration and the lack of threat to the existence of evolving white sanctuaries (which are thought to be free of the problems of the central cities). But now this is beginning to change, even if the perceived magnitude of change, as it relates to the above issues, is likely to be magnified by those expressing one set of focal concerns or another.

In the minds of some, it is in the national best interest to open up areas beyond the margins of the central city to black residents, the logic of which was recently expounded by Downs.[3] Others continue to feel that they have the right to keep blacks out of their neighborhoods.[4] But regardless of the positions taken by various segments of the population, there occurred during the most recent decade the largest movement of black persons ever into non-central city metropolitan residential zones. To be sure, such locations have not previously been devoid of black populations, but they constitute a small percentage of the total population in the metropolitan ring (see Table 1-1).

Blacks have not previously been associated with the mass movement to suburbia that got underway following the end of World War Two. But by 1970, the nation's metropolitan rings were the place of residence of 3.5 million blacks, an increase of almost one million during the decade. An increase of this magnitude could not have occurred without the movement of large numbers of blacks from either elsewhere in the metropolitan area (central city) or nonmetropolitan locations. The evidence shows that the central city was the primary source region for these new ring residents. Nevertheless, the percentage of blacks residing in the metropolitan ring was approximately 5 percent in both 1960 and 1970.

So even though blacks have moved on a scale that is unprecedented, it has been offset by the continuing large scale movement of whites to what represents the principal zone of residence of all white Americans. Thus, as most of the nation's larger central cities have undergone a major change in their racial composition during the previous 20 years,

Table 1–1.   The Size of the Black Suburban Ring Population in the Major Ring Concentrations, 1960 and 1970

	Population	
Metropolitan Ring	*1960*	*1970*
Los Angeles	120,270	240,247
New York	139,694	217,188
Philadelphia	142,064	190,509
Washington	75,446	166,033
Newark	86,049	140,000
Chicago	77,517	128,299
St. Louis	80,496	124,625
Miami	72,086	113,510
San Francisco	68,012	109,319
Detroit	76,647	96,655
Cleveland	6,455	44,773

Source: General Demographic Trends for Metropolitan Areas, 1960 to 1970, PHC (2)—by Individual States.

the metropolitan ring is only now being threatened to become a participant in the process which is familiar to most of the larger central cities. This chapter explores the process of black population growth in noncentral locations and relates new growth zones to old in those rings in which growth is most actively occurring.

The Role of the Major SMSAs

As the population of the United States becomes more and more urban, newer Standard Metropolitan Statistical Areas, with their central cities of 50,000 or more persons, come into existence. In 1970 there existed 243 such units; an additional 31 SMSAs came into existence during the most recent decade. Since 1970, a number of additional SMSAs have come into existence, some of which represent a subdividing of existing SMSAs. Such is the case of the Suffolk-Nassau SMSA, which in 1972 was created by removing this zone from the New York SMSA. While new metropolitan areas continue to emerge, slightly more than half of the nation's population resided within the 65 largest SMSAs in 1970.[5]

The black population is even more urbanized than the total population in terms of character of residence and has a larger share of its population concentrated in fewer SMSAs. In 1970, almost 35 percent of the black population was concentrated in twelve of the nation's larger SMSAs. At the same time, a comparable percentage of the total population was concentrated in 20 SMSAs. Blacks have shown a preference for the older and larger SMSAs, which are now undergoing a reduction in their growth rates. It is in these older growth zones that most of the movement of blacks to the metropolitan ring has taken place. But likewise it was in these SMSAs that a core black ring population previously existed. That core population was generally located in a small black enclave that was politically independent, or in the black residential zone of industrial or dormitory suburbs, which have been described by some as "ghettolets." Thus it is from this locational base that what is currently described as black suburbanization is evolving.

The twelve largest SMSAs in terms of total population do not perfectly coincide with the twelve SMSAs serving as ranking places of residence of black Americans. The incongruence is associated with the differential roles of Houston and Newark as centers with large black concentrations. Nationally, both Boston and Pittsburgh outrank the former SMSAs, but are the sites of smaller black populations. Although black ring growth was most substantial in this set of SMSAs during the previous decade, there does exist a variety of territorial patterns that abetted or slowed this process. In those SMSAs where the central city black community had expanded to the city's edge, spillover into an adjacent political jurisdiction naturally followed. In other instances where there already existed a historic black community in the ring, vacant land adjacent to or within that community was sometimes developed to satisfy the housing demand of a segment of the black population. This latter pattern was much in evidence in Prince Georges County, Maryland during the past decade, as it was Prince Georges County which served as the major target of black movers from the District of Columbia.

Both regional variations and the nature of economic opportunity within individual rings make generalization difficult. The overbound southern city may hamper the process of expansion of black residential development beyond the margins of the central city simply as a function of scale. Although the rings of most southern SMSA's lost a greater number of black residents than they gained during the sixties, Miami was a major exception to this rule. In a number of southern SMSAs, blacks in the ring resided in a semirural environment and ring residence could hardly be associated with the myth of suburbia. In smaller southern SMSAs, higher status whites generally settled in the central city while lower status whites settled in the ring.[6] In some instances in smaller southern SMSAs, blacks also settle in the ring, as the ring communities tend to bear greater similarity to the nonmetropolitan environment from which some of them have moved. The latter point was previously cited by Kirchenbaum in his discussion of the settlement pattern of low status movers to small southern SMSAs.[7]

In a number of larger SMSAs in the North and West, the prevalence of industrial satellites within the SMSA has long led to the presence of a sizeable black population outside the central city, but in environments that were frequently thought to be incompatible with the popularly held notions of what constituted a suburban environment. Thus such northern metropolitan areas as Philadelphia, Pittsburgh, St. Louis, and the southern metropolitan areas of Birmingham, Alabama, have long had a sizeable black population in selected ring communities.

The following statement does much to throw light on the nature of the environment occupied by blacks in the ring of the Philadelphia metropolitan area:

> A roundup of suburban black population on the Pennsylvania side of the Delaware River shows the heaviest concentration in Delaware County which counts 39,000 Negroes among its residents. Of these 21,000 live in Chester City, an old industrial town which now has a black majority and resembles nothing so much as the poor black ghetto of North Philadelphia.[8]

The results of the 1970 census show that the black population in many communities like the one described above is simply growing as a result of natural increase, and a number of such communities suffered an absolute decline in the size of their black population.

The number of blacks found in the metropolitan rings of the nation's larger SMSAs prior to the decade of the sixties were found in employing suburbs and thus their presence was often tied to the availability of employment opportunity rather than environmental amenities. Given the frequent lack of such amenities in the communities in which the largest share of this population resided, they frequently were not thought of as suburban residents. Obviously it was this kind of thinking that led Robert Weaver to make the following statement: "In northern cities the establishment of all-Negro suburbs is usually impossible. This is due to the spatial distribution of nonwhites and the rejection of segregated patterns by nonwhites in the North."[9] Of course it is quite possible that the emphasis was on all-black suburbs, yet even at the time that item appeared, a number of such communities did exist—a fact that Weaver himself acknowledged. In describing black suburbanization in Chicago, he states, "Thus much of the suburban non-white population in the Chicago metropolitan area resided in the all-Negro town of Robbins, Illinois."[10]

In discussing this same phenomenon, Irene Taueber indicated that a sizeable number of blacks had been present in the rings of selected SMSAs at least as far back as 1930, but she refrained from describing this population as suburban. She indicated that by 1950, 25 percent of the black population in northern urbanized areas was located outside the central city. But she was careful to point out that "the growth of Negro populations outside the central cities of the SMSA's cannot be identified with a movement to the quiet lanes of suburbia."[11] However, more recently social scientists, as well as other social commentators, have come to define de facto the population residing within the metropolitan area, but outside the central city, as suburban. Thus the meaning of suburban residence for an increasing number of black Americans is not always clear in terms of its environmental implications.

Early Non-Central City Black Communities

Because the whole notion of what constitutes black suburbanization is so ephemeral, emphasis in this volume focuses on one set of communities which is predominantly black, many of which evolved as black settlements located in the metropolitan ring, and another set which was the target of black ring entry during the decade of the sixties. This grouping accounts for less than half of the black ring population, but it does enable one to ascertain the role of a traditional set of black ring communities vis-à-vis an emerging complex of new zones of black residential development. The boundary between these two universes is not always clear cut, as a number of communities could have been identified with either universe.

The first group of communities was described by this writer during the middle sixties as constituting a viable set of "all-Negro towns," as most were 95 percent or more black and contained a population of more than one thousand residents.[12] Only two of the communities in that study were found beyond the margins of the metropolitan area and they were the communities of Mound Bayou, Mississippi, and Grambling, Louisiana, both of which were located in a rural hinterland. Many of the communities that make up this group had previously been identified by Carter Woodson in his book the *Rural Negro*. These were communities in which Woodson contended that blacks had not given up hope in view of the obstacles which worked against group accomplishment. His chapter describing the character of these communities was entitled "Higher Strivings."[13] Thus some of the communities that were identified as "all-Negro towns" had more than a generation earlier been viewed as places in which blacks sought refuge from a hostile world, and at the same time were places of residence of an enterprising group. Although Woodson was careful to point out the differences among these communities, he tended to emphasize regional differences in terms of community accomplishment. An example of this emphasis can be gleaned from the following statement: "While Brooklyn, Illinois has a population as large as that of Boley, Oklahoma, the latter has accomplished so much more than that isolated town in Illinois."[14] The latter writer seemed convinced that the all-black towns which emerged in the South were of a higher order than those which emerged in the North and West.

It appears, however, that the all-black towns were more commonplace in the North. Of the ten metropolitan ring communities previously identified as "all-Negro towns," six were of northern origin and four were of southern origin. More recently, several additional communities were added to this list by relaxing the definitional constraint bearing on the black percentage. Added to this list of communities were East Chicago Heights, Illinois; Hollydale, Ohio; Roosevelt City, Alabama; Scotlandville, Louisiana; North Fontana, California; Wyandanch, New York; and East Palo Alto, California.[15] The added communities are somewhat diverse in terms of size, economic mix, and political status. The latter two communities could have been included among those communities which are identified here as suburbanizing, and were earlier identified as ghettoizing ring communities as distinguished from colonizing ring communities; the latter mode describes most of the all-black towns.[16]

The decision to include communities such as Wyandanch and East Palo Alto among the all-black towns, even though in 1970 they were only approximately three-fifths black, was based on anticipation of their future racial composition. These, like a number of suburban ring communities, are undergoing a racial transition of the sort which is typical of central city communities, and thus, depending upon the speed at which such change takes place, they will shortly be characterized by a racial composition very much akin to the other all-black towns.

Recent Evidence of Black Suburban Ring Development

Black ring populations have gone virtually unnoticed, as they have essentially occupied vest pocket ghettos, and their presence amidst an ever increasing white population could hardly constitute a threat. A major factor, which no doubt reduced interest in their presence in the suburban ring, was concern with the ever increasing number of blacks in the nation's major central cities and the frequent flight reaction of central city white populations to their increasing presence. Berry has described this phenomenon as follows:

> To illustrate, if we plot in a graph, for each of the central cities of the U.S. areas, the rate of population change on one axis and the number of percentage points by which the black population increased in the same

period on the other axis, a clear inverse relationship appears. The greater the increase in size and concentration of the ghetto, the more rapid the decrease of the central city's total population, the decrease running at about twice the rate of the black increase.[17]

But the phenomena that led to central city abandonment in a number of metropolitan areas are being transferred to the inner rings of those metropolitan areas whose central city environmental accommodations are found increasingly unsatisfactory by a growing segment of the black population. The fight for turf, then, continues in a new arena among another generation of urban residents. To date, this fight is concentrated in those SMSAs with the larger black populations, although some exceptions are evident.

Most black movement to the suburban ring is taking place in only eleven metropolitan areas, which include Los Angeles, New York, Washington, Chicago, Cleveland, Miami, St. Louis, San Francisco, Philadelphia, Detroit, and Newark. But it is evident that a secondary set of SMSAs is becoming involved in the process (see Table 1–2). In 1970, more than two-fifths of all-black ring residents were concentrated in the principal zone, a condition that exceeds by several percentage points the extent to which the central city population is also concentrated in these same places. A rational explanation of this phenomenon seems to revolve around the presence of some threshold population, the proximity of the central city black community to the city's edge, and the stage of development of the central city black community. The latter condition reflects the time a given household has spent in a metropolitan environment.

Yet the nature of this relationship is not fully understood. The

Table 1–2. Secondary Black Suburban Ring Destinations

Ring Identification	Total In-Migrant Population	Total Black In-Migrant Population
Cincinnati, Ohio	78,473	5,170
Dayton, Ohio	78,850	3,894
Atlanta, Ga.	249,816	3,887
Flint, Mich.	42,815	3,622
Jersey City, N.J.	− 6,491	3,300
San Diego, Calif.	124,236	3,113
Baton Rouge, La.	24,336	3,093
Pittsburgh, Pa.	− 61,704	2,786
Baltimore, Md.	170,382	2,719

Source: General Demographic Trends for Metropolitan Areas, 1960–1970, Final Report PHC2 Selected States, U.S. Bureau of the Census, Census of Population and Housing.

extent to which black housholds have found their way to the ring, in either absolute or proportional terms, is generally limited in those metropolitan areas which have been described elsewhere as third generation ghetto centers.[18] Milwaukee, which fits the definition of a third generation ghetto center, included approximately 106,000 blacks in its metropolitan area in 1970; fewer than 1,000 resided in the metropolitan ring. While this is an extreme example, most of the other third generation centers exhibit a similar pattern. Thus, while blacks have been present in selected ring communities for more than a generation, it is the large scale movement that got underway during the mid sixties that is here being defined as black suburbanization.

The principal targets of that movement have often been singled out and data describing them in both economic and social terms has been analyzed in order to acquire insight into the nature of the environment to which this population has found access. The data analyzed generally focused on the principal targets in each metropolitan area in the universe. Most often only three or four communities served as the so-called ports of entry for the largest share of black ring movers. Almost 80 communities in these eleven metropolitan areas captured the lion's share of black ring movement, though fewer than 20 were the primary target of movers (see Figure 1–1). These were communities in which an estimate of net black movers equalled or exceeded 5,000 persons during the decade.[19] Thus the major targets were communities which might be described as medium sized suburban communities in which the modal number was characterized by populations in excess of 25,000.

Most of these communities were already the place of residence of more than a token black population in 1960. The exceptions—those without a core black population in the previous time period—were University City, Missouri; East Cleveland, Ohio; and the Los Angeles ring communities of Inglewood and Carson. Those communities without a significant number of blacks in 1960 found themselves in the path of central city black expansion during the decade. Of the larger SMSAs in which black ring movement was underway, Detroit was one of the least active participants in this process. As a matter of fact, ring to city movement exceeded city to ring movement during the latter half of the decade.

Once again, taking those ring communities with populations in excess of 25,000 as potential targets for black entry, Hermalin and Farley found that of 26 such places in the Detroit ring, 95 percent of the black households were in the four communities of Hamtramck, Highland Park, Inkster, and Pontiac.[20] The location of Hamtramck and Highland Park as political enclaves within the city of Detroit has led

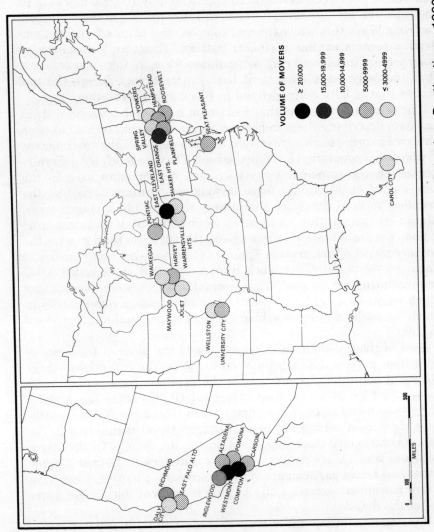

Figure 1–1.   Estimates of Volume of Black Movers to Major Suburban Destinations, 1960–1970

us to exclude them in assessing city to ring movement. When these units are eliminated, it is obvious that the only principal target of entry in the Detroit ring was Pontiac. Hermalin and Farley also found that the actual pattern of distribution of black households was much lower than that expected on the basis of housing value and family income.[21] The absence of blacks from the Detroit suburban ring, in the form of city to ring movers, may be directly related to the availability of attractive housing within the central city made available by white departure from the city. During the sixties, almost ten blacks moved into the central city of Detroit for every one black who settled in the ring. Thus Detroit stands in sharp contrast to St. Louis and Cleveland, where the black movement to the ring exceeded movement to the central city.

A Comparison of Older Black Ring Communities with Newer Ones

In some instances the emerging patterns seem to indicate the rise of the large scale black ring settlement that stands in contrast to the small scale black ring community that evolved during an earlier era. In both instances, though, black movers might have been seeking an environment that stood in contrast to that which was available within the central city during their respective eras of origin. One wishes to point out that the all-black town that evolved during an earlier era might have come into existence for reasons similar to those of the larger scale black ring communities that are evolving during the present era, although support evidence is difficult to uncover.

But the present process seems to be producing in a large number of ring locations the black counterparts to the rising white working class suburbs of Warren, Michigan, Parma, Ohio, and other similar communities, although on a scale that is somewhat more restricted. Thus the Plainfields, the East Clevelands, the Richmonds, and the Comptons may well constitute the black ethnic working class suburbs of the seventies. But given the fact of race and all its many implications, the question becomes whether such communities can survive without deteriorating into environments similar to those the initial mover wished to escape. Sternlieb casts doubt on the future of such communities in his comments, which specifically refer to Plainfield, New Jersey, a suburban ring community located within the Newark metropolitan area. He states:

Such an area is Plainfield, New Jersey, a community which serves as a safety valve for core ghetto areas. Areas such as Plainfield provide a target and a prize in return for following the conventional path of work and saving. Increasingly, minority group members in the North are pursuing the prize. One of the basic questions of our time, however, is whether the goal will be worth the effort; whether Plainfield and other areas similar to it in function can continue to provide the infrastructure of schools, police and all of the other elements which the emigré anticipates at the conclusion of his often difficult escape from the larger city's core.[22]

If the doubts of the latter writer are valid, then the question of the viability of the black ethnic working class suburbs becomes a serious issue, since working class whites have access to environments other than those available in inner city communities. If such communities are not potentially viable, it would seem that the modal environment available to the vast majority of black Americans will be that of the stress-filled type that virtually guarantees a dismal future for most of its residents. This book attempts to validate this notion through an analysis of objective conditions prevailing within the diverse ring environments to which blacks have acquired access.

Most of the communities described as all-black towns are forerunners of the newly emerging black ring developments. While such communities are generally located in those metropolitan areas in which large scale ring movement is currently underway, there are some incongruences in this pattern. The all-black towns are found more often in what has been previously described as first generation ghetto centers. These constitute those metropolitan areas whose black population exceeded 25,000 prior to 1920. Only New York among the major nonsouthern metropolitan center is without such a configuration. On the other hand, second generation ghetto centers such as Newark, Detroit, Cleveland, Los Angeles, and San Francisco are without an original all-black town.[23]

In part this absence no doubt stems both from the nature of the rural-urban fringe during the period of initial black settlement within these urban centers, as well as the orientation of the settlers themselves. Among the pre-World War One settlers, both circumstances and general orientation led a small group of blacks to choose the rural-urban fringe because it permitted one to live in a manner similar to that which prevailed in the rural South. Even today the physical character of a number of these communities still shows strong signs of rural development. Unpaved streets, derelict shacks, weed engulfed plots, and the small vegetable garden oftentimes highlight the anachronism of the presence of these communities in zones in which they are frequently surrounded by new suburban tract developments, or at least communities which exude an urban character. But these communities have persisted, and although some are now undergoing a face lift, there still is much evidence in the physical character of place to reveal the status of its occupants, both now and during an earlier era.

Such communities in southern metropolitan areas are of more recent vintage, and this too is often reflected in the communities' physical character, although diversity abounds in most such places. A possible exception is Richmond Heights, Florida, which is a post-World War Two tract development. Another obvious difference between the southern and nonsouthern towns—provided Washington is excluded from the South—is the political independence of the older northern communities. Thus the all-black town which emerged in the late nineteenth or early twentieth century somewhere along the way acquired a political identity.

Blacks who settled in the ring of those communities which were the sites of heavy industry or upper income white collar workers simply settled in the black quarters of the town, and thus did not develop a separate political entity. Connolly recently pointed out that between 1910 and 1930, New Rochelle, New York, and Pasadena, California, both found in the respective rings of their metropolitan areas, were the third ranking black communities in the states of New York and California.[24] Competition for land in the rural-urban fringe and the growing disaffection with rural life possibly reduced the probability of the evolution of such communities into which blacks moved during a later period. The more recent growth of black settlements in the rings of both first and second generation centers is no doubt induced by an alternate set of forces.

The Spatial Characteristics of the Newer Ring Developments

The volume of black movement to the metropolitan ring during the most recent decade has transformed the character of a number of communities in terms of their racial makeup. It has likewise led to variable patterns of settlement within the zone of occupance. In some instances, blacks tend to be concentrated in a set of spatially contiguous areas, while in others the population is dispersed over a broader spectrum of places. Himes recently illustrated that most black movement to the ring got underway after 1965.[25] This timing also seems to hold for that set of ring communities from which the data in this study were drawn. This would tend to imply that blacks have been present in some individual communities for a relatively short period of time.

The Place of Origin of Black Ring Residents

The largest volume of movement during the five-year period 1965 to 1970 occurred in Los Angeles, San Francisco-Oakland, and Washington, D.C. The central cities of the SMSA were the major contributors to ring growth in each of the eleven SMSAs which constituted the suburban growth centers, with one exception. The exception was Philadelphia, where ring movers were largely drawn from other SMSAs. Ring growth in Cleveland, on the other hand, was the most totally dependent on central movers: here, more than 80 percent of all movers originated in the central city. It appears that central city origins were highest among the cities in which the target community was contiguous to the central city. This simply supports the argument that most housing within the wake of ghetto expansion will eventually be encompassed within its territorial web, given adequate demand.

In those metropolitan areas where suburban ring movement is directed to outlying ring communities, the strength of central city demand is weakened. In both New York and Chicago, moves from nonmetropolitan areas constitute approximately one-fifth of all ring movers. Nowhere else among the target SMSAs did nonmetropolitan movers constitute such a large percentage of black ring movers. This could mean that a growing number of blacks from nonmetropolitan areas are bypassing the central city for selected ring communities. Indeed, five ring communities within the Los Angeles metropolitan area were the targets of more than half of all ring movers during the latter half of the decade.

The location of these communities within the metropolitan area seemed to strongly influence the origin of movers. For instance, Inglewood, which is contiguous to the central city, received almost two-thirds of its movers from the central city, whereas Pomona, which is situated toward the eastern end of the county, derived only 35 percent of its movers from the central city. Altadena, on the other hand, which is contiguous to the older ring community of Pasadena, derived almost three-quarters of its movers from elsewhere in the SMSA. In none of these communities did movers from outside the SMSA constitute as much as a fifth of all movers.

The New York metropolitan ring, which ranks second to Los Angeles in number of black ring residents, stands in sharp contrast to it in the evolving process of the spread of the black ring population. Almost two-thirds of the ring settlers previously lived elsewhere in the ring. The isolated black enclaves that formed in the New York ring during an earlier era now serve as the source regions for the majority of the new target communities that were previously without a sizeable black population. One does find, however, a larger percentage of ring residents originating in the central city as proximity to the central city is increased. Thus centers such as Hemstead and Roosevelt on western

Long Island show more than 25 percent of their black population originating in the central city.

The differenital effect of spillover movement versus the evolution of black colonies which largely draws movers from other ring communities leads to a greater concentration of the black ring population in those SMSAs where spillover development represents the modal form. In Cleveland and Los Angeles, where spillover development is the ranking development, the black ring population is primarily concentrated in a few target communities (approximately 80 percent), while New York and Chicago with its nonspillover development shows black ring populations dispersed over a broader area than that of the primary entry zones.

It appears that the ghettoizing or spillover ring developments evolve out of increased housing demand associated with a single territorial entity, and this often permits the mover to exercise an option favoring one environmental milieu over another within the context of the expanding ghetto community. Among the colonizing black communities it appears that a different set of forces may be at work in terms of the influences responsible for the evolution of such communities. One would conjecture that job opportunities are probably more important than the housing environment in directing people toward these environments. This would be especially true of the large employing suburbs as opposed to the dormitory suburbs of the type frequently located adjacent to the central city. If this is the case, one would expect the higher status movers to settle in the spillover communities, although the distinction between ghettoizing communities and colonizing communities is not always clear cut. In some instances, what started out as colonizing communities became in effect core locations, which then serve as the basis for expansion into contiguous political entities or unincorporated places. Thus location and period of evolution tend to play a significant role in the character of communities in which black outlying settlement occurs.

The All-Black Town as a Suburban Port of Entry

The large scale movement to the suburban ring is most often confined to those communities which were ripe for racial transition. In an earlier review of this phenomenon, Farley describes these communities as the population replacement type.[26] Only a few of the all-black towns were major targets of entry during the decade. This is in part related to the small size of such communities, and in some instances the quality and nature of the available housing stock. In those instances where land was available and developers seized the opportunity to construct attractive housing on these sites, the black population in such communities grew rapidly. Thus individual black towns do possess the potential for providing a small segment of the black population access to a suburban type of environment.

But the size and age of such communities have built-in drawbacks to their serving as major ports of entry to the suburban ring. In those instances where a suburbanlike environment has been superimposed upon these outlying communities, friction between the older residents and the newcomers who do not view themselves as part of the community begins to show itself.[27] Nevertheless, places such as Glenarden, Maryland; Richmond Heights, Florida; and to a lesser extent Lawnside, New Jersey, were black suburban growth communities during the sixties as a result of the construction of attractive single family homes within their zone of identity.

But movements in excess of 4,000 were almost always destined for the larger outlying communities where the presence of blacks was nominal before 1950, and in a few as recently as 1960. Yet even here blacks were generally concentrated in neighborhoods that were predominantly black. Thus it appears that access to residence in the metropolitan ring is essentially confined to those communities that are adjacent to the central city black community or outlying satellite communities, which themselves serve as a core around which employment opportunity is emerging.

Characteristics of the Black Ring Population

A focal concern and question is, who are the black ring-bound movers? This is not an easy question to answer. It is true that the ring population is of higher economic status than that population which remains in the central city; nevertheless the population *is* diverse. This, however, makes them no different from previous nonblack ring movers, who were equally diverse. In viewing the possibility of suburban residence on the part of the black central city resident, much attention has been focused on the plight of the low to moderate income populations.

Anthony Downs, in his *Opening Up the Suburbs*, shows great concern for providing an opportunity for lower income blacks amidst more affluent middle income white populations in order that the deserving poor might be exposed to the values of the white middle class model.[28] Likewise, Weaver notes that even in the traditional suburban developments care will be taken in seeing that only the respectable poor are granted access.[29] Thus the issue of individual orientation as well as socioeconomic status appears to be one that will influence the identity of the mover population. It is not possible from the data at hand to touch directly upon the behavioral modalities of the mover population, but it is possible to categorize that population in terms of social class identity. In most instances mover families earn incomes that would define them as working and lower middle class.

In most of the SMSAs where movement from the central city to the ring was underway during the period 1965–70, almost one-third of the black families involved in the move earned between $10,000–14,999—an earning level that would have placed most in the working to lower middle class stratum. Often another one-fifth of the families had earnings in excess of $15,000 a year, and still another two-fifths of the families earned less than $10,000 per year. Thus it is apparent that all segments of the black population are finding their way to the ring, although the percentage earning less than $3,000 is small. This would tend to imply that only the poorest of the black poor have failed to find a niche in the suburban ring.

The Racial Composition of the Target Neighborhoods

The most affluent black city-to-ring movers were found in Cleveland, New York, and Washington, D.C., while the least affluent movers were found in Detroit and Los Angeles. It can be hypothesized that the nature of available residential opportunities would constrain the income mix of the mover population. But regardless of income category, at least in terms of these broad categories, most black families resided in census tracts in which there were more than 400 blacks. The implication is that blacks principally reside in neighborhoods with other blacks in most suburban ring communities.

The pattern of ring settlement in Cleveland, Washington, Los Angeles, St. Louis, and Miami indicates there are some variations from one SMSA to another. In 1970 Miami and St. Louis had 96 and 90 percent of their black populations, respectively, in tracts with more than 400 blacks, whereas Washington had only 74 percent and Cleveland 86 percent. Among occupational groups, only black professionals tend to be somewhat less territorially segmented than other black groups, but the largest segment of even this population is also territorially segmented. While this represents a rather crude analysis of social class and territorial segmentation, it is only in partial accordance with the following assessment by Robert Weaver: "For middle-class blacks greater dispersion seems probable. In the first place, in moving to the suburbs they are seldom interested in transferring from one racial ghetto to another, and few cities have enough black upper income families to support a separate suburb."[30] No doubt this is true of the more affluent upper income black families, whose income exceeds $25,000 per year, but they constitute a very small percentage of blacks involved in the process of taking up suburban residence.

Only in New York, Chicago, and Washington, D.C. did the $25,000 and over group constitute more than 3 percent of the black movers from the central city to the ring in the five years preceeding 1970. In the Washington ring, where blacks are moving into communities located in both Maryland and Virginia counties, there appears to exist a differential attraction of these locations for those families earning more than $25,000 a year. While most blacks leaving the District of Columbia were destined for Prince Georges County, Maryland, those families earning more than $25,000 a year were more often found in Montgomery County, Maryland. The largest percentage of families in this category, 5.9 percent, resided in Montgomery County; Fairfax City, Virginia, located outside this county, included 8.8 percent of the more affluent group. The vast majority of blacks who currently reside in the suburban ring reside in close proximity to other blacks. It seems that only those blacks who might be identified as upper middle class are less often found in neighborhoods that are predominantly black or in the process of racial transition. This would tend to indicate that for some time to come, blacks who journey to the suburban ring will tend to concentrate in ethnic communities, as is true of other groups possessing similar social class identities.

While most blacks destined for the suburbs tend to choose environments which are, or often become, predominantly black, there is quite a range of variation in the extent to which blacks were found in such environments in 1970. In five of the major suburban rings into which blacks moved during 1965–70, the percentage of the black population found in census tracts with fewer than 400 blacks ranged from approximately 10 percent in St. Louis and Newark, to a high of almost 40 percent in Los Angeles. Twenty-five percent of the Washington black ring population was found in the low percentage black environments, while in Cleveland the level reached only 14 percent.

The patterns described here may reflect the preferences of a segment of the suburbanizing population or a synoptic view of a dynamic process that will subsequently mirror the modal neighborhood makeup that prevails in the central cities. But for the moment, Los Angeles' ring pattern differs from its core pattern, while in St. Louis the ring and core pattern bear a striking resemblance. These patterns may reflect differences in the composition of the mover population, and/or the differential willingness of white and black residents to share a common residential environment. After a closer look at several of these communities, we will attempt to reevaluate the situation.

Differential Growth Rates for Black
Ring Development

The growth of the black population in selected ring communities is essentially related to the movement of blacks from the central city during the previous decade. Among the five cities cited in the previous paragraph, 57 to 80 percent of the new residents lived in the central city of their respective SMSAs five years earlier. In Cleveland, Washington, and Los Angeles, the overwhelming majority were previous central city residents. In the Cleveland case, almost half the 1970 ring population lived outside of the ring five years earlier.

Thus, suburban growth of the black population has been very rapid in some instances and slow in others. The most rapid growth occurred in the Cleveland ring, followed by Washington and Los Angeles. Slow growth typified the rate of change in Detroit, while only moderate growth occurred in the St. Louis ring. The most obvious commonality among the rapid growth rings was the expansion and juxtaposition of the central city black community against an edge of the City.

In Detroit, where the black community is just now approaching the edge of the city, the rate of suburbanization has been slow. In Chicago, whose black territorial configuration is more nearly akin to that of Detroit rather than Los Angeles, a somewhat similar growth pattern prevailed. It is unclear at this point where the Chicago and Detroit spatial pattern will continue to show similarities or soon show signs of divergence. Thus, in some metropolitan areas blacks are penetrating the inner suburbs as white demand is channeled to the outer suburbs. Solomon Sutker has described the communities located within these zones as the zones of emergence of younger and better educated blacks.[31] But even the extent to which blacks participate in this market is seemingly a function of the stage of development of the central city black community.

Considering that Chicago has the second largest black population in the nation, yet ranks sixth in number of black ring residents, the residential configuration argument gains added weight. In 1970 there were only approximately 4,000 fewer black residents in the St. Louis ring than in the Chicago ring. Brian Berry, addressing himself to the Chicago pattern, asserts that almost all the new housing developed in suburban Chicago during the previous decade was developed for a white clientele. He further states, "In contrast to the net increase of 287,000 white families in suburban Chicago, only 13,261 new black families were able to obtain residence in suburbia, and many of these residences were in or contiguous to suburban 'mini-ghettos.'"[32] Thus the fight for housing in the inner suburbs awaits the development of a spillover effect, which leads to the creation of an active black housing market contiguous to zones already perceived as zones of established black residence.

Detroit and Los Angeles: The Polar Cases in the Pattern of Suburban Development?

Detroit and Los Angeles represent the polar extremes in the emerging patterns of residential selection. While both metropolitan areas possess large black populations, a much larger share of the Detroit population is confined to the core city. Likewise, both Detroit and Los Angeles were the leading targets of black migration during the latter sixties, but the Detroit migrants settled more often in the core city than did the migrants to Los Angeles. The large scale movement of blacks to the suburbs stands in contrast to the limited movement beyond the core city of Detroit residents.

The lack of movement into the inner suburbs of Detroit was recently questioned by Farley and Hermalin. The latter writers contend that income was not the barrier that stopped the flow of blacks to the suburbs. They show that a smaller percentage of black families earning $15,000 to $24,999 were found in the Detroit ring than were white families earning $5,000 to $6,999.[33] On the basis of the income characteristics of Detroit black families and prevailing housing values in the 26 Detroit ring communities, Hermalin and Farley projected the number of black families who would be expected to reside in each individual community in 1970. In most instances, there is little congruence between the expected and actual number of black households. While it is obvious that income alone does not serve totally to curtail black movement, it is also true that current income may not be a good proxy for ability to purchase housing. Phoebe Cottingham, in an attempt to compare black and white suburban selection rates in Philadelphia by income class, likewise discovered that blacks possessing the same income status as whites less often chose suburban residence. But she noted that blacks in the same current income class as whites have been found to have smaller wealth accumulations.[34] Thus, this phenomenon should not be overlooked in an analysis of the problem.

Among the 26 Detroit communities identified by Hermalin and Farley, it was expected that ten would possess black occupancy levels of between approximately 9 and 13 percent. This range of occupancy is considered by some to represent substantially integrated communities. But in only one instance did a single community among the ten exceed 2 percent black occupancy; in most other instances the occupancy level was less than 1 percent.

It has been well publicized that Detroit suffered a major loss in its white population during the sixites, but it is also obvious that many of these white residents settled in the inner suburbs. During the 1965–70 period the ten communities which Hermalin and Farley projected would become substantially integrated were the target of large numbers of white movers from the central city (see Figure 1–2). To be sure in most communities, white in-movers from elsewhere in the metropolitan area predominated, but more than 25 percent of all movers in these ten ring communities resided in Detroit in 1965. The substantial white demand for housing in these communities seems to have served as an effective block to the settlement of blacks, while at the same time creating vacancies in various Detroit submarkets that were not previously perceived by blacks as available to them.

Five of these communities (Madison Heights, Dearborn, East Detroit, Southgate, and Warren) were among the nine Detroit suburban communities in which interviews were conducted concerning the causes of the Detroit riot. But what is instructive here are the responses describing the community climate, and support and opposition to suggestions for easing race tensions.[35] In each of these communities, the largest percentage of respondents were opposed to the suggested list of recommendations for reducing race tensions.[36] Warren and Southgate produced the highest negative responses, and Madison Heights the lowest negative responses. The fears and perceptions expressed by the sample make it unlikely that these communities will actively foster black entry.

During the previous decade, the largest number of blacks to ever settle beyond the margins of a central city within a ten-year period took place in the ring of the Los Angeles metropolitan area. However, it should be pointed out that most of this movement was concentrated in those communities contiguous to the central city (see Figure 1–3). Our estimates indicate as many as 20,000 blacks settled in at least two of these communities. Pomona was the only Los Angeles ring community which served as a major receiver of black movers that was not located within close proximity to the City. None of the major entry communities was substantially integrated in 1960, although Compton, with a 40 percent black composition, was already well along the road to becoming a predominantly black community. By 1970, each of the major receiving communities had undergone a significant alteration in its racial composition. Blacks now constituted 14 to 80 percent of all residents in the principal target communities.[37]

While the emerging pattern describing black suburbanization in Detroit and Los Angeles stands in sharp contrast, are these patterns

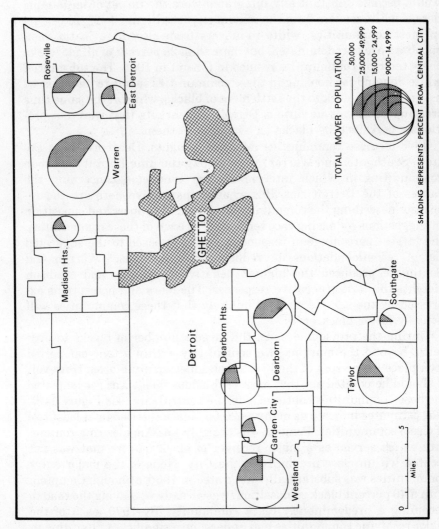

Figure 1–2. White Movement to Selected Detroit Suburbs, 1965–1970

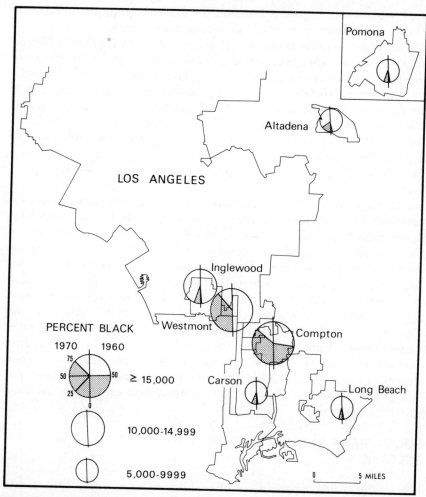

Figure 1–3. Estimates of Volume of Black Movement to Major Los Angeles Suburban Destinations, 1960–1970

the result of differences in black motivation? in white attitudes and responses? Or can they simply be attributed to the spatial arrangements existing at the beginning of the time period and the more or less stable working of the housing market resulting from the allocation of housing to blacks in a comparable manner in both places? No definitive answer is possible in this instance. But Mahlon Straszheim's recent assessment of black housing market behavior in San Francisco indicates that the existing racial residential pattern can be attributed to black response to higher prices and the existence of entry barriers to white submarkets in the form of supply rationing.[38]

One might assume that the entry barriers were higher in Detroit than in Los Angeles because of greater white demand in the communities which were expected to have a larger number of black households than was, in fact, the case. On the other hand, black demand in the Los Angeles case led to the development of housing submarkets that catered to the housing needs of a growing black population. Pettigrew and Vanneman recently demonstrated that whites in Los Angeles held attitudes that might be construed as less racist than those describing the sample representing Newark, Cleveland, and Gary.[39]

But the question of whether the lesser intensity in racist attitudes is sufficient to make a real difference in housing patterns is unclear. Fewer than two-fifths of those in the Los Angeles sample that the previous authors describe as competitive racist (the skilled blue collar worker class) were opposed to the presence of black next door neighbors, when they were perceived as possessing the same objective characteristics as the white residents. In Cleveland, the rate of negative responses to this question was 66 percent.[40] If Pettigrew and Vanneman are correct in their assessment of the distinctions between contact and competitive racism, one should expect blacks with similar characteristics to have little difficulty in acquiring entry into upper level blue collar communities. The attitudes expressed by members of that group in several Detroit ring communities cast doubt on that possibility, however.

SOCIAL RANK AND COMMUNITY SELECTION

Black ring residents are more often blue collar workers than white collar workers. Only Washington, D.C. has a greater percentage of white collar workers. But it should be remembered that in 1960 black ring residents were less well off in terms of current income than were central city blacks. In those metropolitan areas in which large scale black movement to the ring occurred during the sixties, significant changes occurred in the status of the population. But in Detroit, Miami, and St. Louis there is little difference between the incidence of black poverty between the central city and the ring. On the other hand, ring poverty among blacks in Cleveland and Los Angeles is notably below the levels prevailing in their respective central cities.

The economic characteristics of most ring movers clearly lead them to the inner suburbs. Nevertheless, there is obvious sorting out in terms of community character and social status. Four Los Angeles communities can be utilized to highlight this point. Carson and Inglewood both are predominately middle income communities. Since neither had significant numbers of black residents in 1960, it is appropriate to assume that they were largely chosen as residential destinations of lower middle and upper middle class black residents. More than 70 percent of the former community's residents were in this category and 63 percent of the latter. Altadena, with a different locational pattern, had slightly fewer than 50 percent of its residents in this status and a larger low income population than a working class one. And finally, Pomona, a noncontiguous community, was the destination of low income movers, although the combined working and middle income population outnumbered those with lower incomes by a small margin.

Given the social class makeup of black suburban movers, what is the likelihood that they will seek one kind of residential environment over another? Is the lower and working class black population simply seeking an environment that they perceive will provide them an escape from the problems and debilities they experience in the central cities? Is it likely that lower and upper middle income blacks are essentially seeking to upgrade their residential environment in terms of amenities? If the environmental goals of these mover populations differ significantly, is it likely that there will exist suburban environments that can satisfy class based goals if such exist? These are some of the questions for which we will attempt to provide answers.

It is already clear, at this point, that there is a sorting out of persons on the basis of social status in terms of choice of community of residence. But if the choices are expressed within the context of a race-class dichotomy, then the emerging residential pattern is also likely to be expressed spatially in terms of race-class segmentation. The question of who then is juxtaposed against whom in a spatial context is certain to influence neighborhood stability. If the Los Angeles and Detroit models can be employed as prototypes, then the emerging patterns of black suburbanization simply represent an extension of the ghetto process of which most students of urban residential patterns are familiar.

In this chapter, attention has been focused on the residential moving behavior of the black population which has led to the development of zones of black residence in what is generally regarded as the suburban ring. It is evident that small numbers of blacks have been present in the rings of the larger metropolitan areas for one or two generations. But the environments most often occupied by them were seldom identified as suburban. During the most recent decade the tempo of black movement to outlying ring communities has increased appreciably. Peter Labovitz estimated that black movement to the suburbs averaged less than 20,000 per year during the period 1960–66, but in 1967 and 1968, the volume increased more than ten fold.[41] One of the underlying objectives of this book is to attempt to assess the significance of this major breakthrough in terms of tempo. But more important, an attempt will be made to evaluate the gains acquired by those blacks who were the participants in the process.

RESEARCH GOALS

The chapters that follow are structured in such a way as to permit an evaluation of the resources that have become available to a larger segment of the population as a result of the decision to locate in the suburban ring. Emphasis is given to the following attributes associated with the altered location of the mover population: housing; educational benefits; economic security; workplace accessibility; and other social services. As indicated earlier, the communities that were previously identified as all-black towns will serve as the basic point of departure for this study. They span the spectrum of community types in the suburban ring in which the vast majority of blacks have taken up residence. Likewise, there is generally at least one of these community types in each of the major metropolitan systems in which black suburbanization is underway; the ring exceptions include Cleveland, Los Angeles, and Newark.

Primary and secondary data are utilized in assessing the status of these communities, along with secondary data from another 35 communities which have recently become the place of residence of a growing number of blacks. The role of the all-black towns as the direct providers of residential and other advantages is evaluated, as well as their impact on the dispersion of blacks found elsewhere in the suburban ring. Heretofore, most writers have paid only scant attention to these communities, other than to identify them as ghettolets or mini-ghettos, thus making their contribution to the process of black suburbanization little understood. We hope to clarify this.

Chapter Two

The Housing Environment and Black Residential Submarkets in Selected Suburban Ring Communities

Among the services blacks most frequently indicate a dissatisfaction with are housing services.[1] The Kerner Commission found that housing grievances were frequently mentioned as a basis for black discontent. It has been demonstrated that blacks at every income and educational level, with one exception, are more dissatisfied with their housing than are whites possessing similar incomes and levels of educational attainment.[2] Campbell indicates that the differences between the races in the area of housing satisfaction is greater than that associated with any other major urban service.[3] Given the extent of housing dissatisfaction among black Americans, it is only logical to think that those possessing viable options would exercise those options by seeking housing in alternative markets.

ALTERNATIVE HOUSING ENVIRONMENTS

The market with which black Americans have had the least experience is the suburban market, and there is little evidence leading to the conclusion that success will be any greater there than in zones of resistance in the central city. A recent survey indicated that whites in the suburbs are slightly more likely to defend their rights to keep blacks out of their neighborhoods than are central city whites.[4] While these characteristic attitudes exist among whites, counter attitudes exist among blacks; however, the majority of blacks are still willing to reside in interracial residential areas.[5] Yet, as Pettigrew is careful to point out, "there is no widespread desire among black Americans to

27

live in 'mostly' or overwhelmingly white areas."[6] A combination of the attitudes of the two groups has resulted in the evolution of residential zones within the suburbs which are almost exclusively black.

Only recently have blacks begun to seek housing, in relatively large numbers, outside central cities in metropolitan areas. During the most recent decade, between 400,000 to 500,000 black residents became a part of the movement to suburbia. Many of these movers settled in zones of close proximity to older black residential enclaves that were already present in suburban locations, or else they settled in zones that were simply physical extensions of the central city ghetto. We will look first at housing changes that occurred in a set of black suburban enclaves during the previous decade, as these enclaves collectively represent pioneer black communities possessing suburban locations.

Historically, blacks residing in the rings of Standard Metropolitan Statistical Areas have occupied housing of lower quality than that of their central city counterparts. Since the 1970 census of housing dropped the housing question, it is not possible to compare directly those changes in the quality of housing occupied by blacks in the suburbs with those in the central city. In 1960, ten black metropolitan ring enclaves were characterized by levels of substandardness which exceeded that prevailing in a randomly drawn sample of central city neighborhoods with similar objective characterisitics. In only three instances were the suburban enclaves found to have lower levels of substandardness than their central city counterparts.[7] Thus, in the past, residential opportunities outside the central city did not appear to provide an improvement of the quality of housing over that available in central cities. Now, all of this seems to be changing as the social status of metropolitan ring blacks exceeds that of central city blacks for the first time; and this in itself should serve as a crude estimator of the direction of housing quality change.

After having investigated several aspects of the housing attributes of blacks in the original enclaves, our focus will shift to the housing situation of blacks in alternate suburban zones. By 1970, blacks were found to have entered fewer than 80 suburban communities within those metropolitan rings, which accounted for more than half of all the black suburban growth directly related to migration. In each of these communities there had evolved over the decade either a pioneer black enclave or the rapid expansion of an already existing zone of black occupance. In 1960, 52 suburban communities were identified in which 15 percent or more of the population was black,[8] out of more than 800 suburban communities with populations of 10,000 or more. Thus the concentration of blacks in a limited number of suburban communities continues. Selected aspects of the housing situation are detailed for 50 communities, fifteen of which were previously identified as all-black towns.[9] Among these fifteen communities, ten represent the original enclaves previously referred to, while an additional five (whose racial composition will eventually parallel that of the original communities) have been added. The housing information included in this analysis is jointly developed from field surveys and census reports. Field surveys were undertaken in each of the communities identified as all-black towns.

The Traditional Presence of Black Colonies in the Metropolitan Ring

The presence of black colonies in the rings of a number of older Standard Metropolitan Statistical Areas is fairly commonplace, as a number of these communities at the time of their evolution represented rural or rural-urban fringe communities. Since a number of these communities have served as catalysts in promoting the expansion of housing opportunities within the individual communities themselves or within communities in close proximity, they seem to represent a logical group with which to initiate a study focusing on black suburbanization. Since suburbanization is sometimes defined in terms of its locational attributes, few of these communities were previously scrutinized to ascertain if it were valid to describe them as suburban communities.[10]

An analysis of variance was performed using the extent of substandardness as the dependent variable. It was ascertained (using substandardness as an index) that the majority of the black suburban communities more closely resembled a group of central city neighborhoods than a set of communities having similar locational attributes identified as nearest neighbor communities.[11] It was concluded that only one community among the original ten could be categorized as suburban, using a housing attribute as an index of what represents a suburban environment.

The Demand for Housing in Black Colonies

The demand for housing in this set of communities varied during the sixties. The age of the community and the condition of its housing stock in 1960 seem basically to condition its growth potential. Five of the original communities were characterized by growth during the period, while four others suffered population losses. Among the six communities added to the original group only one lost population. The demand for housing in these communities is reflected in both the percentage of the total housing stock built since 1960 and the prevailing vacancy rates (see Table 2–1). New construction might simply

Table 2-1. New Construction as a Percent of the Total Housing Stock in a Set of Black Suburban Ring Communities

Community	Percent Housing Built Since 1960
Urbancrest, Ohio	7.9
Glenarden, Md.	79.6
Brooklyn, Ill.	36.1
Richmond Heights, Fla.	31.0
Lawnside, N.J.	36.8
North Fontana, Cali.	16.0
Hollydale, Ohio	91.0
East Chicago Heights, Ill.	65.2
East Palo Alto, Cali.	15.7
Roosevelt City, Ala.	22.0
Cooper Road, La.	18.2
Kinloch, Missouri	25.9
Lincoln Heights, Ohio	9.1
Robbins, Ill.	26.4
Wyandanch, N.Y.	42.0

Source: Census of Population and Housing: 1970, Census Tracts, Final Report PHC (1)—Individual SMSAs.

reflect perceived demand for housing on the part of housing developers, and the existing vacancy rate should provide a clue to the discrepancy between perceived and actual demand (see Table 2-2). The discrepancy thought to exist is not as apparent as it would appear from the crude data on vacancy, since the extent to which the housing market is segmented in terms of tenure type has not been included in this assessment.

The low vacancy rates prevailing in Richmond Heights, Florida; Lawnside, New Jersey; and Hollydale, Ohio, all indicate the existence of a tight housing market in communities where the single family detached unit is the predominant structural type. In the private rental housing market, the normal vacancy rate is often thought to be roughly 5 percent. In those communities where rental housing accounts for a significant share of the total, only East Chicago Heights is characterized by a significantly less than normal vacancy rate. Urbancrest, Ohio, a low density community whose housing stock was chiefly constructed prior to World War Two, has the highest absolute vacancy rate (2 percent) in the owner occupancy market.[12]

Surprisingly, Glenarden, one of the most rapidly growing communities in Maryland's Prince Georges County, was characterized by a vacancy rate of 5.8 percent. This leads one to speculate that the demand for housing within the zones of new apartment complexes is less strong than that prevailing in the owner occupancy market. This point

Table 2–2. Existing Percent of Housing Stock Vacant in a Set of Black Suburban Ring Communities, 1970

Community	Percent Vacant
Urbancrest, Ohio	17.1
Glenarden, Md.	5.8
Brooklyn, Ill.	1.8
Richmond Heights, Fla.	1.7
Lawnside, N.J.	1.7
North Fontana, Cali.	9.2
Hollydale, Ohio	2.1
East Chicago Heights, Ill.	7.3
East Palo Alto, Cali.	4.2
Roosevelt City, Ala.	3.6
Cooper Road, La.	8.5
Kinloch, Missouri	5.5
Lincoln Heights, Ohio	4.9
Robbins, Ill.	3.2
Wyandanch, N.Y.	3.2

Source: Census of Population and Housing: 1970, Census Tracts, Final Report PHC (1)—Individual SMSAs.

will be raised again at a later time. In general, the demand for housing as expressed by vacancy rates that fall within normal range tends to characterize all these communities, with the exception of Urbancrest, whose rate is more than two standard deviations above the mean for all communities in this universe. North Fontana, California, an isolated rural-urban fringe community whose lack of easy accessibility to a major metropolitan center is a handicap, was on the margin of a plus one standard deviation above the mean vacancy rate.

Vacancies in this universe of communities are positively associated with percent population over 65, and negatively associated with percent population with some college training; an imbalanced sex ratio; and percent of children under ten. Thus, it appears that vacancy rates tend to be lowest in those communities in which the population has high median levels of educational attainment, a balanced sex ratio, and large numbers of children. Even in these communities it appears that the housing demand is greatest in those communities where single family housing predominates and the largest percentage of housing was constructed during the most recent decade. This is in keeping with Frieden's comment regarding the appeal of the suburbs to blacks, which indicates that blacks are more likely to find single family houses that they can buy in the suburbs, and they are also "more likely to be able to find a safe neighborhood in which to live."[13]

The market for housing in this set of predominantly black residen-

tial enclaves appears to be drawn from the black population previously
residing in another metropolitan ring community; at least in terms of
that segment of the population which lived elsewhere in 1965. Glenarden, East Chicago Heights, and Brooklyn led the way in attracting
residents from elsewhere in the same SMSA, whereas East Palo Alto,
North Fontana, and Glenarden were most attractive to residents
originating outside the SMSA. Those communities which drew a significant share of their market from the central city were Hollydale,
Cooper Road, East Chicago Heights, and Wyandanch; and here only
Cooper Road's share of the market was principally dependent upon
attracting residents from the central city. This breakdown seems to
reflect proximity to other communities with blacks in their population
possessing an awareness of alternative housing opportunity, and possibly the image of some of the outlying communities held by residents
of the central city. Some of the older communities are viewed as
"hicktowns" by residents of the metropolitan centers.

The Role of Public Policy in Developing New Housing Demand

In some of these outlying enclaves, low income families have been
able to purchase new housing under the provisions of the government's
235 housing program. What impact this has had upon attracting low
income residents from the central city is unknown at this time. The
235 housing program has been of greatest relative importance in
increasing the housing supply in Cooper Road, Louisiana. Most of
these communities have had some additional housing erected under
the auspices of FHA's 235 program. The only communities which
seemingly have not participated in this program are Hollydale, Ohio;
Roosevelt City, Alabama; Richmond Heights, Florida; and North Fontana, California.

Suburban communities have not generally been supportive of the
235 program, as it was thought that the program would lead to intro-
duction of a segment of the population that suburbanites had often
sought to escape—the poor and the minorities. In communities which
are both poor and minority, barriers to such programs may not exist, or
if they do the opposition may be minimal. Some smaller communities
with limited growth potential, such as Urbancrest, Ohio; Brooklyn,
Illinois; and North Fontana, California may simply have been overlooked as prospective sites for anything other than isolated units under
the provisions of this program, while other communities with land
available for expansion and an active black housing market might
become likely targets.

But under the circumstances, the stigma of publicly subsidized housing and its concommitant opposition does not stop at the gate of black suburban communities. A public official in Robbins, Illinois expressed some dismay over the nature of the housing and its associated market in his community. It is true that the architectural design employed in this instance left much to be desired and bears a strong resemblance to the "shotgun house" occupied by many of the blacks in poor small southern communities.

> In communities where multifamily structures constitute a significant share of the total housing stock, other publicly assisted housing programs have been developed. In Glenarden, Maryland an apartment complex has been built under the sponsorship of the 221 d(3) program, while in Kinloch, Missouri the more recent 236 program has been used to foster the development of multiunit structures. While multiunit housing complexes are becoming less alien to suburban communities, publicly subsidized structures of the type developed under the auspices of the programs just described are still likely to be met with opposition in communities other than those whose divergent economic mix is overshadowed by the more compelling attribute of race. Even in these communities, opposition will not be completely muted.

> The nature of these communities, particularly as it relates to size and location, impacts upon its housing market. The most active markets are associated with those communities in which land does not represent a scarce item and new housing construction represents a significant share of the communities' total housing stock. Thus the physical environment in a number of communities precludes the development of an active housing market. A five-factor, factor analysis model employing a principal components procedure was employed to detect the latent housing dimension, describing variations in the nature of the housing market prevailing within this group of communities. Factor four, which accounts for 10.5 percent of the total explained variance, is basically correlated with those variables directly linked to housing market attributes. Eighteen of the 47 variables included in the analysis load high on this factor (see Table 2-3).

A number of variables that load high appear ambiguous in their effect on the factor scores that emerge for each community. Those communities characterized by high positive factor scores are also characterized by rapid growth, few female headed households, higher than average income, few persons from other suburbs in the SMSA, and a small number of in-migrants from the South. Conversely, those communities with high negative scores are characterized by a high

Table 2-3. Factor Loadings: Factor 4 Environment of Previous Residence

Number of Variable	Name of Variable	
44	Home value	.831
9	Sex ratio	.791
23	Ratio of central city black community to median income of this community	.747
13	Number of children in school	.739
26	Percent unemployed	.715
46	Occupied housing built since 1960	.633
38	Outside this SMSA in 1965	.591
29	Percent professionals	.579
34	Percent same house as 1965	.438
39	Percent in South 1965	−.935
18	Median family income	−.950
37	Percent living in another suburb in this SMSA in 1965	−.925
11	Percent female household head	−.691
20	Percent poor receiving public assistance	−.659
1	Population size	−.639
2	Percent growth 60–70	−.550
12	Female heads with children under 18	−.452
7	Percent age 65 or over	−.432

percent of their residents previously living in other suburbs in the SMSA, a higher percent of residents living in the South in 1965, and higher home values. The strength of the variables associated with previous place of residence has led this factor to be labeled "Environment of Previous Residence."

The Social Class Mix of the Movers to the Black Colonies

The market for housing in a number of these communities continues strong, while in others it shows sign of waning. Glenarden and East Chicago Heights, both communities with slightly fewer than 5,000 persons in 1970, continue to show signs of market strength, although in the two years following 1970, Glenarden's market was less strong than during the previous four-year period, while that of East Chicago Heights had increased by 40 percent. Both communities showed an increase in their share of entrants whose annual family income was less than $4,000 and a decline in the percent of entering households whose income was greater than $12,000.

Nearly half of East Chicago Heights' new residents fell into the less than $4,000 category in 1972, whereas during the latter sixties approximately the same percent of entering families earned between $8,000 and $11,999. Glenarden, on the other hand, attracted the largest share (63.8 percent) of its residents from the $12,000 and above income category in the latter sixties, but saw this share dwindle to just more than 30 percent by 1972. In both instances a change occurred in the demand for housing based on tenure type. Glenarden's post-1970 market has essentially revolved around the increased availability of moderate cost apartment units.

Almost 90 percent of that community's recent movers were occupants of apartment dwellings. While this population was the predominant one during the latter sixties, its advantage was closer to 60 percent. Figure 2–1 illustrates the spatial segmentation of the rental and owner occupancy markets in Glenarden and, implicitly, the social class differentiation between these two markets. Some subliminal friction is thought to exist between these two tenancy groups. Residential differentiation is easily demarcated by the physical nature of the accommodations (see Fig. 2–2). The rental occupants in the latter community are concentrated in a series of moderate rise apartment clusters, which vary in their extent of physical isolation from the rest of the community. East Chicago Heights, unlike Glenarden, does not have its rental and owner occupancy populations highly spatially segmented.

Both these communities were characterized by high negative scores on factor four in the factor model. These scores were thought to stem in large part from the high percentage of in-movers from other suburban communities in the SMSA and residence in the South in 1965. Glenarden continues to draw residents from other suburban communities within the SMSA, but movers from the District of Columbia exceeded all nonlocal movers. Almost one-third of the families occupying a different residential unit since 1970 were intracommunity movers. The intracommunity mover group accounted for one-half of all movers in East Chicago Heights, with Chicago representing the overwhelming place of former residence of the nonlocal movers.

Among those communities scoring highly positive on factor four, Wyandanch and Richmond Heights were characterized by the most active markets. The Wyandanch market was strong in both the late sixties and early seventies, with the rental market showing gains but with a preponderance of all residents still residing in purchased units. In both time periods approximately three-fifths of the mover population had annual incomes in excess of $8,000. The Richmond Heights housing market has been slightly more active in the early seventies than it was in the late sixties, although there has been a slight decrease in owner occupance transactions. Multiunit structures represent a very small percentage of the total residential units in Richmond

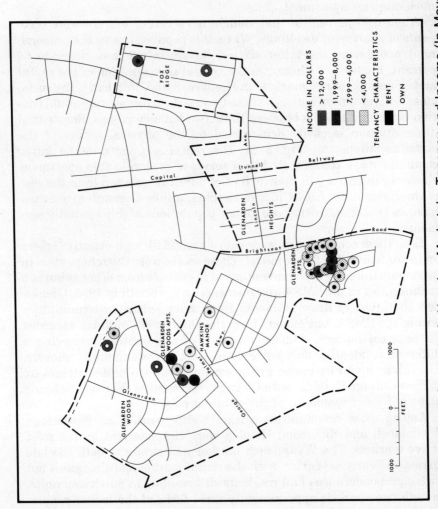

Figure 2–1. Internal Variations in Glenarden's Housing Market, by Tenancy and Income (In-Movers since 1970)

Figure 2–2. Variations in the Physical Design of Housing Units in Glenarden

Heights, but a growing number of single family detached structures are occupied by renters. The spatial segmentation of these two tenancy types is not always readily apparent, as is the case of Glenarden. Yet several low rise multiunit structures have been developed in Richmond Heights that constitute one of the physically least attractive areas in the community. In the latter community there has been an increase in the percent of families with annual earnings in excess of $12,000.

In each community, it is possible to detect from the survey data the modal income group that individual communities are able to attract. It might be assumed that the modal income group is likely to influence the housing that will be developed in the future, as it is they who tend to establish the character of the community in terms of its external imagery. Since 1970, East Palo Alto and Wyandanch have largely catered to families whose annual earnings are in the range of $8,000 to $12,000; Kinloch, Cooper Road, and East Chicago Heights, on the other hand, have attracted the largest number of their residents from the less than $4,000 category. Richmond Heights, during the most recent period, has attracted families largely from the upper end of the income spectrum for this universe, $12,000 and above. And finally, Glenarden, which during the late sixties attracted more than 60 percent of its new residents from the upper end of the spectrum, shifted to a bimodal split, with 41 percent representing families in the $4,000 to $8,000 bracket and 31 percent in the greater than $12,000 income group.

The future economic and social character of these communities will be influenced by the choices of housing developers and those community groups who choose the nature of the housing to be developed. In those instances where the communities are politically unincorporated, the decision will rest chiefly with the developer and his appraisal of effective housing demand. The smaller and/or older communities, which are already characterized by high density, cannot be expected to have their housing stock seriously altered without a land clearing effort that would result in the removal of substandard units, which have a blighting influence on the landscape, and thus subjecting the cleared area for possible redevelopment. In some instances, parcels of this and land of similar character have already begun to be redeveloped. Communities that fall into the latter category are Hollydale, Ohio; Lawnside, New Jersey; Roosevelt City, Alabama; Kinloch, Missouri; Brooklyn, Illinois; and Lincoln Heights, Ohio. Both Urbancrest, Ohio and North Fontana, California possess the physical potential for residential development, but their location and/or imagery could hamper their development.

The Condition of the Housing Stock *Good*

Suburban housing in general is likely to represent housing of sound quality. This is largely true because a disproportionate volume of suburban housing has not yet reached the age at which evidence of deterioration is visually apparent. Residents of suburbia are generally financially able to provide preventive maintenance. The continued pattern of building most of the nation's new housing units in the suburbs will have the effect of upgrading the total housing stock. During the fifties, two-thirds of all new housing was built in metropolitan areas, and, according to Frieden, most of this was built in the suburbs.[14] But in the seventies, many older suburban communities will have reached a state of architectural obsolescence, as many of the housing units built for an emerging middle class of a generation ago are likely to be minus many of the features which are standard items in the newer units built for today's same (relative) economic status population. Such communities are unlikely to be able to retain their former levels of attractiveness. Because of their declining attractiveness, they are likely to become ripe for black entry.

Prior to the most recent period, blacks residing within metropolitan areas but outside central cities occupied lower quality housing than their central city counterparts. A recent Census Bureau estimate of this situation indicated that 16 percent of the housing occupied by blacks in the suburbs was considered substandard, whereas only 9 percent of that occupied by central city blacks was so categorized.[15] Since this was a recent census estimate, it is not apparent what criteria were involved in making this assessment.

While the black population is almost universally found in central cities throughout the nation, their pattern of suburban distribution is highly selective. In 1970 it was demonstrated that suburban blacks had incomes which exceeded those of central city blacks for the first time, and consequently one would suppose that there had been a corresponding improvement in housing quality. The post-1965 movement of blacks into zones in which they had previously been excluded, and the rapid abandonment by blacks in rural-urban fringe locations in a number of major southern metropolitan areas, should have done much to reverse the central city–suburban housing quality pattern.

Part of the difficulty associated with attempts to assess the condition of the nation's housing stock revolves around the definitions employed to describe the status of that stock. The Douglas Commission, in an attempt to assess the extent to which the nation was making good on its effort to see that every American lived in a decent home, arrived at the conclusion that there are no suitable definitions of what constitutes a decent home and a suitable living environment[16]—a condition that made their task all the more difficult. Most often, attempts to assess housing quality are forced to rely on the definitions employed by the Census Bureau. However, most housing analysts seem to agree that the census definitions leave much to be desired, and thus generally conclude the lack of safe and sanitary housing is far more widespread than we are led to believe.

In 1960, 44 percent of all nonwhites resided in housing units that were defined by the Census Bureau as substandard—and this was a major improvement over the previous decade. At the same time only 13 percent of all white Americans resided in structures described in this manner. One might safely assume that all Americans experienced an improvement in their housing environment during the sixties, based on the Census Bureau's definition of substandard housing. The simple construction of new units and the removal of elements from the original substandard stock would reduce the percent of housing identified as substandard.

Also in 1960, six of the ten original all-black communities that are a part of this study were characterized by levels of substandardness that was equal to or above that which represented the average housing quality condition for black Americans. Only in Robbins, Illinois; Lawnside, New Jersey; Lincoln Heights, Ohio; and Richmond Heights, Florida were housing quality conditions better than those confronting most black Americans, and in the case of Robbins the difference was marginal at best.

One of the drawbacks of the census definition is that it describes the extent of substandardness rather than the intensity or seriousness of the problem. Nevertheless most attempts at appraisal have had to rely on this set of data. Now that the Bureau of the Census has abandoned the task of assessing the structural characteristics of the housing of the American population, other agencies and groups are being forced to devise schemes to satisfy their goal.

The current interest in the quality of the environment has prompted the development of schemes which are more comprehensive than that previously employed by the Census Bureau. Kain and Quigley, who recently undertook such a task, remarked that "Difficulty in measuring the physical and environmental quality of the dwelling unit and surrounding residential environment is perhaps the most vexing problem encountered in evaluating the several attributes of the bundles of residential services."[17] A similar scheme was recently developed by the Department of Housing and Urban Development and is entitled, "Neighborhood Environmental Evaluation and Decision System." Both of the latter attempts to assess residential quality transcend a simple assessment of the visual quality of the residential unit.

The current attempt to evaluate housing conditions in the fifteen survey communities includes aspects of the newer, more comprehensive residential quality schemes, as well as housing quality variables previously employed by the Census Bureau. The latter scheme, however, was easier to follow, as the Bureau's guide to its enumerators were readily accessible and easy to follow. Thus the evaluation of the individual residential unit is based on the criteria employed by the Census enumerators in 1960. The evaluators were instructed to identify housing units as falling into the following categories: Excellent, Good, Fair, and Poor. This four-category description permits a slightly finer expression of quality at the upper end of the scale than is possible using the old three-division evaluation scale employed by the Bureau, which includes the categories standard, deteriorating, and dilapidated.

A dichotomous categorization of standard and substandard would show that of the fifteen communities surveyed only two are characterized by having more than half its housing within the substandard end of the spectrum. The two communities in which substandard housing predominates is Cooper Road, Louisiana, and Roosevelt City, Alabama (see Fig. 2–3). Fair housing—a category which is suggestive of the category deteriorating used by the Census Bureau—varies widely among these communities. Seven communities have more than 30 percent of their housing in a state requiring some rehabilitation if it is not to slip further down the quality ladder. The leaders in this category are Roosevelt City, Alabama; Lincoln Heights, Ohio; and Kinloch, Missouri (Fig. 2–4). Top of the line housing or that without any serious visible defects is concentrated in Hollydale, Ohio; Lawnside, New Jersey; and Glenarden, Maryland. (See also Figure 2–5).

In some of these communities there was no evidence of housing in the excellent category in the sample, while in others there was no evidence of poor or dilapidated housing in the sample, but most communities included elements in each category. The greatest diversity in housing quality variations were found in East Palo Alto, California; Wyandanch, New York; Robbins, Illinois; and Cooper Road, Louisiana. So even in communities whose areal expanse is highly restricted, there exists housing that might be described as slum housing only short distances from housing of recent vintage. This situation is made possible by a set of forces not generally at work in communities described as suburban.

There are signs of housing quality improvements, at least in terms of the proportion of the total housing stock classed as standard, in each of the communities for which there was data available in 1960. Table 2–4 provides a comparative measure of housing quality change during

A

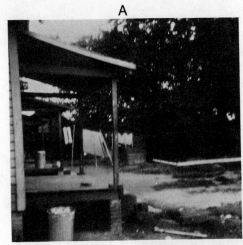

B

C

Figure 2–3. Examples of Low Quality Housing in Roosevelt City, Alabama (A and B), and North Fontana, California (C)

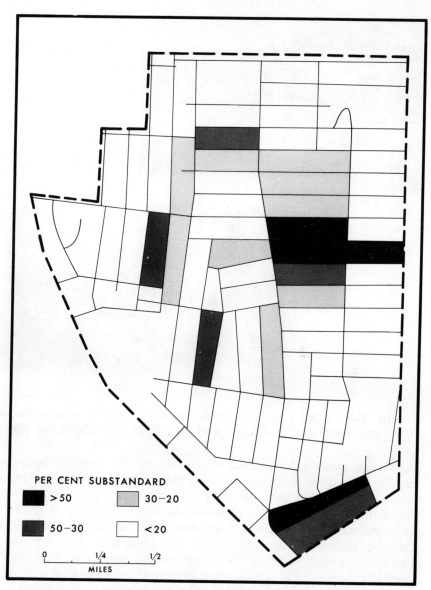

Figure 2–4. Housing Quality Variations in Kinloch, Missouri

A

B

Figure 2–5. Illustrations of High Quality Housing Available in Richmond Heights, Florida (A), and East Palo Alto, California (B)

the sixties. Among the original communities, only one experienced a negative change in quality. Richmond Heights, Florida, a community whose housing stock was basically developed during the fifties, was characterized by a minimum of substandardness in 1960. But by 1970, fully one-third of its housing was categorized as substandard.[18] The greatest improvements took place in Glenarden, Brooklyn, and Lawnside. In each instance, these represented communities in which more than one-third of the standing stock was constructed during the decade. In Glenarden, fully 80 percent of the housing available in 1970 had not been present in 1960. The least progress was made in Urbancrest and Robbins, with Lincoln Heights, Cooper Road, and Kinloch showing only minimal improvement.

Table 2–4.   A Comparison of Changes in Housing Quality in a Selected Set of All-Black Towns, 1960–70

Community	Substandardness Percentage		Change in Quality (In Per Cent)
	1960	*1972*	
Brooklyn	81	44	+37
Kinloch	62	46	+16
Glenarden	53	7	+46
Urbancrest	52	45	+ 7
Cooper Road	49	33	+16
Robbins	43	37	+ 6
Lawnside	34	6	+27
Lincoln Heights	27	40	+13
Richmond Heights	1	33	−32

Sources: Census of Population and Housing: 1960, Census Tracts, Final Report PHC (1) Individual States; and 1972 All-Black Towns and Field Survey Report

Among those communities which joined this universe for the first time in 1970, Roosevelt City, Alabama suffered the poorest quality housing in the entire fifteen-community group, with 60 percent of its housing categorized as substandard in 1970. An independent group surveyed the structural conditions prevailing in Roosevelt City in 1970 and concluded only about one-third of that community's housing was substandard (see Fig. 2–6). The independent survey employed the same criteria as had been recommended by the Bureau of the Census in 1960, yet their estimate turned up almost one-third fewer substandard units than did the 1972 Census survey. Part of the difference in the results can possibly be explained by enumerator error, and part on the grounds that the earlier survey evaluated each household, whereas the latter survey only canvassed a 3.5 percent sample of the total housing stock.

Among the remaining communities in which no temporal comparison of qualitative changes in structural conditions were undertaken, Hollydale had the lowest percentage of substandard housing of any community in the universe with 6 percent; Wyandanch and East Palo Alto, both of which are in the process of racial change, had approximately one-fifth of their units requiring some rehabilitation and/or maintenance; and East Chicago Heights, which had been ignored a decade earlier (for at that time it was only 82 percent nonwhite), had slightly more than one-third of its housing stock requiring the elimination of a variety of physical defects. The latter community is similar to Cooper Road and Richmond Heights in the extent to which substandard housing is found to exist, but has much less substandard housing which is described as dilapidated than occurs in Cooper Road.

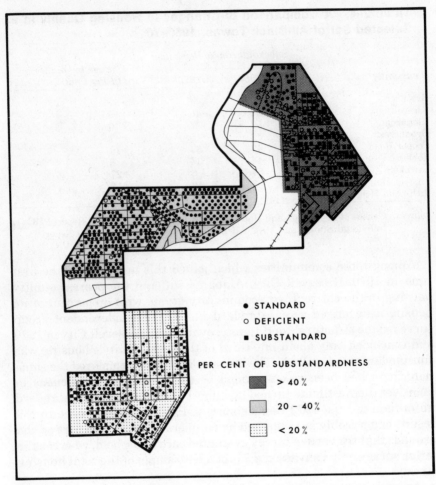

STANDARD

DEFICIENT

SUBSTANDARD

PER CENT OF SUBSTANDARDNESS

> 40 %

20 - 40 %

< 20 %

Figure 2–6. Internal Variations in the Structural Conditions of Housing in Roosevelt City, Alabama, 1970

On the question of the structural quality of housing as ascertained by a cursory visual appraisal of visible defects, it appears that the residential unit that blacks occupy in non-central city locations within the metropolitan areas is showing signs of improvement. But even so, some physical rehabilitation will be required in most to deter fair housing from declining into poor housing.

The Residents' Perception of Their Residential Environment

There was no direct attempt to compare the field investigator's appraisal of housing quality with those of the housing occupant, but each sample respondent (household head or surrogate) was asked if his or her unit required major physical maintenance. The responses to this question should provide indirect evidence of the general congruence of these two sets of housing quality assessments. In general, the resident response indicating the need for major physical maintenance exceeded the level of substandardness reported by the field investigators. Thus, if the residents' response is accepted as reflecting a more accurate appraisal of the extent of substandardness, then the improvements previously described would vanish. The most frequently cited maintenance requirement was the need to paint. Since painting essentially reflects a measure of aesthetic appeal rather than structural defect, the residents' perception of substandardness might be inflated.

In only one instance was the residents' appraisal of the need for major physical maintenance lower than the substandardness index derived by the field investigators, and this occurred in Kinloch. The range in the differences as expressed in percentages varied from 2 to 32. Some of the most glaring differences in the two sets of appraisals occurred in two of the communities whose level of substandardness was regarded as low by the field investigators. It is clear that the two groups were not measuring the same qualities, although both represented an aspect of residential quality. A previous attempt to compare evaluation of neighborhood quality, which is a more comprehensive concept than housing quality, as undertaken by neighborhood residents and a group of professional planners, resulted in only a moderate degree of agreement.[19] In that instance a correlation coefficient of .35 described the degree of association between the planners' evaluation of the neighborhood, using the extent of "pleasantness" as an index, and a set of neighborhood residents' evaluation of how well they liked their neighborhood.[20] In our sample, the discrepancy is widespread when the percent of substandardness is used as an index.

In attempting to move one step beyond a simple appraisal of housing quality to that of neighborhood quality, the household head was requested to compare the community of present residence with that of most recent residence. The possible responses were superior, same, and unfavorable. Roughly one-half of the communities were ranked as superior to the communities of last residence. This group of communities includes Richmond Heights (75 percent), Hollydale (73 percent), Lawnside (61 percent), Glenarden (59 percent), Cooper Road (58 percent), East Palo Alto (54 percent), and North Fontana (52 percent).

In two communities, Roosevelt City and East Chicago Heights, the residents were equally divided on the superiority of the present community. In all other communities the residents were less enthusiastic about the present community of residence than were those in the communities just enumerated. As a matter of fact, only 32 percent of

the residents in Robbins considered it superior to the last place of
residence, and only 34 percent in Wyandanch. Hollydale, Lawnside,
and Glenarden, which ranked high on the community superiority
question, were also communities with little substandard housing. But
Wyandanch, with only one-fifth of its housing rated as substandard,
compared less favorably on the community of previous residence question than did Richmond Heights. The latter community had a substandardness level of 33 percent. These two communities were at
opposite poles on the issue of superiority to previous community of
residence.

In terms of residents' evaluation of the present place of residence
vis-à-vis the last, the communities of Richmond Heights, Hollydale,
Lawnside, and Glenarden might be thought of as communities of first
resort, or communities which attract movers from other environments,
while Wyandanch, Robbins, and Kinloch are communities of last re-
sport, or communities into which people are pushed. This assessment
was partially verified by the residents' response to the question, "If you
were to change your place of residence within the next twelve months,
what mover action would you take?" Among those residents who rated
the present community as superior, the choice was to seek another
place of residence within this community. Residents whose appraisal of
the present community was basically negative more often indicated
that they would move to another community. Wyandanch is an apparent anomaly, as it is evident that its housing environment must be
rated at least good, and yet there was an overwhelming percent of the
respondents who viewed it as being no different from their previous
place of residence. Most of the criticisms seems to revolve around the
nature of the social environment rather than the housing environment
per se. Thus, statements that "it is becoming more like Harlem" were
fairly common. This latter point tends to highlight the nonhousing
aspect of residential satisfaction.

In thirteen of the survey communities the enumerators·were asked
to observe qualities of the residential environment that transcended
observed physical defects in the unit itself: an appraisal of the maintenance of the yard, as reflected by the nature of the grass cover, as well
as an appraisal of the condition and/or presence of adjacent sidewalks.
These measures were designed to appraise physical qualities of the
environment that provide esthetic appeal and, in the latter instance,
an element of safety. In addition to the variables just described, the
enumerators noted the presence of glass and other debris on the residential property, on an adjacent sidewalk, or in the street.

Likewise, a similar evaluation was made of the presence or absence
of junked or inoperable automobiles in the yards, in the streets or

alleys, in close proximity to residential properties. The latter reflects a set of behavioral characteristics that denote value status and/or the effectiveness of the communities to provide the necessary maintenance to minimize the presence of materials that detract from the overall physical quality of the environment. This measure also illustrates the need for powers to prevent the accumulation of such physically unattractive materials. A rating scale was devised which enabled the enumerators to derive a landscape score for each community. Properties would receive a negative value if glass and other debris, along with the presence of junked autos, were present on or in close proximity to an individual property. A maximum of 30 points could be assigned each residential property and a minimum of minus 20. The average score for the thirteen-community group ranged from 27.3 in Glenarden to 8.9 for Cooper Road (see Table 2-5).

The rank of communities on the landscape index bears a striking resemblance to the community ranking on the substandardness index, although there are a few deviant cases. Most noticeable among these is East Chicago Heights. East Chicago Heights shows up as having a very pleasant landscape, although approximately one-third of its housing was rated substandard. Most of the housing in East Chicago Heights which has been described as substandard would fit the Census classification of deteriorating. Nevertheless, some physical maintenance is necessary to maintain this stock in its current state.

The landscape characteristics seem to reflect first the age and poverty characteristics of individual communities. While not a single community merited a negative score on this index, negative scores

Table 2–5. An Evaluation of Landscape Quality in Thirteen Black Suburban Communities

Community	Landscape Score	Qualitative Description
Glenarden, Maryland	27.3	Very Pleasing
Lawnside, New Jersey	26.8	Very Pleasing
Hollydale, Ohio	24.9	Very Pleasing
East Chicago Heights, Ill.	23.1	Very Pleasing
Wyandanch, New York	18.3	Moderately Pleasing
Richmond Heights, Florida	17.7	Moderately Pleasing
Robbins, Illinois	15.5	Moderately Pleasing
Lincoln Heights, Ohio	14.2	Moderately Pleasing
Urbancrest, Ohio	10.3	Moderately Pleasing
Roosevelt City, Alabama	9.7	Weakly Pleasing
Brooklyn, Illinois	9.6	Weakly Pleasing
Kinloch, Missouri	9.3	Weakly Pleasing
Cooper Road, Louisiana	8.9	Weakly Pleasing

Source: Information Derived from 1972 Survey of All-Black Towns.

were assigned individual properties within the community. In Kinloch, Missouri, an older community which was described as weakly pleasant, it was found that negative scores were most often assigned to properties with large families, where the head was elderly, and where the head of the household was the single occupant. The use of the landscape index is simply one attempt to move beyond the residential unit itself as a means of assessing the quality of the residential environment. This is a crude first attempt and its utility as an index of environmental evaluation will have to be scrutinized. But Frank Kristoff, a noted housing analyst, was quoted by Marcuse as saying the following in terms of the weakness of current measures employed to evaluate housing quality:

In addition this measure does not encompass environmental deficiencies that are today accepted as contributing to lack of livability of a given neighborhood. Examples of such deficiencies are garbage-littered streets arising from poor sanitation services, cracked and broken sidewalks, unpaved or broken streets, missing or ineffective street lights, inadequate sewage and drainage facilities, and the mixture of noxious, noisy and heavy traffic generating commercial and industrial usage for residential areas. Others would add social disabilities, such as the danger of assault, mugging and robbery in "high hazard" neighborhoods with high concentration of unemployment, juvenile delinquency, and narcotics traffic and addiction.[21]

Some of the elements which have been identified by Kristoff are incorporated in the Landscape Index developed for this study. None of the social variables mentioned by Kristoff was utilized here, although the previous reference to the response of the residents of Wyandanch suggest that social variables should be included in such an evaluation.

The Housing Environment and Human Response: An Unresolved Issue

Having arrived at a series of measures that can be used to evaluate the residential environment of this set of communities, one still does not know how these relate to what has been described as housing outputs. Peter Marcuse has identified housing outputs as health, comfort, economic well-being, security, status, and esthetic enjoyment.[22] From the results of the present assessment, it is not possible to say with any degree of precision the extent to which the housing environment has contributed to each of these individual goals, yet in a loose fashion it is possible to make statements that reflect the residents' perception of how well these goals have been satisfied. This is an area in which little progress has been made, for the nation's housing policy has revolved around inputs rather than outputs. Burns and Mittelbach, who recently attempted to evaluate housing inputs to benefits accrued, had this to say:

> The quantity and price of housing actually produced in the market, therefore, are not necessarily good indicators of the "correct" amount and quality. Accurate prescriptions of the "correct" amounts and quality cannot be determined until the evidence on housing outputs has been augmented considerably. Clearly, of the external returns from improved housing—including physical and mental health, deviant behavior, and other quality of life measures—are substantial, even currently high levels of investment in upgrading housing quality may be too low.[23]

Like Marcuse, the above writers exhibit concerns for housing outputs, which are expressed in terms other than the structural conditions of the unit. Yet our total experience in evaluating housing output is related simply to producing housing that is structurally sound. Oscar Newman, who recently developed a treatise that addressed itself to the role of the housing environment on crime prevention, had some thoughts on the matter of housing design and the human response (output), which are expressed as follows:

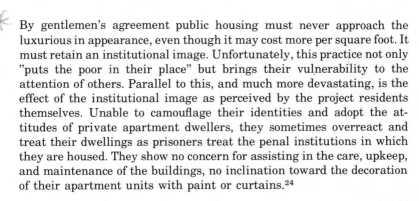

> By gentlemen's agreement public housing must never approach the luxurious in appearance, even though it may cost more per square foot. It must retain an institutional image. Unfortunately, this practice not only "puts the poor in their place" but brings their vulnerability to the attention of others. Parallel to this, and much more devastating, is the effect of the institutional image as perceived by the project residents themselves. Unable to camouflage their identities and adopt the attitudes of private apartment dwellers, they sometimes overreact and treat their dwellings as prisoners treat the penal institutions in which they are housed. They show no concern for assisting in the care, upkeep, and maintenance of the buildings, no inclination toward the decoration of their apartment units with paint or curtains.[24]

While Newman refers to a specific housing design phenomenon, the ingredients present in the previous discussion are present. His discussion gets at the heart of evaluating housing outputs in cost per square foot of floor space, as opposed to long run cost, which might be expressed in individual productivity as measured by a sense of individual accomplishment, as well as the individual's contribution to the development of the larger society. The Newman orientation to the housing environment is essentially related to the growing interest in the spread of crime.

Individual Spacing Within the Urban Milieu

One condition of the residential environment which has received increased attention during the recent period is the spacing of individuals within the urban milieu. One measure which has traditionally distinguished suburban residence from residence in the central city has been the low density character of most suburban communities. High density and a sometimes parallel phenomenon of crowding has frequently led central city residents to flee the densely settled zones of the central city to the large lot, low density zone of the city's periphery.

The density characteristics of the survey communities varies from less than 1,000 per square mile in Hollydale and Urbancrest to more than 8,000 per square mile in East Palo Alto (see Table 2–6). Most of these outlying black communities are land poor and thus the number of persons that they can possibly accommodate is a function of housing design. In most instances these communities seldom exceed one square mile in area, with 0.9 square miles representing the modal size class. The largest of these communities are Cooper Road and Wyandanch, both of which are located on the margin of the zone of suburban development. They include 5.8 and 3.8 square miles, respectively. Among the nongrowth communities in the group, gross residential density is declining, while in those communities in which active housing markets were previously identified, gross residential density was on the increase. Density increases occurred in Cooper Road, Wyandanch, Glenarden, Robbins, and Richmond Heights. The lowest density communities generally tend to be physically isolated, and in fact the residents of three of these communities perceive them to be rural communities rather than suburban communities. The extreme case occurs in the dispersed settlement of North Fontana, California, where

Table 2–6. Relative Density Variations in Black Suburban Ring Communities

Low Density Communities (<2,000 persons/sq.mi.)	Medium Density Communities (>3,000<6,000 persons/sq.mi.)	High Density Communities (>6,000<10,000 persons/sq.mi.)
Hollydale	Wyandanch	Lincoln Heights
Urbancrest	Glenarden	Robbins
North Fontana	East Chicago Heights	Richmond Heights
Brooklyn	Kinloch	East Palo Alto
Roosevelt City		
Cooper Road		
Lawnside		

Source: U.S. Census Bureau.

more than 90 percent of the population sample responded that they thought the community was rural in character.

From the perspective of outputs of the residential environment, the concept of density is probably less meaningful than the concept of crowding. While density, simply put, describes the number of persons per unit of area, crowding is a much more complex concept. Crowding is a condition that implies a restriction of the individual's space requirement. Thus one's perception of a condition is a combined outgrowth of the personal psychology and set of learned traditions that might be identified as culture. According to Stokols, crowding may have both a social and nonsocial basis.[25] In the former case a condition of or feeling of crowding is elicited by the presence of other persons and their relationship to the perceiver. In the latter instance, a feeling of crowding is usually associated with the effect of a physical variable on the restriction of space.

It has been demonstrated by a number of scientists that crowding creates stress in lower animal populations. There have been serious attempts recently to project what has been learned from the animal environment to that of the human environment as it relates to crowding as a stress factor. Bruno Bettleheim suggests that there are inherent dangers in this type of analogy.[26] Nevertheless, research continues in this area that could lead to a major breakthrough in understanding how the human population adjusts to a set of environmental conditions.

It is widely known, however, that human populations have specific tastes for environmental quality and that among some of the valued environmental attributes, spaciousness frequently shows up. Many writers who have devoted much energy to understanding the rationale for the development of suburban communities suggest that the demand for spaciousness and openness, along with a distaste for the congestion that sometimes characterized life in large cities, is often of great importance. Interest here, then, relates to the extent to which non-central city residence provides black residents in this select set of communities a freedom from spatial restrictions or limitations that might be defined as a condition of crowding.

Attempts were made to evaluate the adequacy of spatial requirements as described by floor space in the residential unit, external space as described by adequacy of yard size, and a feeling of neighborhood crowding. Furthermore, an attempt was made to evaluate a strictly social definition of crowding by determining the number of persons gathered in one's household for the purpose of a social get-together that would generate a feeling of crowding on the part of the host. In the latter instance the respondent was asked to indicate which room in the household was normally used for social gathering.

The absence of satisfactory interior living space as reflected by inadequacy of room size was present to some extent in each community. Whether this represents rising aspirations or a response to a physical condition that is entirely related to social status is unknown at this point. The greatest dissatisfaction associated with inadequate interior residential space occurs in Richmond Heights, Florida. Here 47 percent of all household heads indicated that their residential unit contained too little space. Following Richmond Heights were Brooklyn (36.4 percent) and Cooper Road (35.7 percent), both low density communities. Those communities in which fewer than 10 percent of the population (household heads) viewed their housing units as containing too little space were Lawnside (4.5 percent), Glenarden (7.9 percent), North Fontana (8.4 percent), and East Palo Alto (8.8 percent).

All other communities ranged from just over 10 percent on the limitations of their interior dimensions to just under 30 percent. Among those communities with the highest expressed levels of spatial inadequacy are those in which housing was built originally for a black market, and two communities which rank high on the poverty scale. Richmond Heights, unlike the previous two communities, is much more recent in terms of the age of its housing stock. Much of the original post-World War Two housing developed in this community was characterized by somewhat restrictive dimensions.

The Relationship Between Density and Crowding

There seems to exist only a limited relationship between density and crowding in this instance. East Palo Alto and Richmond Heights, possessing similar densities, are at opposite poles on this specific measure of crowding. Likewise Cooper Road, with one of the lower crude densities of all communities, shows up very poorly when measured against Glenarden, which is a medium density community. From the results reported here one might question the notion that rural populations, especially black rural populations, live under conditions of lower crowding than some urban populations. For on this index of crowding, a number of communities which have a strong rural flavor show up as suffering the most extensive inadequacy of interior residential space.

Adequacy of external residential space as defined by the dimensions of the yard seem to be of lesser concern to household heads. Nor does external space seem to be directly related to interior space. Robbins, Kinloch and Brooklyn are the communities in which the response to the question of adequacy of yard space was most negative and here fewer than 20 percent of the household heads in the community of greatest dissatisfaction expressed concern with this segment of space. Thus crowding as simply reflected by physical dimensions of space tends to show up most often in those communities which are poor, and aging—with the exception of Richmond Heights. East Chicago Heights, Lincoln Heights, and Robbins represented the middle range in crowding on this measure.

This lack of satisfactory physical space does much to lessen the suburban emphasis that has been employed in describing these communities. It tends to imply that shelter rather than space has historically been of overriding importance in the black citizen's quest for a minimally satisfactory living environment. Given the absence of previous studies focused on this topic, it is difficult to discuss its meaning in terms of housing outputs.

When crowding is viewed from still a third perspective, another set of results emerge. In the latter instance household heads were asked to evaluate their neighborhoods in terms of whether they perceived them to be crowded or uncrowded. Having previously asked questions which bore directly on the spatial adequacy of the residential property, the respondent was now being asked to evaluate a larger milieu, which represents a direct extension of his residential unit. Neighborhood crowding was most often reported by those communities which were old and in which the possibility for physical expansion was minimal. The spacing of the individual residential unit appears to bear an important influence on this response. Among the land poor communities, housing is sited on small lots and a packing effect emerges. Brooklyn, with a 40 percent response rate on the neighborhood crowding index, is perceived as the most crowded in this set of communities. It is followed by Kinloch (34.8 percent), East Chicago Heights (34.7 percent) and Lincoln Heights (33.3 percent). Glenarden, one of the more recently developed housing environments, also ranked high on this index (29.8 percent). A closer look at the Glenarden response surface reveals that two-thirds of the respondents residing in the high rise apartment complex known as the Glenarden Apartments view their neighborhoods as crowded, in contrast to the household heads in the Fox Ridge single family detached housing neighborhood. Paradoxically, the respondents in a second apartment complex in Glendarden, which was physically less isolated from a single family occupance neighborhood, viewed neighborhood crowding to be much less extensive than that prevailing in the Glenarden Apartments complex.

None of the respondents in Hollydale, Lawnside, and Urbancrest reported their neighborhoods to be crowded. Only minimum responses of neighborhood crowding were noted in East Palo Alto and North

Fontana. Almost one-third of the residents of Urbancrest complained of inadequate interior residential space, but none perceived their neighborhood as being crowded. This is probably the result of the spacing pattern of residential units and the presence of few children. It is clear that the first dimension of crowding is related to nonsocial phenomena, while one's perception of neighborhood crowding is likely to be influenced by social as well as nonsocial stimuli. In those communities where interior and exterior residential spaces are limited, socializing in public spaces will likely result. The demand for playgrounds and other outdoor recreational spaces will be required for children, while bars and lounges are likely to be found more frequently to provide outlets for a segment of the adult population.

Whatever psychological and physiological stresses that are usually associated with crowding should be less severe than those thought to be prevalent in many central city environments. Carey's description of the crowding effect on black central city populations in general seems to be only mildly descriptive of the crowding situation of the black communities investigated here.

> Thus, the plight of the Negro resident of our segregated urban residential neighborhoods is not only acute in terms of the stresses of crowding to which he is subjected, but also to the density effects of both residence and employment in noisy and polluted workplaces where he is subjected to environmental insult.[27]

The future perception of neighborhood crowding is likely to be influenced by the population composition of the neighborhood in terms of social class and ethnic identification, the design and spacing of residential units, and the esthetic qualities of the environment itself. Among the varying hierarchies of crowding it is not clear which is likely to generate the most stressful conditions—the lack of interior residential space or the condition of neighborhood crowding. Obviously, in some instances the two are directly related.

The final note on crowding relates totally to the social component of crowding. In this instance one was attempting to arrive at some general conclusion regarding the number of persons one feels comfortable with while entertaining in a single room of his residential unit. Stokols has previously pointed out the effect of the activity engaged in with others on one's view of limited space.[28] Here it was asked how many persons (friends or relatives) constituted a threshold population beyond which one no longer felt comfortable while entertaining in the room in his residence normally set aside for this purpose.

The modal crowding threshold varied from community to community and does not seem to provide an easily discernible pattern. Almost half the communities reported ten or more persons assembled for a social gathering constituted the crowding threshold. Only three communities reported seven to eight persons as representing the crowding threshold, while another five communities most often reported nine to ten persons as representing the number beyond which social crowding could be identified. The question of what the physiological or psychological response was when this threshold was transgressed was not solicited. It is suspected that the response will vary with the personality structure of the individual participant, but nevertheless the identification of a threshold implies the occurrence of some individual discomfort. But at this point it is impossible to imbue these threshold levels with definitive meaning.

The previous discussion represents an in-depth analysis of the housing situation in fifteen suburban ring communities in which blacks constitute the majority population. Those communities among the group which are politically incorporated represented until recently the only communities in the nation in which blacks were in complete control of local government, and in fact may still represent the sole source of "black power" in America. The communities in which primary data were collected represent a cross-section of the kinds of outlying residential developments to which blacks have access. In no way, though, can the growing demand by blacks for housing accommodations outside the central city be satisfied in the context of evolving black colonies of the sort that characterized most of the communities previously described.

This has given rise to black entry into outlying residential environments which were previously white, or zones within a larger predominantly white community in which housing was built with the black residential market in mind. Some of these newly emerging black residential zones abut the central city black community, while others represent enclaves whose location is remote from the central city zone of black residence. In the next section a brief assessment is made of the residential characteristics of the black population in an additional 30 communities in which black entry is basically a product of the sixties. These communities are the chief targets of black suburbanization in their respective metropolitan areas. It is the purpose of this appraisal to ascertain what the black newcomer is getting as he changes his old environment for one generally assumed to offer greater rewards. Limitations abound, as the conclusions derived are based on secondary rather than primary sources.

HOUSING IN COMMUNITIES OF MORE
RECENT ENTRY

> Black suburbanization was essentially confined to fewer than a dozen Standard Metropolitan Statistical Areas during the sixties. Those involved represented metropolitan areas with large central city black populations and cities in which blacks had been present in relatively large numbers for two or more generations. The significance of the latter point is speculative at the moment. The primary focus here is on communities which were recipients of at least 1,000 or more black residents during the previous decade. However, it should be noted that the outlying communities with a black core population failed to attract a significant number of black residents. They simply grew as a function of natural increase. A number of them, in fact, experienced net losses in their black population.

Metropolitan Areas with Old Core Black Communities

In metropolitan areas such as New York, Philadelphia, Pittsburgh, and Birmingham, where blacks have resided in non-central city communities for at least a generation, change was evident. In the New York metropolitan area such older established black suburban cores as those of Mt. Vernon and New Rochelle suffered a net population loss. A similar experience was typical of the older outlying communities of Philadelphia. Only New York and Philadelphia among the metropolitan areas with established outlying communities participated in the process of what might be recognized as a major drive toward black suburbanization. Both Pittsburgh and Birmingham experienced a net loss in their black population in both the central city and the ring during the decade. Even though Philadelphia must be considered one of the leaders in this process, many of its smaller black enclaves suffered a net loss during this period.

Leonard Blumberg had previously looked at patterns of black suburbanization in the Philadelphia metropolitan area and because of the dispersed nature and physical condition of these enclaves had described them as "Little Ghettos."[29] Although Philadelphia ranked among the leading SMSAs in its increase in the number of blacks in non-central city locations, it is difficult to delineate clearly the volume of migration on a community by community basis. Thus, no community from the Philadelphia metropolitan area was included in this analysis.

Among the ten metropolitan areas described by Reynolds Farley as being the centers of black suburban growth during the fifties,[30] two can now be deleted and three additional SMSAs added. Los Angeles, Cleveland, and San Francisco can now be added to this group. Cleveland underwent the most phenomenal increase in its suburban black population, for prior to the sixties, blacks had been unable to acquire sizeable residential accommodations in outlying areas in the Cleveland ring in any meaningful way.

Variations in Size of Communities of Entry

The 30 communities of recent entry, which will be central to this discussion, are situated in the following SMSAs identified in the previous chapter: (1) New York, (2) Los Angeles, (3) Washington, (4) Newark, (5) Cleveland, (6) St. Louis, (7) San Francisco, (8) Chicago, (9) Detroit, and (10) Miami. Detroit was the only metropolitan area among these in which black movement was essentially confined to one principal target zone. Farley recently indicated that during the late fifties, movement from the ring to the city was the modal pattern of black movement in the Detroit metropolitan area.[31] A number of outlying communities in the Detroit region suffered an absolute or net loss in their black population during the sixties; among those hardest hit by black out-movement were Ecorse, Hamtramck, River Rouge, and Royal Oak Township.

Among the target communities almost two-thirds were in the size category of 10,000–50,000 population, being about equally divided among the 10,000–24,999 and the 25,000–49,999 categories. Six of the principal target communities were places with more than 75,000 residents but fewer than 100,000 (see Fig. 2–7). Thus the places chosen for relocation ran the gamut from small villages such as Seat Pleasant, Maryland and Wellston, Missouri to the sprawling community of Hayward, California, with almost 100,000 residents. Obviously these communities differ in size from the all-black towns, which seldom included a community with more than 10,000 residents.

> The racial composition of these principal target zones includes in most instances a white majority, although that majority is often tenuous if a given community was a community of black entry during the decades of the fifties and the sixties (see Fig. 2–8). But obviously the status of a community's racial composition at the end of the period is more complex than the previous statement infers. Such factors as distance from the central city ghetto, the size of the community area, the structural design of the units available—as well as other factors— influence racial composition. A number of the entry communities abut the central city black community and are thus in the wake of black residential expansion (see Fig. 2–9).

> Communities of this type have been described previously as spill-

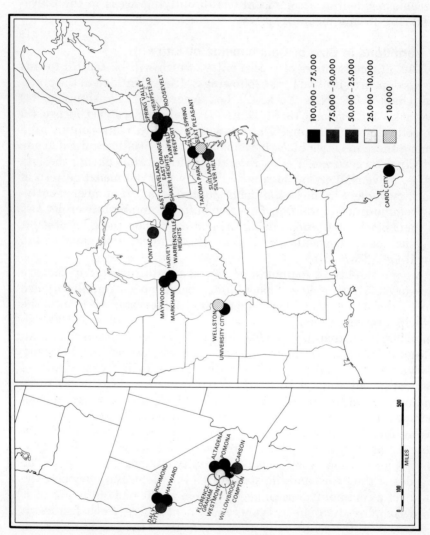

Figure 2–7. Population of Black Suburban Target Zones, 1970

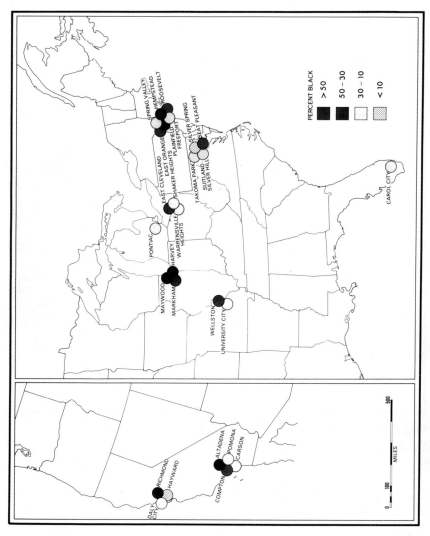

Figure 2–8. Racial Composition of Principal Suburban Target Zones, 1970

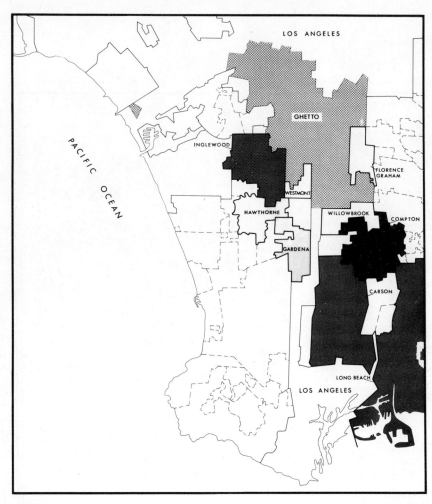

Figure 2–9. Primary and Secondary Mover Destinations in Relationship to the Los Angeles Ghetto

over communities.[32] Examples of this type are most commonplace in Cleveland, St. Louis and Washington (Fig. 2–10). Among the communities which now have a black majority, only Roosevelt, New York and Markham, Illinois represent the non-central city spillover variety. The communities in which blacks constitute more than 30 percent, but less than 50 percent are all communities which might be described as black colonies. The latter communities are physically remote from the central city black community. Those communities in which the per-

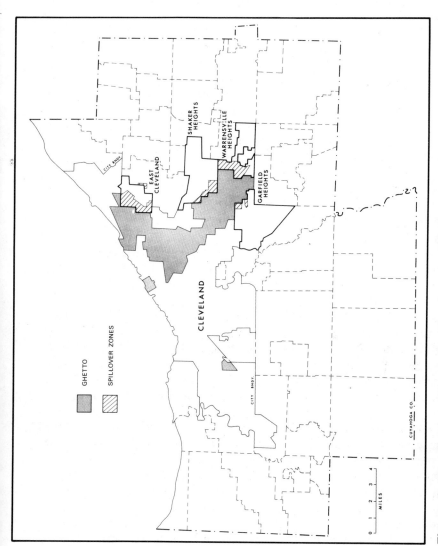

Figure 2–10. Primary Mover Destinations in Relationship to the Cleveland Ghetto: An Example of the Spillover Effect

centage of blacks is less than 30 possess a variety of patterns of locations and thus their racial composition is not directly related to their location.

Black majorities seem to be attained most quickly when the community of entry is physically small. Seldom, though, did communities which had a negligible number of blacks in 1960 move to the 30 percent and beyond category during the decade, although in a few instances this did happen. Altadena, California; Harvey, Illinois; and East Cleveland, Ohio, all with relatively small black population bases at the beginning of the period, experienced major shifts during that period. The most dramatic shift to occur in any of the larger of these communities was represented by the 2.4 percent black population in East Cleveland in 1960 which by 1970 had become 59.8 percent black. These shifts in racial composition are somewhat indicative of the absence of white competition in the housing market in zones of black entry.

Distinctions in the Housing Environment
Based on Location

A five-factor, factor analysis model was also run using data describing these communities in the same way as previously described. Just as in the former case, one factor loaded high on variables that both directly and indirectly related to housing. In this instance, factor five instead of factor four loaded on the housing variables. Twenty-five variables were characterized by loadings of 0.4 or above, but only 6.7 percent of the total variance was explained by this factor. In the previous factor run, using only the data for the fifteen survey communities, this factor was labelled "environment of previous residence." This label seems appropriate in most cases, as it clearly distinguishes communities which have drawn their principal market from the central city from those drawn from elsewhere in the SMSA. But a more descriptive label would seem to be age of housing. Communities scoring highly positive represent places in which most of the housing was developed during the sixties, while those communities scoring highly negative are places in which most of the housing was built prior to 1949.

Another trait which is highly associated with the factor scores is location. Those communities characterized by positive scores are most often black colonies which are not contiguous to the central city ghetto. Communities scoring negatively are most often associated with the spillover effect of the central city ghetto. No consistent pattern describing tenancy characteristics was associated with the factor scores. The original communities had scores on this dimension that were akin to those of the black colonies, the exceptions being Urbancrest and Cooper Road.

Among this dichotomous community group, largely differentiated on the basis of continuity to the central city, the aggregate volume of net in-migration showed remarkable similarity. While the derivation of these estimates are crude, they represent a first attempt at assessing the attractiveness of these communities to persons who previously lived elsewhere. The older suburban communities on the city's inner edge were the targets of more than 100,000 black residents during the decade. Almost 90,000 new residents settled in those communities that were somewhat further removed from the city's edge during this period. Factor scores describing the social rank of these individual communities show that those on the city's inner edge were generally the higher status communities. Since few of these communities were the place of residence of blacks in 1960, there is an indication that these new residential zones simply represent middle income extensions of the central city black community.

Among the outlying communities, few score high on the social rank dimension, indicating that residents previously residing elsewhere in the SMSA or from outside the SMSA are possibly a lower status population. This contention was noted previously. Thus it appears that higher social rank blacks who previously lived in the central city have sought to upgrade their housing environment by selecting residential accommodations within their awareness space. On the other hand, black ring residents who previously lived in another suburban cluster likewise chose a place of residence in a nearby ring development.

An example of the latter situation is best typified by the probable relationship between Hempstead and Freeport, New York, and Pasadena and Altadena, California. In both instances these represent contiguous communities in which housing demand shifted from the former to the latter during the decade. Both Hempstead and Pasadena had a black core population in 1960, while their near neighbors were the place of residence of only a very small black population at that date. Carson, California (which is considered here as being noncontiguous to the city of Los Angeles) ranks third highest among the communities on the social rank dimension. While Carson is technically not contiguous to that edge of Los Angeles that is predominantly black, it is contiguous to other communities which are extensions of the Los Angeles black community. Thus it more appropriately fits the pattern of spillover communities, rather than that of the quasi-isolated black colonies.

The spillover communities exhibit a residential sorting out along social class lines. This is probably best illustrated in the Cleveland case, which shows the highest ranking blacks have settled in War-rensville Heights and Shaker Heights and lower ranking blacks in East Cleveland. The original black communities can be distinguished from this group of communities generally on the basis of both social rank and distance from the city's edge. The original communities, with possibly three exceptions, were developed for black residential occu-pance. None of these emerging black communities was developed in this manner, but a number could easily be transformed into com-munities with a black majority in a short period of time. Even now, East Cleveland, Wellston, Markham, and Roosevelt have become pre-dominantly black within a rather short time period. In no single community of entry do blacks live outside of zones of black concentra-tion. Thus the areas of black entry soon become areas that function as part of the black housing market (see Fig. 2–11).

The tenancy characteristics of the two community types, based on distance from the city edge, show a distinguishing mix. Among the spillover communities there is a predominance of owner occupancy settlement in the colonies. Rental occupance predominates in three spillover communities: East Orange, New Jersey; Silver Spring, Mary-land; and Takoma Park, Maryland. Among the colonies there is only a single community with an overwhelming proportion of the population residing in rental housing and that is Spring Valley, New York. The Spring Valley black community was recently described in the follow-ing way.

> The Spring Valley ghetto has been described as containing some of the most wretched housing to be found anywhere in the nation, including the deepest South. It consists of 1920's vintage summer bungalows of one or two rooms that have been overcrowded by Negro families in desperate need of shelter. It is an anomaly that relatively well-paid Ford employ-ees, who can afford a new car and a color television set, are confined in housing described as that of a quality "most farmers would not use for their livestock."[33]

If the above statement is an accurate description of the housing oc-cupied by a segment of the black population in Spring Valley, it is evident that more than income is responsible for black occupancy of substandard housing. The fact that blacks residing in outlying colonies have traditionally included in their population a high percentage of persons whose income were below the poverty level has led to their being ill housed.

Roosevelt, Hempstead, Freeport, North Amityville, and Wy-andanch—all communities on Long Island with sizeable black resi-dential concentrations—have been described as pockets of poverty.

A

B

C

Figure 2-11. The Nature of Housing Available to Black Movers in Westmont, California (A), Carson, California (B), and East Cleveland, Ohio (C)

More than two-fifths of the nonwhite families in both Nassau and Suffolk counties, in which those communities are located, were described as residing in pockets of poverty in 1960.[34] However, by 1970 the percentage of the population whose earnings placed them in the poverty category had been reduced by more than half. Spring Valley, the community whose housing was described above, had fewer than 10 percent of its black families described as having incomes that would place them in the poverty category in 1970. In each instance, however, the extent of home ownership appears to be directly associated with the extent to which blacks constitute a given percentage of the total population.

In Freeport and Hempstead where blacks still constitute the minority population, there is a good mix between owners and renters. Roosevelt and North Amityville, both of which possess black majorities, are predominantly owner occupancy communities. Obvious improvements have occurred in the economic status of the Long Island group, and this has possibly led to an increase in the owner occupancy mix in the communities under review. But it is apparent that only a restricted supply of housing is available to blacks in these individual colonies. There is further evidence of this in Sternlieb and Beaton's assessment of the Plainfield, New Jersey housing market wherein they conjecture:

> Is minority-group purchasing geographically concentrated within the community? At first glance a wide distribution of minority purchasers seemed evident. Where, however, the blighted sections of the city are superimposed on areas of minority group purchase, a much more distinctive pattern emerges. The bulk of these purchases are immediately peripheral to the blighted sections of the city. The reverse is true for white purchases.[35]

Everywhere the evidence shows that suburban blacks are buying into the system, if increases in home ownership rates can be used to support this contention. There is even less ownership in outlying colonies that are not yet predominantly black than is the case of the tenancy pattern characterizing communities on the city's edge. This might simply reflect differences in the economic status of the populations who confine their residential search pattern to one community type or another.

Housing Value Changes in a Selected Set of Communities of Black Entry

A question that frequently arises in regard to outcomes associated with black neighborhood entry is the question of the new population's impact on housing values. From among the spate of studies conducted during the last fifteen years a variety of conflicting answers have been set forth. Interest in value change in this instance is significantly different from that of previous researchers. As a matter of fact value change is viewed in this instance simply as a measure designed to determine the relative attractiveness of the zone of residential entry and changes in that attractiveness over time.

> An in-depth assessment of changes in the relative value of housing was undertaken in a sample of 23 communities. Among the 23 communities chosen for this particular examination, ten were identified as colonies, eight as city edge or spillover communities, and five were from the original survey group. In all but two instances a relative decline in value was evident. Value change was measured by examining shifts in the median value of housing in zones of black entry away from the median value of all housing in the suburban county of residence during the ten-year interval (see Fig. 2–12). If there was no change in value, a given zone of entry would maintain the same distance, expressed in thousand dollars, from the median in both time periods. This amounts to setting the median at zero and then observing the relationship of housing value movement around it over time.

In no way is this kind of ecological description of housing value change to be viewed as synonymous with changes in value of individual properties. But it is important to note the status position of housing value in zones of black entry, as these home purchasers should be aware of the dynamics of the real estate market in which they are participants. Kain and Quigley recently reported that the equity invested in the purchase of housing represents the largest share of the savings of most low and middle income households.[36] Given this situation the question arises, to what extent is the black home purchaser concerned with the future of his investment, or is his demand for decent shelter the overriding concern?

Information available at this point will not permit one to arrive at a definitive conclusion, but it appears that the latter dimension is the overriding one. This is not meant to ignore the economic plight of the prospective home buyer, who may only have a limited down payment and thus is restricted to markets in which assistance in purchasing is made available through real estate and auxiliary institutions. An example of the type of institutional intervention to which the previous statement refers was recently reported by Labovitz in describing the East Cleveland phenomena. East Cleveland is one of the edge communities included in this analysis and one of those that has undergone the most rapid racial transition. Labovitz describes the real estate transactions in the following way:

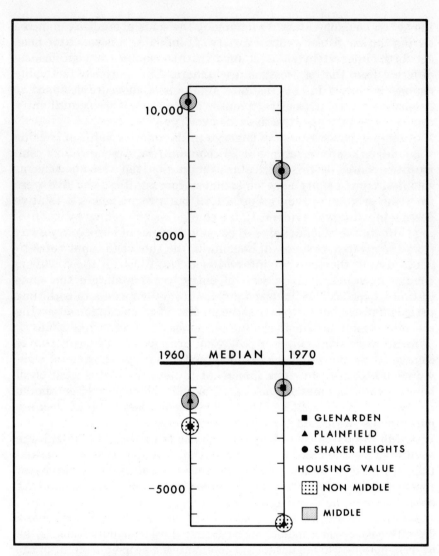

Figure 2-12. Shifts in Housing Value and Class Composition in Selected Communities, 1960–1970

The rapid changes often involved "land contract" sales, with blacks who had fewer opportunities to escape the Cleveland ghettos and few other sources of financing the purchase of a home assuming exhorbitant interest rates.[37]

Data collected during the early sixties showed that blacks had a mean net worth that was considerably less than that for whites in every age category. In those age categories in which home purchases most often occur, the mean net worth of blacks is approximately one-fourth that of whites. Lansing and others concluded from this "that a Negro couple seeking to buy a new home is likely to have difficulty raising a large down payment. They themselves may not have the needed capital, and they may not be able to obtain it by such expedients as borrowing from their parents."[38] This situation obviously forces black home buyers to participate in that market that permits them to acquire for sale the housing most readily available. But further, as Kain and Quigley previously pointed out, operating in this market is likely to negatively affect assets held by the black purchaser group, as a result of purchasing in a depreciating market rather than in an appreciating market.

In 1960, ten of the 23 zones of entry could be described as middle income housing areas in keeping with the definition employed by Davies. In an article in which he undertook to illustrate the change in the geography of middle income housing in several large central cities during the sixties, Davies defined middle class housing zones as those areas in which the median housing value fell within a range of a +$2,000 to a −$2,000 of the city's median.[39] While middle income housing and middle class populations are not synonymous, Davies suggests that the two are highly correlated. The housing areas identified as middle income in 1960 were Plainfield, New Jersey; East Cleveland, Ohio; Westmont and Altadena, California; Freeport, Roosevelt, and Wyandanch, New York; Shaker Heights, Ohio; University City, Missouri; and Carol City, Florida.

The thirteen other zones of entry fell on the low side of the boundary separating middle income housing from low income housing. It might be assumed that these communities provided a housing environment no better than that which is becoming increasingly common in the nation's larger central cities. The non-middle income housing environments were represented by the following communities: Glenarden, Seat Pleasant, and Takoma Park, Maryland; Pomona, East Palo Alto, and Richmond, California; Harvey, Maywood, and East Chicago Heights, Illinois; North Amityville, New York; East Orange, New Jersey; Richmond Heights, Florida; and Wellston, Missouri. Keep in mind that this represented the status of the housing environment in 1960. Lower income housing in this instance simply reflects the fact that housing in these areas could be distinguished from that previously described in terms of cost.

During the ten-year interval between 1960 and 1970 six of the original ten middle class housing zones had shifted downward, such that the middle class designation was no longer appropriate. The communities which were transformed from middle class housing areas to non-middle class housing areas include Plainfield, East Cleveland, Seat Pleasant, Westmont, Freeport, and Richmond. Thus the housing class change was equally distributed among city edge communities and spillover communities. Those middle income housing areas that retained their original status were Wyandanch, Carol City, Shaker Heights, and University City. The latter communities, with the exception of Wyandanch, were the places of residence of black population of high social rank in 1970, as is reflected in the factor scores on the dimension labelled "social rank" in the previously mentioned factor analysis. Paradoxically, Wyandanch ranked nineteenth on the social rank dimension of the communities under investigation in this instance.

For some reason apparently unrelated to the status of the community's population, housing value shifts around the median were minor, thus permitting no change in housing class designation. There was one instance, however, in which the housing value shift was to the right, indicating a movement toward the median. This resulted in housing in a zone described as non-middle class in 1960 being moved into the middle class category by 1970. The community in which this change occurred was Glenarden, Maryland. A similar pattern prevailed in East Chicago Heights, Illinois. The relative improvements in housing value occurred in those communities which were essentially all-black during the base year. The extensive number of new housing starts in the latter two communities obviously shifted their median values in the direction of the median for the county.

A crude attempt has been made to explain the relative change in value of housing in this set of sample communities through the use of a multiple regression model. Initially five variables were regressed upon the absolute value shift away from the county median during the ten-year interval. An example of this technique is described as follows: in 1960 the median value of housing in the zone of black settlement in East Palo Alto, California, was $5,400 below the county median, but by 1970 it was $10,900 below the county median. Thus during the interval a value shift of $5,500 further away from the county median occurred. The initial independent variables included only variables that might be described as internal to the community of entry. They included volume of new construction (houses built 1960–1970) (x_1); percent housing built before 1940 (x_2); percent housing substandard in 1960 (x_3); change in the size of the black population: 1960–1970 (x_4); and change in the size of the total population: 1960–1970 (x_5). A change in the size of the total population was the only significant variable at the 10 percent level (variable x_5).

Five additional variables were later added to the original set. The added variables included four external variables and·one internal variable. Additional variables included: the number of units built in the county between 1960–1970 (x_6); the number of black migrants to the ring, 1960–1970 (x_7); the number of white migrants to the ring, 1960–1970 (x_8); percent units owner occupied 1960–1970 (x_9); percent change in rental occupancy in individual communities, 1960–1970 (x_{10}). The expansion of the number of variables led to two variables being identified as significant at the 10 percent level. In this model run the significant variables were percent housing built before 1940 and percent units owner occupied. Both variables were negatively associated with relative value shifts. The multiple correlation coefficient was raised in the later effort from .650 to .803. Thus while the linear relationship proved weak, the correlation between the observed changes in value in the individual communities and the predicted values were high. The coefficient of determination in the ten-variable model was .65.

Among the 23 sample communities there were nine in which the predicted declines exceeded the observed declines and twelve communities in which the predicted declines were less than the observed declines. As previously mentioned, value increases characterized Glenarden and East Chicago Heights. Among those communities in which the computed decline was greater than the observed decline, there was almost an even distribution between edge communities and colonies. This tends to indicate a somewhat stronger tendency for the edge communities to be negatively influenced by the incorporated variables. The implication here might reflect the greater demand for housing in close proximity to existing black community or the absence of knowledge of housing opportunities remote from the central city, even though that housing has a tendency to be of more recent vintage.

There seems to be a slight tendency for the communities whose value decline was less than the predicted to have a higher black percentage in their total population. But similarly, the largest dollar shifts were generally associated with communities possessing a black majority or near majority, with the exception of the two extreme cases of Takoma Park, Maryland, and Pomona, California, both of which were approximately 12 percent black in 1970. A seeming paradox occurs in the latter two instances, since these are second and seventh ranked communities on the social rank dimension of the communities in this restricted sample. On the other hand, two of the lower social rank communities were among those experiencing the greatest relative decline in value: East Palo Alto and Plainfield. The smallest dollar shifts were generally associated with city edge communities and the largest with the black colonies.

The predicted outcomes in value shifts differ among individual communities as a function of the model used. The ten-variable model generally provided an improvement in the ratio of predicted value shift to the observed value shift, but no evident improvement was discernible in the predicted outcome in seven cases. The best predictions were for the communities of Freeport and Roosevelt, New York; Maywood and Harvey, Illinois; Seat Pleasant, Maryland; and Richmond Heights, Florida. All but two of these were identified as lower income communities in 1960. It is not clear from this examination what additional forces might have been at work that impinged upon value shifts in these individual communities.

THE PROCESS OF BLACK ACQUISITION OF
SUBURBAN HOUSING

If the notion that has been promoted by some economists is correct, then the change in the racial composition of selected inner suburban communities is a natural phenomenon. A number of economists contend that various income groups express a preference for residing in neighborhoods with others of similar economic status, and thus this leads to housing segregation. This thinking has been employed in the development of an arbitrage model of housing market development. Nourse and Phares define arbitrage "to denote the shift in the usage of housing stock from one income stratum to another, the motivating force being profitability."[40] The spillover effect, which describes the suburbanization process leading to the presence of an increasing number of black households in the ring, represents an example of the operation of the arbitrage model. The expression of customer preference is thought to stand at the core of the arbitrage model. The outcome of this expression is a segmented housing market, usually translated in terms of socioeconomic status but frequently also in terms of race.

An Example of the Operation of the Process   No
in a Single Community
James Little recently employed the arbitrage model to analyze the economic and racial transition that is underway in University City, Missouri.[41] Little, in describing the conditions which led to racial transition in University City, had this to say:

> In the decade following the second stage of development, University City underwent changes which foreshadowed the racial change which was to

occur in the latter half of the sixties. Several neighborhoods experienced a slow but steady decline in the mean income ranks of neighborhood occupants, while market prices for housing in neighborhoods fell in response to the increased supply of housing produced by post war building boom. (At the same time, the areas of the city of St. Louis immediately to the east were beginning to experience racial transition. During the latter half of the sixties, racial transition concentrated in the northern neighborhoods of University City occurred at a rapid rate.)[42]

Nourse and Phares have also applied the arbitrage model to the same residential area, although their emphasis was on income transition. They contend that as the housing market operates, new housing is not constructed for the poor, and thus they must bid for already existing housing. The growth of this population leads to increased demand for housing in adjacent zones. This results in a boundary shift between discrete housing markets, leading to the sale of housing to the poor in what was previously a higher income market. These writers, in describing the income transition, indicate that "Normandy, Wellston, West End, and University City lie directly in line with the main thrust of low income movement out from the city."[43] The income transition is thought to lead to a relative decline in housing value, thereby increasing the availability of housing to lower income groups.

Emphasis on the arbitrage process is designed to illustrate how the largest number of black suburban residents have been permitted to acquire suburban housing. The rate and speed of acquisition is a function of demand in the zone contiguous to the target area and the social distance separating the two populations. Given the current income characteristics of the black population, one can expect that the arbitrage process will continue to allocate the largest percentage of suburban housing to that sector of the population. While it is true that upper income blacks are likely to be less constrained by this process, they constitute such a small percentage of the mover population as to have little influence on the emerging pattern.

Mahlon Straszheim concludes that "Increases in black family incomes in the context of a continued segregated market of the type prevailing in 1965 will not solve blacks' housing problems."[44] On the other hand, Brian Berry contends that filtering growing out of the arbitrage process permits blacks to upgrade their housing opportunities. He admittedly qualifies his position by indicating that this outcome was witnessed during a housing boom period.[45] With a downturn in the economy and a slowdown in the number of housing starts, what is the probability that a prospective black homeowner will be more or less likely to purchase housing in a segmented market?

The Segmented Housing Market Versus the
Dual Housing Market

The empirical evidence describing the evolution of some outlying black communities tends to indicate that in some instances blacks are indeed operating in a dual as opposed to a segmented market. In a number of black colonies it appears more reasonable to support the existence of a dual market. This is particularly true of the all-black towns which were previously described—indeed, these colonies constituted traditionally a source of simple shelter. But the acumen displayed by some developers and construction firms in developing middle income housing within these colonies, especially for a black market, is evidence of the operation of a dual market.

It seems that the conceptual support for the arbitrage model rests solely on the transfer of the existing stock of housing from one group to another for reasons previously described, while the case of developing new stock for a race-specific clientele is ignored. It is not known to what extent some of the newer suburban colonies which have emerged recently are the product of the existence of a dual housing market as opposed to a segmented market. Paradoxically, the only positive housing value changes in the 23 communities previously described took place in a dual housing market. This statement is not made in support of dual housing markets, but to simply point up the paradox associated with the modal housing allocation process and how blacks are served by it.

Not much information exists to allow the same type of analysis of the housing environment of the principal communities of black entry as was employed in describing such conditions in the all-black towns. A few studies, though, are beginning to emerge where the principal focus is on individual communities. Among this set, Little's work on University City is one of the better examples. University City was the place of residence of fewer than 1,000 black residents in 1960, but had a population of almost 10,000 blacks by 1970. Blacks were concentrated in the three northern neighborhoods of the city, as these were located adjacent to neighborhoods in St. Louis and Wellston, which had already undergone racial transition (see Fig. 2–13).

The neighborhoods of entry represented zones of newer housing but lower social status than the neighborhoods to the South. Little carefully points out that while racial transition was taking place in the relatively lower status neighborhoods, these neighborhoods were not low income neighborhoods. His view is "that it is the upper middle class blacks who are the leading edge of racial exchange."[46] The latter statement is probably true in those situations where the community of

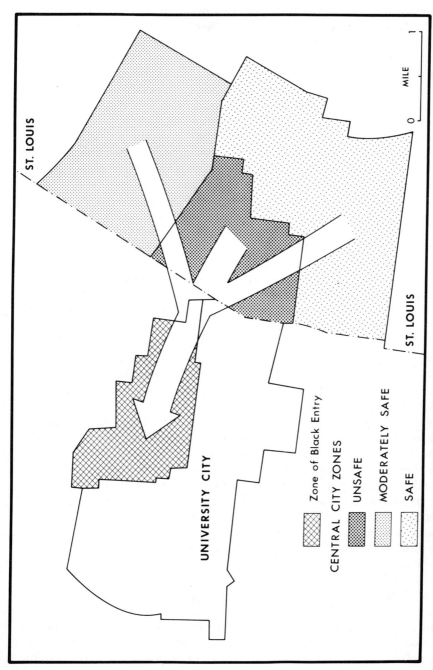

ST. LOUIS

ST. LOUIS

UNIVERSITY CITY

Zone of Black Entry

CENTRAL CITY ZONES

UNSAFE

MODERATELY SAFE

SAFE

0   MILE   1

Figure 2–13. Movement from the Central City to the Suburbs: Another Example of the Spillover Effect

entry is middle class, but certainly not true when the racial transition is taking place in lower status communities.

The level of substandardness prevailing in University City in 1960 was 3.2 percent. This was one of the lower levels of substandardness prevailing among the major entry communities, especially when one considers that much of the housing in this community was built before 1949. But most of the higher status communities of black entry were characterized by only a minimum volume of substandard housing. While substandardness ranged from low to a level that might be considered moderate, seldom did the level approach that prevailing in the all-black towns. Wellston, Missouri, with 47 percent of its housing stock considered substandard, represents an exception.

The general conclusion is that blacks who abandoned the central city for the ring upgraded their housing stock, although other strands of the housing bundle may be equally as important as the physical quality of housing. A 1969 survey of movers to Plainfield, New Jersey, which included black and white movers, revealed that employment opportunity (access) was the single largest reason given by persons choosing to reside in Plainfield.[47] This same survey revealed that more than 70 percent of the black purchasers settled in a deteriorated zone, while only 24 percent of the white movers settled in such zones.

From the data available it is not possible to directly compare the environmental characteristics between communities, even where some data exists which describe these communities of entry. For instance, Little has identified the community of origin of a sample of recent movers to University City. But one does not know what the differences were between the community of origin and that of destination that led to the move. Little implies that since the community of origin was in the second stage of the income-race transition, this might have motivated the movers.[48] A more recent survey of the mover population sheds little additional light on the situation. Approximately 30 percent of the interviewed group originated in the same zone of origin previously described by Little. Recent movers to University City from St. Louis's West End were apparently attracted by their perception of environmental amenities in the target community rather than being repelled by conditions in the previous community.[49]

No more than 30 percent of the movers expressed dissatisfaction with housing conditions in the community of prior residence, although almost 90 percent expressed satisfaction with housing conditions in the entry community. Concern with community safety has been expressed by some blacks as motivating feelings of neighborhood dissatisfaction, but less than one-third of the respondents in this sample indicated that crime was a motivating force in the decision to move. As a matter of fact, the largest majority of movers considered only University City as their choice of a place to live. Most of those indicating that they considered other communities most often mentioned other inner suburbs. Whether this simply represented the awareness space of this population or a careful appraisal of a wide range of choices is unknown. However, it is clear that the characteristics of their previous neighbors was not the overriding factor prompting the move.

SUMMING UP

The all-black towns have usually represented the initial environment of black residence in metropolitan ring communities, but the housing environment in a number of these communities is so unsatisfactory as to make them unlikely targets for future growth. In those instances where such communities have included sizeable segments of vacant land and where there is an apparent demand for new housing for blacks, developers have capitalized on the situation. In a number of instances these communities have been employed to promulgate the dual housing market, as opposed to the segmented housing market. But, likewise, the all-black towns and quasi all-black towns have provided a core for the future of suburban movers; that is, persons growing up in a metropolitan ring environment are likely to move elsewhere in the ring at some future date. There is already evidence that this is occurring within the black population. Most white ring movers already represent other ring locations as the principal source of origin of movers to individual suburban communities.

To date, only a few in-depth studies exist on the character of the residential environment in the areas of newer black settlement in the ring. As the black presence in the ring becomes more pronounced research interest in such communities is likely to grow. It is clear, though, that in most of these communities blacks have become homeowners and are generally expressing their option to live in environments which they perceive as superior to those available to them in central cities. At this point, most blacks are participating in housing markets that are sensitive to their identity as blacks. Thus the arbitrage model well describes the process by which the majority of blacks acquire access to suburban housing markets. A very small percentage of the black population now participates in what Straszheim defines as the white housing sub market (fewer than 15 percent black)—a situation that generally leads to blacks acquiring older housing. It is frequently only in the dual housing market that new housing is available

to blacks who have not attained upper middle class status. The following statement no doubt sums up black attitudes regarding participation in the white submarkets:

> Although the majority of residents questioned in the Chicago study
> believed that better housing and neighborhood facilities existed in white
> areas, only 26.7 percent had ever seriously considered moving out of the
> black community. The deterrents are both economic and psychological,
> the latter in the form of anticipated feelings of isolation and fear of
> personal violence.[50]

The issue of whether blacks should seek residential accommodations outside of a black context is one that has received a good deal of
attention in recent years as some black leaders have advocated a
separatist existence. On this issue Kain was led to comment:

> Increasing numbers of individual black households are finding their way
> out of the ghetto but they do so in general without the active support of
> black leaders and intellectuals. Indeed in some instances they encounter
> hostility from the black community for their efforts to obtain a better life
> for themselves and their families.[51]

Whether Kain's comment on this issue is accurate is open to some
question, but more in terms of intensity than in the crux of the notion.
But if blacks are to continue to secure housing through the arbitrage
process, can residential environments exist in which most black
households are not found in segregated environments?

Under these conditions, how is the abandonment-decay cycle described by Nourse and Phares to be altered? Writing in the early
sixties, the Griers after reviewing population shifts during the previous decade, said, "To eradicate residential segregation in the United
States will require community planning of scope not previously accepted by Americans, plus a level of governmental involvement in
housing and other 'private' areas of the nations economy far exceeding
that which now exists."[52] That statement appears equally appropriate
today if black suburbanization is to represent anything other than a
stage along the abandonment-decay cycle.

Chapter Three

The Educational Environment and Educational Output in Selected Suburban Ring Communities

Most residents, when polled on why they moved to the suburbs, will generally cite some environmental quality that attracted them, such as the style of housing, or openness, lack of congestion, etc.; or the absence of similar qualities in their old neighborhood. But another quality that frequently emerges as a prime motivator is the quality of the schools—expressed either in terms of educational achievement or social class mix, or some combination of the two, depending upon the class identity of the respondent.

More than a decade ago Robert C. Weaver, Secretary of Housing and Urban Development during the Johnson Administration, stated that both white and black middle income families would change their place of residence if middle class schools were not available to their children.[1] Thus, one question we attempt to answer in this chapter is the following: Are blacks who have recently moved into the suburban ring gaining access to good education, such that they can anticipate the life chances of their children to be substantially improved as a result of establishing residence in these locations?

BLACK SUBURBANIZATION AND EDUCATIONAL EXPECTATIONS

There are some mixed feelings in terms of the prospective outcome of such actions if good education is to be measured by average expenditure per pupil. Bernard Frieden recently showed that the average expenditure per pupil in some Los Angeles suburban districts was lower than that for the central city itself.[2] As a matter of record, two of the suburban zones of recent black entry were among those described by Frieden as characterized by average expenditures per pupil that were lower than those for the central city. The gross figure for Los Angeles may disguise the actual allocation to predominantly black schools in the city and thus invalidate the suburban–central city differences, even in the low expenditure suburban zones. Nevertheless, if Weaver correctly assessed the move of a number of blacks from Cleveland's Glenville section to the higher status community of Shaker Heights as a search for superior schools,[3] then the role of schools and its impact on black suburban movement should be examined. Whether the schools which serve these outlying populations actually provide the quality education this mover population is seeking becomes a question of some importance.

AN ASSESSMENT OF EDUCATIONAL QUALITY AND CHARACTER IN THE ALL-BLACK TOWN

As in the previous chapter, the initial and most complete analysis will be directed toward those fifteen communities previously identified as all-black towns. The extent to which these communities fit the suburban image has not yet been thoroughly treated, but it was indicated that these communities are very diverse. If their housing environment can serve as a clue to the extent to which they might be viewed as suburban, many would have to be identified in some alternative fashion. Similarly, the social status of these communities can be differentiated along an axis extending from high to low. When the factor analysis model was used with data for these communities only, the resulting scores were different from those obtained from the entire universe of 50 communities.

However, while the scores differed, there was very little change in the internal ranking of these communities on the social status variable. The higher ranking communities are Glenarden and Hollydale, while the lower ranking communities are Roosevelt City and Cooper Road. It would be most difficult to attempt to identify these communities in terms of social class status from this set of factor scores, as they only compare each community in this small universe in terms of its relative position. Of the fifteen communities, six were assigned scores indicating that they were the least prestigious of the lot. These include Lincoln Heights, Brooklyn, Kinloch, Urbancrest, Roosevelt City, and Cooper Road.

It is assumed that there should exist a differential response to the question of satisfaction with the educational quality provided in the

schools as a function of social rank. While black parents show a relatively high level of dissatisfaction with the education their children
receive nationally, the level of this response has generally been associated with social class. If the response of these parents follows that
of the larger black population, then a more critical assessment of the
quality of education should emerge from those parents who reside in
the communities of higher social rank.

→ Another issue frequently associated with educational quality in the
minds of black parents is that of having their children attend racially
integrated schools. There is some evidence suggesting that the issue of
racially integrated education has received a setback among the
priorities of black parents; nevertheless, this is still thought to represent a desirable goal of a substantial segment of the black population.
Unfortunately, the means available to reduce racial imbalance in the
schools are seldom supported by white parents, and of late they have
been joined by segments of the black population who view schemes to
integrate the schools as educationally irrelevant and in some instances
demeaning. However, the data available will allow us to show the
extent to which residence in these outlying communities has affected
the racial makeup of the schools in terms of both student and faculty
mix.

The parental view of the quality of education available to their
children is almost as diverse as the communities themselves, but in no
instance did fewer than half the respondents feel that their children
were receiving less than a good education.[4] The greatest parental
satisfaction based on the belief that their children were receiving a
high quality education was found in Hollydale, North Fontana, Lincoln Heights, and Glenarden. The greatest dissatisfaction with quality
of education was found in Robbins, East Chicago Heights, Kinloch,
East Palo Alto, and Wyandanch. The latter communities responded
that 20 to 40 percent of their children were receiving a poor education.
Strangely enough, in none of the communities located in the South did
parents view the education their children received as being substantially subpar. As a matter of fact, among the three Deep South communities the overwhelming response was that the education their
children received was good.

What variables influenced the parental perceptions of quality of
education is unknown, but on the basis of a subjective assessment the
amount of dissatisfaction with the schools is generally limited. In those
communities in which a disproportionate percentage of the respondents showed dissatisfaction with the schools, they recommended that
the hiring of better teachers was the best solution to the problem of
poor quality education. The implications of this response are unclear,

as they do not specify what are thought to be the weaknesses of the existing teaching staff. Objective data on school quality is missing for most of the school districts in this universe. The most extensive objective information available for a single school was that which described the schools of North Fontana, California.

The Case of North Fontana

The black children of North Fontana, an unincorporated settlement beyond the margins of the city of Fontana, California, attend school in the latter community. The black population of North Fontana is small and concentrated, and is similarly concentrated in a single school in the Fontana Unified School District. Most of North Fontana's black children of elementary school age are enrolled in the Juniper School. In 1972 slightly less than one-third of the enrollment at Juniper School was black, thus, while blacks are highly segregated in terms of their residential pattern in the community, they do not attend schools that are racially imbalanced. The latter is no doubt an outgrowth of their small numbers rather than an indication of a policy favoring racially balanced schools.

A variety of tests are given in the nation's schools annually as a means of evaluating the development of cognitive skills. One such test is designed to test reading comprehension. In the fall of 1971 there were four sixth grade classes at Juniper Elementary School, all of which included black enrollment. The level of black enrollment in any given class is unknown, but the reading scores for these four groups ranged from an average reading level, by group, of 2.8 to 5.8 years in achievement. Thus in one class the average reading level fell only slightly below grade, while in another class sixth grade pupils were performing at approximately the third grade level. (There is some indication that these scores reflected the use of a tracking system.) Interestingly, the response of the black parents in North Fontana to the quality of education question was that their children were receiving an excellent education.

It is difficult to determine from this data whether the parents' view of the quality of education their children were receiving was accurate or inaccurate. It could be that the parents were responding to the perceived educational progress of their children from out of their own educational backgrounds, or from the absence of problems in the schools, or the absence of racial isolation in the schools, or some combination of these. Nevertheless, it is evident that black sixth graders from North Fontana were involved with their peers in an education experience in which performance varied from slightly to well below expected grade level. Again, it is not clear what the racial or ethnic composition was in any of these four groups.

The Level of Education Provided in the Home Community

The amount and level of education received in the home community is generally related to its size, and in some instances its political status. Among the fifteen communities included in this study, four basic patterns emerge. The dominant pattern is one that finds elementary schooling being provided in the home community, while pupils travel outside the home community to secure a secondary education. Communities in this group include Lawnside, East Chicago Heights, Urbancrest, Brooklyn, and Roosevelt City, all of which were communities of fewer than 5,000 residents in 1970.

The second most frequently observed pattern was that in which the individual communities provided both elementary and secondary education for their children. This pattern is associated with communities of larger size than the previous group. None of the communities in this group had fewer than 5,000 residents in 1970, and most were closer to 10,000. Among this group of communities are Cooper Road, East Palo Alto, Wyandanch, and Kinloch. All but the latter community are large, politically unincorporated tracts of rather recent origin, at least in terms of a black presence. The third pattern includes those communities in which some of the pupils attend elementary school within the home community, while others journey to schools in nearby communities to attend elementary school. All children receive their secondary schooling outside the home community.

Finally, there are two communities in which all schooling is provided outside the zone of black residence. These communities are Hollydale and North Fontana, both small, unincorporated settlements whose satisfaction with their educational system exceeds that of all other communities in the group. Two obvious questions arise: (1) Which of these patterns produces the most responses of satisfaction from residents; and (2) To what extent do these patterns lead to racial isolation or racial balance in the schools?

Parental Satisfaction

The highest level of parental satisfaction with the quality of education that their children receive occurs in those communities in which all education is received outside the community proper. Communities in which some elementary facilities are located within the community and some outside rank second highest in level of satisfaction. The lowest level of satisfaction is expressed by parents in whose communities both elementary and secondary educational programs are available. It is reasonable to assume that it is not the patterns themselves that promote dissatisfaction, but the variety of conditions associated with these patterns. The social class mix of the student population, the racial composition of the schools, and the racial composition of the teaching staff are all related to the locational characteristics of the school vis-à-vis the school population, the racial and class character of the adjacent population, and the regional effect.

The Social Class Mix of the School Population

There is a growing body of literature which suggests that the achievement of blacks on standardized tests purporting to measure cognitive development are directly related to the social class of the school population. A government publication of a few years ago stated that "a predominantly Negro school is generally a predominantly lower class school. If we classify the elementary schools on the basis of proportion of lower class students in the school instead of the proportion of Negroes, we find that the contrasts in achievement are even stronger."[5] Thus, it has been suggested that cognitive achievement is a function of the social class composition of the school when other significant inputs are held constant.

In most instances the child attends elementary school in his home community, and thus the social class of the school reflects the social class mix of the local community. In some instances the communities are very homogeneous in terms of their socioeconomic mix, while in others greater socioeconomic diversity prevails. In those communities which are large enough to support more than a single elementary school it is possible for the schools to be characterized by differences in social class. Whether or not this shows up in the school achievement levels is unknown at this point. Likewise, if the secondary educational facilities are located beyond the margins of the community, then the social class mix of the school will be influenced by the nature of the school feeder patterns. Thus it is possible for children who have attended elementary school in a district where most of the children are from low social rank homes to attend junior high school or high school in an environment wherein the social class mix is more diverse.

An example of the latter situation might best be illustrated by comparing the patterns of educational arrangements for children in Lincoln Heights and Kinloch, both old, low status, nongrowth communities. In Lincoln Heights the children attend secondary schools located outside the home community whose feeder patterns allow them to draw upon a socially diverse student population, with a sizeable percentage of students from higher status backgrounds in attendance. On the other hand, Kinloch students attend grades K–12 within the home community.[6] If what some educators have portrayed as an advantageous school environment is valid, then those students from Lincoln Heights should have an educational advantage, if other variables remain constant.

Racial Composition of Schools— Four Patterns

The racial composition of the school generally reflects the racial composition of the community of residence if there is no direct effort to alter the situation. Where no interventionist strategy has been introduced in the case of school pattern one, where all education is provided within the home community, then racially imbalanced schools will be the rule. In the case of school pattern two, which sends the children outside the home community for secondary training, the racial composition of the schools will be influenced by the racial composition of the adjacent communities. When the black community represents an isolated exclave, such as Urbancrest or Lawnside, its children will in all likelihood receive their secondary schooling in a non-racially isolated school environment.

Normally the third pattern (some elementary schooling provided inside the local community and some outside) reflects a direct intervention on the part of some level of government to accomplish some desired end. This might be an attempt to eliminate de jure or de facto school segregation, to improve the economic efficiency of school operations by a consolidating technique, or to achieve one of a number of other possible goals. Robbins, Richmond Heights, and Glenarden reflect this pattern. In the first two cases there has been a reduction in the intensity of the single race school. The recent court mandate to desegregate the schools in Maryland's Prince Georges County has had the effect of reducing the racial imbalance in the schools in Glenarden and adjacent areas. Pattern four, which has children receiving all of their schooling beyond the margins of the home community, has generally been characterized by little de facto school segregation. The four patterns of organization of education for children from predominantly black residential environments influence the extent to which they also attend schools that are predominantly black.

There is no way of determining how the racial composition of the schools influenced the parents' perception of the quality of education received by their children. When parents were asked to specify what they thought to be the racial composition of the schools, there was often a diversity of opinion on what the racial composition was for a given school, although there was general agreement that the school either was or was not predominantly black. In one instance there seemed to be a tendency to underestimate the actual percentage blacks constituted in the population as a whole. In 1971–72, fewer than two-thirds of the parents of children in Glenarden's Glenardenwoods School thought it to be more than 80 percent black, when in fact it was 99.8 percent black. A similar pattern prevailed with parents at other Glenarden schools (see Table 3–1).

There is no consistent pattern of parental response in terms of school quality related to their perceptions of the racial composition of the schools. Obviously a number of other factors might influence parental perception of school quality. Among these might be the racial composition of the teaching staff, the means by which pupils travel to school, the extent to which teachers reside in the community, as well as any of many other variables. When parents were asked to specify the racial makeup of the teacher corps, they indicated that in eight of the fifteen communities half or more of the teachers were black. Black teachers were thought to be in the majority in those communities which previously were de jure segregated, were old established black communities, and/or which provided all education within the community itself.

SOME SOCIAL ATTRIBUTES OF THE SCHOOL ENVIRONMENT

Qualities of the teaching staff are often included among those attributes that are significant for educational success. Among those objective qualities most often taken into consideration as factors bearing on the achievements of students are: percentage of teachers with advanced training, years of teaching experience, verbal skills, and so forth. In a few instances, selected subjective attributes have also been considered.

Table 3–1. Perceived and Actual Racial Composition of Glenarden Schools, 1971–1972

School	Perceived Racial Composition (% Black)				Actual Racial Composition (% Black)
	20–39	*40–59*	*60–79*	*80–100*	
Glenardenwoods	7.4	11.1	18.5	62.9	99.8
Kenmoor		60.0	40.0		88.3
Ardmore	35.7	50.0	7.1	7.1	96.2

Source: Results of 1972 Field Survey and Prince Georges County Board of Education

James Guthrie and others attempted to measure the effect of teacher attitudes on achievement. They found that in those instances where the teacher indicated satisfaction with his choice of a career and satisfaction with his or her current assignment at a given school, student achievement was significantly higher.[7] Likewise they found if teachers did not think the staff worked well together student achievement was lower.[8]

School Tone

The impact of teacher attitude on the students' academic performance as well as other overt forms of behavior is not well understood, or at least is not as readily measurable as some of the other individual and environmental relationships. A very incisive view of teacher attitudes on student behavior was recently described from a clinical perspective by Robert Coles. Unlike the work of Guthrie and others, there is no way of arriving at statistically significant relationships using the methods employed by Coles, but the power of the subjective analysis employed by him is highly illuminating. In attempting to assess teacher-student relationships, Coles seeks to pinpoint, among other things, an intangible element in the school which he describes as tone. He describes "tone" as:

> . . . a product, immediately, of a particular principal and set of teachers and group of children, and even the climate of opinion that characterizes a given region, a state, a city, a neighborhood, then a street, a classroom, eventually emerging in a teacher who teaches in a certain way, and across the room, a child who responds to it all in a certain way.[9]

The tone that characterizes a given school is believed to be critical to the expected educational outcome. The established tone becomes even more critical in those school settings where both racial and cultural differences lead to conflict between pupils and teachers. Under such circumstances, tone is believed to intervene in the successful outcome of the learning process. Just as Coles has previously stated, the tone which prevails within the school districts under investigation here is likely to be diverse, reflecting an amalgam of variables that produce a series of unique educational outcomes. This should be expected when we consider that the communities range from those which are Old South in tone to those where the initial presence of black students in the school possibly created anxiety for both parents and school officials.

The parental perception of the racial composition of the teaching staff indicates that the older communities in which the schools were formerly de jure segregated still maintain predominantly black faculty. Brooklyn, which is 99 percent black, is perceived to have a teaching staff which is 98 percent black. Kinloch, with a similar population composition, also has a faculty that is perceived to be 85 percent black. These two schools represent one end of the spectrum of faculty racial imbalance. On the other end of the spectrum is the very small percentage of black teachers in the schools attended by North Fontana children. It likewise appears that these communities are doing little to change the racial imbalance of their faculties. Parents reported that more faculty integration was taking place in Glenarden, East Palo Alto, Lincoln Heights, Cooper Road, Richmond Heights, Robbins, and Urbancrest.

The impact of this type of alteration on the learning environment is unknown, but will no doubt be governed by the overt hostilities and mutual sensitivities of both faculty and students who might have been thrown together for the first time. The success of this experience will in large measure be related to the emergence of Coles's previously described tone. One might contend that the expected outcome might be more favorable in the Southern school districts, provided that previous antipathies fail to emerge. This contention is predicated on the cultural commonalities that prevail among white and black southerners, although class differentials might void some of the assumed cultural commonality.

Wyandanch and East Palo Alto: An Example
of Divergent Inputs

The two communities which deviate most from the fifteen survey communities are Wyandanch, New York and East Palo Alto, California. Unlike most of the other communities in the group, these two communities are undergoing a racial transition. While they both possessed a small black core population in 1960, blacks constituted an inordinately small percentage of the total population. But by 1970, approximately 60 and 65 percent of the population in these respective communities were black. Thus, Wyandanch and East Palo Alto are more nearly akin to the group of communities which have previously been described as black colonies. They are both similar in population size, and are somewhat isolated, politically unincorporated communities which constitute black islands in an area surrounded by a white majority. While these communities possess a number of objective commonalities, there are some differences in the way their schools are perceived by parents.

In evaluating the quality of the local elementary schools, the parents of Wyandanch introduced a fourth quality measure to the three included in the survey instrument. This additional measure was "fair."

It is apparent that this group of parents tends to view "fair" as representing a quality that is less positive than "good." Fair then becomes the modal quality describing Wyandanch schools. In both instances the bulk of the parents reporting had children attending three separate elementary schools. In each of the elementary schools serving the largest share of Wyandanch's black children the category fair was used most often to describe the quality of education dispensed. In only a single instance did a respondent describe the quality as excellent. It was assumed that the social class background of the parents in the individual neighborhoods might have played a role in their assessment of school quality. There were only slight identifiable differences in the respondent population by school as measured by the level of educational attainment of household head and wife, and the occupation of head. Likewise, there was no discernible difference in response to the quality issue from school to school.

If the same measures are employed to ascertain the class status of the parents in East Palo Alto, it will be discovered that they rank slightly higher than those of Wyandanch. This difference also shows up in the data on social rank emanating from the previously described factor model. Slight differences do distinguish the response relating to individual schools in East Palo Alto, but they do not appear to be related to the social class of the respondents. In one instance, 30 percent of the respondents thought the quality of education available at one school was excellent, but it must be remembered that our sample is comprised of small numbers. Nevertheless, no fewer than 60 percent of the respondents view the quality of education available to their children in local public elementary schools as being good or better. On an individual school basis, those who viewed the school as poor ranged from approximately 8 percent to almost 29 percent.

One group of residents in East Palo Alto who thought the local public schools were failing their children eventually set about to establish an alternative school, which they named Nairobi Day Schools, Inc.[10] This attempt was initiated after parental efforts to place their children in what they considered superior schools in nearby communities led to unfortunate results. They perceived that their children were the victims of psychic abuse in the all-white environments that characterized the nearby communities. The Nairobi Day School was recently described as an example of a school which is developing a unique Afro-American educational model, based on corporate commonality.[11] Professor Wilson, in describing this model, states:

> The first posited value, grounded in Afro-American folkways, aids in defining a basically Afro-American school, the school district as a

community-family. This "community" is conceived of as that group of persons, diverse in aspirations, motivations, and skills, who identify with each other and who function as an extended family in order to encourage the overall development of the community's children.[12]

The schema described by Professor Wilson is a construct born out of the sense of futility of black parents who see the European-American educational system failing their children. The Nairobi Day School emerged full bloom only after it was learned that black children in good schools may be prevented from learning because of the hostility projected upon them in a culturally alien environment. The extent to which this experiment is likely to be replicated is unknown, but chances are that they are small. The success of such programs is difficult to measure, as the educational objectives of the program differ from those established for most schools. Nevertheless, the establishment of such a program probably implies that there is some element present in the East Palo Alto community that is missing in Wyandanch. Just what that element is is unknown at this point, although there are some differences that may or may not contribute to the differential response to the educational system by these two sets of parents. Two obvious differences relating to the educational infrastructure of the two school systems is the racial composition of the teaching staffs, and the mode of journey to school.

The Wyandanch parents' perception of the racial composition of the teaching staff in their children's school showed that they believed the teaching staff to be approximately 70 percent white. There was only slight variation around this value from school to school. One might question what the school tone might be in a set of predominantly black suburban schools which are isolated enclaves of lower to working class populations. Depending upon the sensitivity of the teachers in this conflict-prone setting, the learning environment might be reduced to one in which the principal effort is to police rather than teach. It was mentioned earlier that the hiring of better teachers was the most frequent response by parents who perceived their children to be receiving a poor education. In Wyandanch, 66 percent of the respondents suggested this solution, while 8.3 percent suggested better discipline and another 8.3 percent suggested hiring guards. Neither of the latter two responses appeared on the survey instrument but represent parental write-in items.

It is possible that the racial composition of the schools' teachers influence their identification with the schools' clients. The parents of Wyandanch perceived that only 5 percent of the teachers in their schools resided in the community, a factor that might contribute to a lack of community understanding. One might suspect that the black students and white teachers in Wyandanch are "strangers when they meet." Wyandanch is physically spread out so that most pupils are bused to school. No children in the sample population walked to school. There seems to be no opposition to this practice on the part of black parents, as busing in this instance is unrelated to attempts to reduce the level of racial imbalance in the schools. Thus busing is not an issue, as it is carried out simply to facilitate the movement of children to satisfy a basic educational goal.

On the attributes just discussed, East Palo Alto stands at the opposite pole. Parents perceive that 72 percent of the teaching staff are black, approximately 46 percent reside in the community, and roughly 75 percent of all pupils walk to school. Just what these differences mean in terms of parental perception or objective accomplishments is unknown. But in two communities which are quite similar in racial composition and location within a metropolitan area, they differ significantly in terms of the previously specified educational inputs. As a community which has become predominantly black, East Palo Alto's schools reflect this fact in both the student and teacher makeup of those units. However, a predominantly black faculty did not grant assurance to the parents that their children would receive a quality education. For had that been the case, the Nairobi Day School would not have come into existence.

In East Palo Alto only 32.2 percent of the parents thought that the hiring of better teachers would improve the quality of education in their children's school. This is approximately one-half the ratio of the response level on this item as was given by Wyandanch parents. Almost 30 percent of the East Palo Alto parents thought the quality of education could be raised by upgrading teachers' salaries, while another 22.7 percent thought that busing pupils to other districts would aid in providing their children with a higher quality education.

In these two school systems, which are essentially self-contained and have all levels of education available, a different set of practices have evolved which may have some bearing on the school tone. In some ways this is a very precarious concept, but yet it can and does appear to affect the learning environment in which pupils and teachers interact, and subsequently the outcome of that interaction is reflected in school performance and parental satisfaction. If tone is to be objectively measured as a cluster of attitudes and behaviors, an evaluation profile employed by the Cincinnati public schools probably would come close to providing an index against which school performance might be measured.

Among the many items appearing in the Cincinnati school profile are survey items designed to elicit a student response illustrating his attitude toward himself and his school, and a parental response aimed at evaluating the school atmosphere, quality of the school program, and school-pupil relations and educational issues. The profile also includes a group of items eliciting a response from teachers relative to staff morale, pupil characteristics, working conditions, and community and parent contact. The racial composition of the school and its staff is also given, along with information designed to allow the school to be identified in terms of its socioeconomic status. It is possible that a schema of the sort devised by the Cincinnati school system could lead to more effective pinpointing of those inputs that are most significant in enhancing educational achievement.

For whatever reason, the school tone appears to be more favorable in East Palo Alto than in Wyandanch, when measured against parental response. But without objective school achievement results, it is difficult to ascertain if parental response is correlated with level of school achievement, or if this reflects a response to a more general school situation.

The issue of busing was not an "issue" in the schools just described. It was practiced extensively in one situation and was absent in the other. In the community where it was practiced it was unrelated to racial issues. In the remaining communities in the survey group there were variations in the extent to which students were bused to school. In East Chicago Heights and Brooklyn no children were reported bused to school, and among the remainder, only three communities reported that more than half the children from the sample households were being bused. The three communities in which busing was the principal mode of conveying students to school were North Fontana (88 percent), Hollydale (88 percent), and Richmond Heights (51.2 percent). Likewise the quality-of-education response of these parents was generally good. It is clear that in the schools in which students are largely bused there is a general absence of racial imbalance. On the other hand, those schools in which busing is employed only on a limited scale or not at all are most severely imbalanced. The latter include Brooklyn, Lawnside, Kinloch, Roosevelt City, and East Chicago Heights.

THE ISSUE OF RACIAL IMBALANCE AND BUSING: ONE PERSPECTIVE

The issue of the educational value of racially mixed schools and the subsequent necessity for busing remain unresolved, although Robert Crain recently demonstrated from survey data a strong case in favor of integrated education. His data indicate that school integration leads to an increase in self-control among blacks and the adoption of values that lead to school success and friendships, which aid in securing employment opportunities that were previously unavailable to blacks.[13] However, he was very careful to point out under what conditions these advantages accrue, and how they vary between regions. In regards to the use of busing as a technique to facilitate integration, Crain states that: "Even if busing has some negative consequences, these are probably outweighed by the various benefits from education which the bused child would receive."[14] David Armor, on the other hand, was less enthusiastic than Crain about the positive benefits of what he calls "induced integration." Reviewing the data from a number of cases of suburban school integration, he found that achievement gaps between black and white children remained after the experience had been underway; that bused students did not improve their aspirations for college; nor was black self-esteem heightened by the experience.[15] One of Armor's policy conclusions after reviewing the data is as follows: ". . . that massive mandatory busing for purposes of improving student achievement and interracial harmony is not effective and should not be adopted at this time."[16]

On the surface, the conflicting statements of Crain and Armor are indicative of the complexity of the matter and the difficulty involved in producing research results that have universal applicability. Thomas Pettigrew and others have accused Armor of presenting a distorted and incomplete review in his article, "The Evidence on Busing," which, they claim, is supported by a weak methodological structure.[17] This kind of argument is not uncommon, and counter arguments can be expected to emerge which will support the alternative position. Gordon Foster's recent statement on this whole issue tends to sum it up well. He states that, "Research on the cognitive and affective results of desegregation will, and should continue, but it may never really tell us much except what we want to hear."[18]

For almost two decades now, the issue of eliminating racially segregated schools has concerned not only schoolmen, various special purpose groups, local, state, and national government, but most of all, parents. Some progress has been made in this area, especially in those de jure segregated school districts to which the 1954 Supreme Court decision directly addressed itself. But that progress has been slow, with most of it occurring within the last five years. In the more troublesome and intractable area of de facto segregation, less progress has been made, but district courts are beginning to hear such cases. The court decrees to date have been mixed.

In the communities involved in this study, the level of racial imbalance is less in those districts which were previously de jure segregated, but even here some resistance is evident. Much of the difficulty growing out of attempts to desegregate schools is that desegregation is defined in terms of legal interpretations, which revolve around a racially dichotomous population described as white or nonwhite. This interpretation might have been satisfactory when the segregation issue was totally confined to the southern United States, but once the issue and attempts at resolution were extended beyond the borders of the South, this legalistic view of race created additional problems. One example was the resistance of integration attempts on the part of a segment of San Francisco's Chinese population, which is racially nonwhite.

School Segregation: The Southern Model

Blacks residing in the South were historically provided education inferior to that of their white neighbors—if educational quality is to be measured by the availability of educational facilities, the training of teachers, and a host of other educational inputs. Not only that, but the loss of self-esteem growing out of a social system designed to demonstrate the inherent inferiority of a group, of which these inadequate facilities were but a simple reminder, was further evidence of an intangible message, not only of inferior education but inferior status as well.

This left no course other than a legal one in seeking to redress this grievance. Out of this legal recourse and the opposition of white citizens, particularly in the South but by no means confined to this region, attempts at successful school integration have often left much to be desired. Some of this lack of success can be attributed to the mechanistic way in which the problem has been handled as a means of satisfying the law. For those who have attributed failure to such programs, as did Armor, Foster reminds us that, "Desegregation alone does not guarantee quality education, but then desegregation is not only a commitment to improve test scores—it is a pledge to provide equality and justice in a society plagued by racism."[19] It is now evident that the whole notion of what constitutes racially integrated schools needs to be reviewed, and a more realistic means of perfecting this end established.

To date, most schools defined as being racially balanced are schools which have been desegregated as a result of court action or are in the process of being transformed from racially imbalanced schools to racially balanced ones. In either instance the problems attendant upon such situations promote an atmosphere that often leads to mutual feelings of disdain and the mutual intensification of stereotypic images. This simply means that demographic integration in and of itself cannot be expected to produce the academic achievements expected by black parents, nor the lessening of white achievement oftentimes expected by white parents. Since so many of the attempts at school desegregation are engaged in without community support, special efforts must be made to reduce the probability of the occurrence of the self-fulfilling prophecy. This means that the attributes of the individual student should be considered when the decision is made to place him in a given social environment in order to predict his or her behavior in that given social context. Thus the appropriate racial mix that might define an integrated rather than simply a desegregated situation would vary as a function of the individual attributes that would permit two racially dichotomous populations to function successfully in an environment characterized by a minimum of stress. This would require a kind of attention seldom devoted to the problem.

That the problem of producing a maximally successful experiment is likely to be difficult is an understatement. It has been indicated that summer workshops designed to ease the task of middle class teachers confronted with the problem of teaching students described as disadvantaged have often led to little in the way of educational accomplishment. If programs such as these have failed to produce valid results, this is indicative of the difficulty involved in a program frequently undergirded by parental hostilities. In the early years of school desegregation in a number of southern school districts, care was taken to select the black pupils who would serve as the "guinea pigs" in a limited experiment designed to enable the district to be viewed as satisfying minimal compliance with the law. While this selection process no doubt led to the success of the program, it was engaged in for questionable reasons, which had little to do with providing mutual benefits to both the black and white students enrolled.

Black and White Responses

Philosophical changes among segments of the black community, which have grown out of a heightened interest in black pride and black belonging, have led to the surfacing of some strange bedfellows. An example of one such new alliance in opposition to attempts to further desegregate the nation's schools is that which found CORE's Roy Innis joining forces with Governor McKeithen of Louisiana to slow down the process of desegregation in that state. Even Governor Wallace found some support in the black community from a segment of the cultural nationalists. This is indicative of the frustration growing out of repeated attempts on the part of black people to alter their status in American society by becoming a part of the nation's dominant institutions, where white schools were historically viewed as the mechanism which could best aid in the reduction of the income gap separating whites from blacks.

White parents have been equally protective in maintaining control over this resource which, it is believed, provides their children with an added advantage. This has been especially true of working class and lower middle class white parents. Lillian Rubin, who recently analyzed the class struggle aimed at limiting busing in a western school district, shows that lower class white parents who were identified as conservatives are basically interested in their children learning the three Rs and the maintenance of discipline in the classrooms.[20] It was learned in this situation that this was also a principal educational goal of black parents. Thus these two groups of parents, who seem to share the greatest commonality in terms of educational philosophy, are the ones who are most often thrust into the roles of antagonists in attempts at school desegregation.

Many blacks have now reversed their position on the merits of school integration and are frequently heard to remark that it is not necessary for their children to sit in the classroom with white children to get a good education. This is obviously true if one means by a good education simply the transmission of a basic set of skills that persons with a given level of training are expected to have. But education is obviously more than that, and if blacks and whites are not expected to maintain parallel institutions in all facets of American life, then some meaningful form of school integration appears necessary. This is said even in the face of the growing movement in the black community for control of its institutions and some of the perceived advantages that flow from it.

For this, too, is simply another strategy designed to cope with racism and a kind of economic imperialism and protectionism fostered by those currently in power. This attitude can be seen from a memorandum prepared by one of the President's speech writers in February 1970. This memorandum has been titled, "The Ship of Integration Is Going Down."[21] The writer states, "In short, integration appears to damage rather than advance both the cause of education and the cause of racial harmony . . ." and states further, "it is not our ship; it belongs to national liberalism—and we cannot salvage it; and we ought not be aboard."[22] Thus it appears that the politics of education at this time is amassing a divergent set of supporters to maintain essentially the status quo.

SCHOOL LIFE STYLE AND COGNITIVE DEVELOPMENT

An additional facet of school life, which impinges both upon educational achievement as well as racial balance, is the prevailing life style of the pupils as reflected in the way that they interact both with one another and the faculty. School tone was previously discussed almost totally from the perspective of the student-teacher interaction. While this is important, it is equally important how students relate to one another and how this relationship establishes the principal life style dimension of the school.

Schools which are predominantly black are frequently labeled lower class schools, even though objective data might prove otherwise. Such descriptive labels more appropriately define the school's life style. This style may be expressed in terms of the basic mode of conduct, which establishes a set of values or affectations to which a significant number of students will aspire. Thus a school's life style might be characterized by specific language patterns, informal dress codes (peer group accepted styles), defiance of authority, violence, and other forms of antisocial behavior. A given mix of these attributes could lead to the lower class labeling so commonplace in identifying schools which include a significant percentage of black or other minority populations. It appears that even when a majority of the students are not lower class in terms of the objective characteristics of the households of which they are a part, the school's life style is established by a small minority of students whose values tend to dominate the total school atmosphere. Such an atmosphere leads other students to adopt, or at least passively condone, these life style dimensions as a means of either peer group acceptance or sheer survival in what becomes a hostile environment. The prevailing school life style often impinges upon the achievement results of that school.

The complexity of the latter issue makes its resolution difficult. This may be explained as being related to the effect of the nonschool environment on the school as it is reflected in patterns of teacher-student interaction and the general lessening of parental authority in society at large, coupled with individual efforts to survive in a highly economically competitive society—a situation that often results in the weakening of familial bonds. To what extent the latter set of conditions prevails in the communities under review is not known. But it is conjectured that elements of this life style would be least often found in the more traditional communities, but found more frequently in those communities in which recent movement from the central city is a principal characteristic. Thus a nongrowth, low income community would be less likely than a moderate income community to show signs of the lower class life style in the schools.

Parental Educational Achievement

One issue that has not yet been examined is the educational character of the adult population of the survey communities themselves. The educational background of this group probably affects their own outlook in terms of expressed satisfaction with the quality of education their children are receiving, their realistic aspirations for their children, and their willingness to support the cost of education as reflected in increasing tax burdens. If the black communities which lie beyond the margins of the central city are to be equated with other suburban communities in what has grown to represent the suburban myth, then this should be reflected in a variety of social and economic measures of their population, with level of education representing a sensitive one.

It is generally conceded that the most highly trained individuals in American society are today's residents of suburbia. Among the communities under review there is considerable variation in level of educational attainment of the adult population. It is apparent, when level of educational attainment of these communities is examined, that the achieved level of education in a number of instances is extremely low. Blacks nationwide gained almost two years in median educational attainment during the sixties, bringing the group median to ten years of formal education. In seven instances the survey communities failed to register levels of educational attainment on a par with national levels of black educational attainment. When one takes into consideration the fact that the great majority of blacks are residents of the central city, it is clear that the black population in almost half the survey communities has achieved educational levels below those characterizing the central city black populations.

The prevailing level of educational attainment in these communities should permit one to typecast them in terms of their outlook as it relates to educational aspirations and achievement for their children. It was previously noted that the best educated segment of the American population resides in suburbia, but likewise there are variations in the level of educational attainment that characterize suburbs of a given type. Leo Schnore, sometime ago, developed a suburban classification scheme that identified suburbs in terms of the ratio of their labor forces which resided within the community. He identified these suburbs as employing, intermediate, and residential.[23] Schnore investigated 300 suburban communities and found that employing suburbs had the smallest percentage of the adult population having completed high school (43.2 percent). The intermediate and residential suburbs showed higher levels of educational attainment than the employing: 48.2 and 55.8 percent of their respective adult populations had completed high school.[24]

Of the fifteen survey communities involved in our study, all must be identified as residential suburbs. Five of the communities in the present sample were characterized by higher levels of educational attainment than the Schnore group; they include Glenarden, Lawnside,

Hollydale, East Palo Alto, and Wyandanch. Another four communities were characterized by having a similar level of high school graduates, with a smaller percentage of the population of the remaining communities having attained this educational goal. It should be remembered, however, that the earlier sample was based on 1960 information. There is some discrepancy in the reported level of educational attainment derived from the field survey and the 1970 census. Lawnside, New Jersey represents an extreme deviation between the two data sources. The 1970 census shows that only 32.2 percent of Lawnside's population had completed high school, while the 1972 field survey revealed that 46 percent of the adult population had completed high school. One possible reason for this large discrepancy might be a post-1970 migration of higher status blacks to the community. This migration was associated with the development of a new housing tract within the community.

Levittown, in Nassau County, New York, one of the first of the new breed of post-World War Two suburban communities, was characterized by a median level of educational attainment of 12.2 years in 1960.[25] Only two of the survey communities fared this well, Glenarden and Hollydale appearing to possess populations which are similar in educational attainment to that of one of America's suburban prototypes in 1960. Employing median levels of educational attainment, the survey communities have been divided into four groups. The critical levels of median educational attainment employed were $\geq$ 11.5 years; 10.0–11.4 years; 9.0–9.9 years; and < 9.0 years.

Group I includes Glenarden, Hollydale, East Palo Alto, and Wyandanch. Group II includes North Fontana, Lawnside, Robbins, and Richmond Heights. Group III includes Urbancrest, Lincoln Heights, East Chicago Heights, and Kinloch. Group IV includes Brooklyn, Roosevelt City, and Cooper Road. It was decided to assign a descriptive terminology to each of these educational classes that implicitly describes the manner in which parents might be expected to respond to the local educational system, and the corresponding reaction of the communities' children to the educational program of which they are a part.

Group I communities are described as modern, as they represent communities in which most adults have graduated from high school. These are communities in which parental expectations as they relate to the educational system are probably highest. But at the same time these are communities in which the pupils are probably most independent and assertive and thereby express the greatest willingness to exert themselves as individuals. Groups II communities might be thought of as emerging, showing some of the characteristics of the communities in the modern group but still plagued by some of the drawbacks of the traditional group (Group III). Nevertheless, parents in communities such as these should be expected to place greater emphasis on the value of the quality of education that their children receive. The greatest differences among the two might be the latter group's inability to precisely evaluate the kind of education that is available to their children. The children themselves, having been socialized largely in a more conservative environment, are likely to be less assertive and possibly more amenable to conforming to the institutional guidelines established by the schools.

Group III communities are those in which the parental median level of educational attainment is less than ten years. The modal educational class in three of these communities was less than eight years of training. This, coupled with the fact that these are communities which have long existed in their present form, makes it unlikely that they view education as a panacea designed to alter one's status. Here, neither parents nor students are expected to place great faith in education, but both are likely to show greater respect for the institution of education simply as function of their obedience to authority. The pre-traditional communities (Group IV) might be expected to behave much as the traditional communities behave, with little expectation that quality of education is likely to influence their children's life chances. Here, the students are likely to be less assertive, nondisruptive, and to conform to a code of conduct that emphasizes respect for authority. The schools, then, might be assumed to provide a ritualistic experience for most of those students who remain there until they are forced out or choose to detour from this experience to others that might be considered more meaningful in terms of their immediate goals.

The cost of supporting educational systems continues to soar. Many states and other units are now engaged in a review of alternative modes of providing financial support for local educational systems without going directly to the taxpayer. This action is partially induced by what is generally described as the taxpayers' revolt. During the last half dozen years, taxpayers exhibited a growing unwillingness to pass referenda that would approve new bonding proposals in support of educational facilities. Jennings and Milstein report that such citizen behavior was rare prior to the late sixties.[26] A more careful review of the responses of citizen support of education systems reveals that each response was usually associated with a specific set of social or economic attributes. These authors found, for instance, that lower income populations were less supportive of increased school taxes than others.[27]

In communities such as those involved in this survey, a mixed reaction should be expected in terms of their willingness to support a tax increase to help defray the rising cost of educating their children. As a means of assessing support for increasing the tax burden to support the local educational system, each respondent was asked if there had been an increase in local property taxes for the purpose of providing additional funds to support the local educational system. This was followed by a question eliciting their reaction to this phenomenon if it had occurred. While admittedly this is a different issue from that of the bond issue previously mentioned, it nevertheless gets at the question of willingness to support the local educational system.

Among the fifteen communities involved in this phase of the investigation, ten indicated that there had been an increase in property taxes for the purpose of providing additional funds to support the local school system. Respondents in two communities were ambiguous in their response to this question, and in the other three the majority of the respondents indicated that taxes had not been raised for this purpose. The absence of an increase in taxes was generally confined to the poorer communities, including the Group IV communities of Brooklyn and Roosevelt City. The third community among this group was North Fontana. There was not a clear concensus among the respondents of Cooper Road and Glenarden on the question of a tax increase. In the latter instance, it is suspected that the nearly balanced renter-owner mix prompted an ambiguous response.

Generally there was support for a tax increase to support the local educational system in the survey communities. The highest level of support was to be found in Hollydale and East Palo Alto (Group I): they were among the communities previously described as modern and in which parental expectation was likely to be high. The largest number of communities (eight) favored a moderate increase in taxes. Among these communities 50–74 percent of the respondents favored a tax increase. The single Group I community found among this group was Glenarden. Less than majority support for a tax increase occurred in Wyandanch, Cooper Road, and Kinloch. Wyandanch, a Group I community, was the only community of its type to exhibit an unwillingness to provide additional financial support for its local educational system. This no doubt reflects a contextual situation, and thus one would be hard pressed to explain the local citizens' response.

The preceding discussion has emphasized the educational outlook of residents of the all-black town because of the richness of the data available for that purpose. In many instances the uniqueness of individual all-black towns will not allow one to generalize to the problems of the black suburbanizing communities, where little information is available that describes their residents' views. Occasionally the issue of altering the racial imbalance of some of these communities emerges and their response allows the national news media to focus upon them momentarily, as was the case in Pontiac, Michigan in 1971.

Objective data which measure the performance levels of schools, on the other hand, are seldom made available to persons who do not have a direct involvement with the individual school system. Of the fifteen all-black towns, indexes of cognitive development could be secured for only three communities—Richmond Heights, Florida and East Palo Alto and North Fontana, California. A similar level of response characterized efforts to secure the same kind of information for black suburbanizing communities. Thus it is possible to ascertain the level of cognitive development in only a limited number of schools attended by blacks in the metropolitan ring.

READING ACHIEVEMENT AS A MEASURE OF EDUCATIONAL QUALITY

Parental expectations regarding school performance, as measured by cognitive development, is expected to vary as a function of parental level of educational attainment. Since most of these communities are considered modernizing, it is assumed that the parents will have high levels of expectation for their children. However, there is some evidence that cognitive developmental levels in outlying schools with significant black enrollment are lower than what parents might expect in terms of their belief in the superiority of suburban schools versus central city schools.

There are also weaknesses in employing certain cognitive outputs as measures of the quality of the academic program in a given school, but this seems to be the simplest way to judge educational quality. Admittedly, this is a crude index. The fear that an individual school might fare poorly under this kind of scrutiny no doubt prompts school authorities to be very protective of information that would facilitate such scrutiny. Nevertheless, the monumental educational study.popularly referred to as the Coleman Report has seemingly institutionalized the use of verbal achievement as the single most important measure of cognitive development and thus the measure most often employed in evaluating school quality.

It has been concluded that among the various factors which influence cognitive development, none is as important as social class background. Coleman carries this position even further as he states that:

> . . . schools bring little influence to bear on a child's achievement that is independent of his background and general social context, and that this very lack of an independent effect means that the inequalities

imposed on children by their home, neighborhood, and peer environment are carried along to become the inequalities with which they confront adult life at the end of school.[28]

If the Coleman assessment is correct, is it rational for working class black families who move into black suburbanizing communities to assume that the level of cognitive skills to be derived in outer city school systems should transcend those which would have accrued in inner city systems? This question cannot be answered simply, for other kinds of outputs from the educational system may assume an importance equal in rank to cognitive development. Furthermore, is it possible that school inputs might be made more effective in overcoming the influence of nonschool characteristics on cognitive development, or at least in minimizing the probability of promoting a more positive cognitive outcome? Along the latter line, Herbert Gintis has taken the position that cognitive output is directly related to affective style, and thus teacher-student interaction patterns are more important than we have been led to believe.[29] It should be pointed out, however, that Gintis's output measure was worker earnings. But if school tone is important in cognitive development, how does one evaluate the contribution of aspects of tone?

School Tone and Cognitive Development

It is generally assumed that what is here being referred to as tone is of little statistical significance in explaining the level of cognitive achievement. The qualities that go into establishing school tone were investigated by Coleman and others, who found individually that such attributes did not explain very much of the variance in school achievement. However, Coleman did note that teacher characteristics had a more significant impact on black and other minority students' performance than they had on white student performance, and this effect was thought to vary by grade, becoming more significant as one progressed in school.[30] He states that teacher sensitivity in the school environment is the second most important teacher effect on school performance, with black students being more responsive to this effect than white students.[31]

VARIATIONS IN COGNITIVE OUTPUT: THE CINCINNATI EXPERIMENT

As a means of gaining additional insight into the problem of cognitive development and school tone, a set of variables extracted from the data collected by the Cincinnati public schools was employed in a multiple regression format where sixth grade verbal achievement was the dependent variable. Data from the Cincinnati school system was employed simply because of its availability on a school by school basis and thus data could be combined with other objective information for purposes of analysis.

Sixteen schools in the city of Cincinnati were selected as units of observation. Ten of these schools were situated in Cincinnati's black community and maintained predominantly black student enrollments, while the remaining six were predominantly white schools. One school was located on the margin of the black community and, in fact, the neighborhood in which it was located was predominantly black, yet its school population was overwhelmingly white. The sample schools were drawn from the range of social class backgrounds, as reflected by the level of median family income, that were representative of neighborhoods of black and white residence in Cincinnati. The black schools ranged across the socioeconomic spectrum, with three schools in lower income neighborhoods, four in working class neighborhoods, one lower middle class, and two in upper middle class neighborhoods. There were no schools in Cincinnati outside the black community which were located in lower income neighborhoods. Two of the predominantly white schools were in working class neighborhoods, one in a lower middle class neighborhood, and two in the upper middle class neighborhoods (see Fig. 3-1).

The Selection of Variables

Initially, 24 variables were employed in the experiment to ascertain their contribution to sixth grade verbal achievement in each of the sixteen schools. The maximum number of variables entered in any single multiple regression model was fourteen. These fourteen variables generated a multiple correlation coefficient of .986 and a corrected coefficient of determination of .588. The fourteen variables employed are:

1. IQ
2. Percent black enrollment
3. Transfer out
4. Transfer in
5. Pupil characteristics
6. School program quality factor
7. Percent black teachers
8. School-pupil relations factor
9. Percent students from non-low income households
10. Voting for tax levy
11. Total days of employee absence

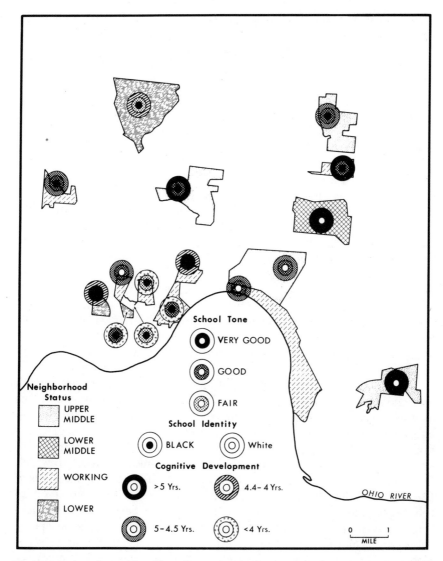

Figure 3–1. Cognitive Development in Sample of Cincinnati Schools

12. Staff morale factor
13. PTA membership factor
14. Average years of teaching experience

Of the fourteen variables included in the model, none describe school facilities or programs. (Coleman has previously demonstrated that facilities and curriculum contributed least to student academic achievement.[32]) Since the principal emphasis here is on school tone, the variables selected for inclusion represent those that reflect the interaction potential of significant factors in the educational process.

Pupil Characteristics

The fourteen independent variables essentially describe pupil characteristics, teacher characteristics, parent characteristics, and parent attitudes. Among pupil attributes, IQ and a factor described as "pupil characteristics" (no. 5) contribute most to developing verbal skills. The latter factor represents the teachers' perception of the students' behavior. Marshal Smith was critical of Coleman for employing teacher perceptions in his study as a student body attribute.[33] His position was that teacher perceptions reflected their knowledge of student achievement based on their familiarity with the students' performance on a number of standardized tests, and thus knowledge of achievement should not be used to explain achievement.[34] While this criticism could be partially leveled here, teacher perception in this instance is made up of several factors, most of which impinge upon student conduct.

Some examples of the items which are incorporated in this factor are specified thus: (1) Students get along pretty well together; (2) self-image of my pupils; (3) behavior of my pupils in school; (4) punctuality of my students; and (5) freedom from physical threat in and around my school. Each of the items which go to make up the "pupil characteristic" factor are assigned a score that can vary from one to seven. The average score is close to the middle of what the school system describes as the average score for all schools. It is possible to partition the aggregate score to determine which items are having the greatest impact upon the aggregate score. From the teacher's perception of student characteristics it is possible to determine the extent to which the behavior of the students is in conflict with the norm expectations of the teachers. Both IQ and pupil characteristics contribute positively to the development of verbal skills, with the latter being somewhat less important than the former. Racial identity, the third explanatory pupil attribute, is not as important as either of the former characteristics, although the percentage of black students does show a small negative association with verbal achievement.

Teacher Characteristics

Among teacher characteristics, years of teaching experience and teacher morale are the principal contributors to verbal achievement. Teaching experience contributes positively to cognitive development, whereas teacher morale is characterized by a negative coefficient. In the latter case, teacher morale can be partitioned in the same manner as pupil characteristics. In those schools where student behavior deviates least from teacher norms regarding conduct, a high positive correlation exists. One item included under the staff morale factor is satisfaction with assignment. This item is a crude surrogate for the teacher preference of student body in the Coleman data. Although Smith contends that teacher characteristics do not explain very much of the unique contribution to the explanation of variance in achievement, he does concede that teachers seem to help those students whom they say they prefer to teach.[35] This factor has been shown in previous research to make a positive contribution to the cognitive development of black children.

The racial characteristics of the teacher have been previously shown to play a significant role in black verbal achievement. The Coleman data showed that the higher the percentage of black teachers in schools attended by black students, the lower the level of verbal achievement. He and others have attributed this outcome to the lower quality preparation of black teachers in terms of their own mastery of verbal competence. Eric Hanushek also included this variable in his model of the education process wherein he attempted to derive a black production function. He interprets this as a measure of teacher quality distribution.[36]

If facility with language is linked to social class, then it would be somewhat irrational to assume that the largest share of the cadre of black teachers would have overcome this handicap. But needless to say, if black teachers expressing a greater willingness to work in environments with a majority of black students are able to minimize the level of alienation and the subsequent withdrawal to the streets, the loss of a fraction of a point in verbal achievement might be acceptable. The Cincinnati outcome may be influenced in part by not partitioning the influence of black teachers on performance separately between black and white schools. However, Ray Rist has shown that in some instances black teachers, like white teachers whose values reflect their social class orientation, engage in classroom behavior which penalizes a large share of their students whose conduct conflicts with their norm expectations.[37] In this instance, it might be useful to consider data describing the achievement level in three predominantly black schools and then view how the children are perceived by their teachers, and subsequently how the children view their school. (See Table 3-2; in each instance the school is identified by a fictitious name.)

Brown Elementary School is a lower income school, as reflected by percent of pupils from families above low income, but so are each of the other schools described in Table 3-2. School data indicates, though,

Table 3–2.   School Performance and Student-Teacher Perceptions in Three Lower Income Inner City Schools

Elementary School	Reading Level at Grade Six	Pupil Characteristic	Teacher Morale	Student Attitude Toward School	% Black Teachers
Brown	3.6	2.2 (Negative)	3.4 (Moderately Low)	Unfavorable	28
Jones	4.4	5.4 (Positive)	5.4 (Moderately High)	Highly Favorable	42
Stevens	4.1	4.6 (Positive)	5.5 (Moderately High)	Weakly Favorable	54

Source: Cincinnati Public School Information System, Division of Program Research and Design, 1972.

that the social status in the Brown district is slightly higher than in the other two districts. These three schools have the lowest social status of any in the sixteen-school group chosen for investigation. In 1971–72, the median sixth grade verbal achievement level reported for the Cincinnati Public Schools was 5.1 years. Each of these schools as shown in Table 3–2 falls below that level, with Brown Elementary showing 1.5 years gap in median performance. Nine of the ten predominantly black schools in the sample fall below the city's median reading level, whereas four of the six predominantly white schools show the same tendency. Although black higher status schools are often found nearer the median, there exists a substantial gap between the performance level of those schools and white schools of similar status, using the school system's measure of status.

Brown Elementary School was in the throes of racial transition in 1971, and at that time was 55 percent black. The other two schools were 99 and 100 percent black, respectively. The most obvious relationship between achievement and school characteristics is the score describing the pupil characteristics of Brown School. Not only was it lowest for this group of schools, it was lowest for the entire sixteen group universe. The teachers at Brown School generally viewed the conduct of their students negatively, while in the other two schools, student conduct was viewed as being positive. The performance level at the Brown Elementary School accords well with the following statement made recently by Coles:

> Moreover, in most instances, what teachers predicted and deemed possible for children about what life in the long run would bring them, about what schooling meant and would mean to them had come true. The children had already, even at say, six or seven, acceded to their teachers' judgments about themselves, about what would happen to them, sooner or later.[38]

What is being proposed here is that teachers and students at the Brown Elementary School were ill prepared for their encounter and that this was probably further aggravated by the increase in tension associated with the process of racial transition occurring in the school. If the teacher morale factor is disaggregated in this instance, the one item that receives the lowest score is assistance in handling the discipline problem. The Brown School administration was thought by the teachers to be doing a poor job in this area, whereas in the latter two schools assistance in this area was thought to be excellent.

A recent assessment of the school environment in a small southern community, in which a systemwide school desegregation program had been initiated during the previous year, showed that the most significant difficulties evolving out of this experience had to do with teaching. Robert Mayer and others reported that 63 percent of the white teachers mentioned such difficulties, while only 28 percent of the black teachers reported this as a major problem.[39] These writers likewise showed morale to be lower among white teachers.[40] The situation at Brown Elementary School is probably commonplace at many schools around the country and shows in part the impact of cultural differences growing out of racial isolation and social class differences. In major urban centers white teachers are found most often in schools whose enrollment is predominantly white, and black teachers in schools whose enrollment is predominantly black, although white teachers are more often exposed to black students than are black teachers to white students.[41] This situation is even more highly exaggerated in suburban school districts.

When a multiple regression model was employed with only eight independent variables, the observed level of achievement was essentially congruent with the predicted level of achievement for Brown Elementary School. The residual was .092. When teacher morale, years of teaching experience, and PTA membership were added to the model, the gap between the observed and the predicted achievement level widened in the direction of lower achievement. The inclusion of the morale variable, which was strongly negative in its association with achievement, coupled with low PTA involvement, reduced the predicted achievement level even more. The addition of these variables had only a slight positive effect on the other two schools in the sample.

Student attitudes were not directly measured in terms of their impact on achievement. Generally, a student's self-confidence was positively associated with his attitude toward himself and negatively with support for increased school taxes and school atmosphere. These two measures are both associated with aspects of parental behavior and perception. The student's attitude toward himself was positively associated with IQ, PTA membership, and learning environment. Attitudes toward school were associated with income, IQ, and reading achievement. Ability and social class, then, largely determine to what extent the school environment is compatible with the perceived needs of the student.

At Brown Elementary School, only one-third of the students indicated that they liked their school, although almost half like school generally. On the other hand, of the students at Jones and Stevens elementary schools (96 percent and 44 percent, respectively) liked their schools. The students did not differ greatly in the level of expressed liking for their teachers, although the Jones School again showed the more positive view (75 percent), while 61 and 64 percent expressed this view at Stevens and Brown schools. Although almost two-thirds of the students at Brown School indicated that they liked their teachers, only 36 percent felt that their teachers cared about them. The value for the Jones School was only slightly higher, but at the Stevens School more than half the children felt that their teachers cared about them. To what extent these attributes influence achievement is unknown, but Hanushek indicates something he called a quasi-teacher effect—time spent disciplining students lowered class achievement.[42]

In the Mayer study, attention was focused on teacher-pupil interaction and the amount of that time spent on discipline or reprimand. It was found that teacher interaction time with black students was less than for white students, but a greater proportion of these limited interactions was devoted to reprimand.[43] It pointed out also that the black teacher was more likely to engage in reprimand behavior than the white teacher.[44] Among the teachers in the Brown Elementary School in Cincinnati who showed much dissatisfaction with their school administration for not assisting them with the problem of discipline, we can expect low teacher morale. Consequently, these teachers may take a dim view of student behavior, leading to rapid teacher turnover, or simply the development of attitudes which support the position that these students are unteachable and thus are not deserving of the effort.

In interracial settings, white teachers seem to indicate a reluctance to discipline black students, and these students seem to realize this very early. In describing the manner in which one white teacher in a northeastern school handled the problem, Coles revealed that this teacher was herself from the South and was familiar with aspects of black culture. This teacher's comments, while showing signs of southern attitudes, also showed signs of feelings and empathy. The following poignant comments show this:

> "I'm not afraid of what they know, what they can do well: music and art and athletics. I show them I know about their history, their speech, their everything, I hope—and they catch on. Oh, it's not all that deliberate. It sounds it, now that I am talking, but the truth is I feel close to a lot of those children, and I guess they pick that up. Then they also pick up that I want them to move on, get ahead in the world."[45]

She further commented, "We should recruit different kinds of people to be teachers. It's what you feel that counts, not only what you've learned in education schools. . . ."[46] Given the complexity of the problem, what can those black families, some of whom for the first time are acquiring access to suburban schools, expect in the way of an improvement in the kind of education their children will receive as measured by cognitive development?

COGNITIVE DEVELOPMENT IN SELECTED SCHOOLS

Within individual schools found in the suburban ring, black student ratios reflect the presence of black families in the immediate catchment area. The absence of large numbers of blacks in most suburban communities limits their presence in the schools unless a given school district is engaged in a busing program with some inner city school system. While black students are generally present in suburban schools in very small numbers, the rapid increase in the black population in selected suburban target communities has resulted in altering the racial composition in selected schools in those districts. The evidence shows that unless some special effort is introduced to maintain some predetermined racial composition in the schools, suburban school districts, like their central city counterparts, tend to reflect the changing residential character of the neighborhood.

The evidence describing the cognitive characteristics of these schools is difficult to come by, and that which is available is sometimes derived using a variety of instruments, which makes comparison difficult. It was previously indicated that data describing the cognitive character of the schools attended by children of the all-black towns were available for only three communities—East Palo Alto, California; North Fontana, California; and Richmond Heights, Florida. The number of schools in each district serving black students varies as a result of the racial makeup of the district or a public policy decision that has as its goal a predetermined level of black participation. The Richmond Heights community represents the latter pattern, as its children have been assigned to schools in keeping with the objectives of the desegregation efforts of the Dade County public school system. The Ravenswood City school district, which serves East Palo Alto, is more than four-fifths black—a fact that led an official of that district to comment that "our district, unlike other districts, has a majority of third world population." In this instance he meant unlike other surrounding suburban school districts. The third district for which cognitive data is available is the Fontana Unified School District, which serves the small semirural community of North Fontana as well as the larger urban center of Fontana. In neither instance does the school district coincide with a political entity that might be described as a town.

If the cognitive output, as reflected in reading achievement, that characterizes the two California school districts is typical of that to which blacks have access in suburban ring communities, then one might be prompted to question the notion that these schools will provide blacks with the higher quality education which one assumes is being sought. But to pass judgment simply on the basis of a single educational output, at just one point in time, would be harsh judgment indeed.

The Fontana Schools

In the Fontana Unified School District, blacks are found in largest numbers in three elementary schools, but even in the school where they are most numerous they constitute slightly less than one-third the total enrollment. Even so, the school district views this school as racially imbalanced, along with another which has a slightly larger percentage of Spanish surname pupils. The school which has the largest black enrollment was characterized by median reading achievement level of 4.2 years for pupils enrolled in the sixth grade. In the Fontana district school which enrolled only 15.6 percent black pupils, the achievement level was only 4.3 years. As was indicated earlier, tracking within grades might have occurred at Fontana's racially imbalanced school, as it was the only district to show a wide range of variation in individual sixth grade class performances within a school. At this particular school, five sixth grade groups were tested, with the following levels of achievement evolving: 3.0 years, 4.5 years, 3.7 years, 4.4 years, and 5.5 years. Thus there was one group in this school which was performing above the California norm, but none at or above the national norm.

These achievement levels may simply represent a diversity of levels of student preparation not characteristic of other schools in the district. It was stated earlier that none of the black parents interviewed expressed negative opinions regarding the quality of education their children received, even though all children from the survey homes were enrolled in the school showing the lowest level of cognitive achievement. Of course it is possible for children to be receiving satisfactory ratings in their day-to-day school work, ratings that reflect the teacher's appraisal of the level at which individual students are expected to perform. If one refers to the three Cincinnati schools identified above in Table 3–2, one finds that only two-thirds of the children at Brown Elementary School—the school with the lowest cognitive achievement level—state that their teachers think they should be doing better in school. Compared with the other two schools in the sample, where 72 and 81 percent of the students report that their teachers express this position, this seems to imply that teacher expectations are based on objective evidence of ability. The parental response to this same question is quite similar to that of the teachers in each instance, although the parental perception of the student's ability is generally slightly higher than that of the teachers. The median level of parental education in the North Fontana community places them in the traditional category (Group III), a situation that might lead them to expect less from the educational system.

The East Palo Alto Schools

The Ravenswood City School District which provides for the educational needs of East Palo Alto has also encountered difficulty in having their children perform at the California norm on reading achievement. The black families interviewed indicated that their children are concentrated in only three of the eight elementary schools operated by the district. In the schools their children attend, sixth grade reading achievement levels in the fall of 1972 were 4.0 years and 4.8 years. Thus reading achievements in each school ranged from 1.1 years in two instances, to 0.3 years in the third—below the state norm for sixth grade reading achievement in that year. Only one school in the district showed achievement surpassing the state norm, and it was located in an upper middle income neighborhood.

Almost 30 percent of the parents at one school reported that they thought the quality of education their children received was poor, while only 8 percent of the parents reported the same attitude at a second school; yet the same median level of achievement prevailed. At the latter school, 3 percent of the parents thought the education their children received was excellent; but most often, parents expressed the belief that their children were receiving a good education at each of the three schools. A review of the parents' educational background shows that slightly fewer than half the household heads in one instance were themselves high school graduates, and a similar educational pattern of attainment was evident in another. These parents had incomes that placed them in the working class category. In the third school, where the reading level was closer to that of the state norm, the parents might be described as lower middle income. Of these parents, 85 percent thought that their children were getting a good education. In indicating how the quality of education might be improved in the latter community, most parents suggested the hiring of black teachers and busing to other districts as possible means of accomplishing that task.

The Richmond Heights Children

The third community for which there is a congnitive description of the schools in our sample is Richmond Heights, Florida, a working class community in metropolitan Dade County. The children of elementary school age are found largely in six schools in the South County area. The large number of schools attended, given the size of the community, basically reflects county desegregation efforts. Blacks seldom comprise more than 25 percent of the enrollment in any of these six schools, although the one elementary school, physically located in Richmond Heights, is almost two-fifths black. But in 1969 this school was 100 percent black, and the shift in the racial composition represents a stipulation by the Department of Health, Education, and Welfare to the Dade County Board of Education to speed up the process of school desegregation in that year.

The cognitive output of these schools in most instances represents the level of achievement one year after school desegregation had been underway. The level of cognitive development in these South Dade County elementary schools is higher than that describing the level of achievement in either of the previous two systems described. Only two of these schools are K–6, while the other four are K–5. In each instance the reading achievement level for each school exceeds the level for that grade by almost a full year, and in most instances more than one year.

While the level of reading achievement is high for each of these schools, the results are not as good for black students. The Dade County Board of Education makes data on cognitive achievement available by ethnic identity. This data reveals that black students have reading scores two years or more below those of white students, but even so, these data indicate that blacks are closer to grade in reading achievement than in either of the two school systems previously described. The higher level of black cognitive development found here than in the previous environments does not lend itself to an easy explanation. If Coleman's thesis regarding the social class mix is valid, one might assume that the presence of higher social status white students, with their evident, highly developed reading skills, aided in boosting the level of black cognitive development. But when one considers that the higher status whites and somewhat lower status blacks had shared a common learning environment for only one year, this tends to become questionable.

The parents with children in these schools generally agreed that the children were provided a good education. In four schools a small number of parents felt that the education their children were receiving was excellent, while in three schools a similar number stated that the education was poor. It appears that the parental perception of reality in this instance conforms more nearly with the objective case. This is particularly true with the racial composition of the teaching staff. Perceptions tend to be slightly distorted regarding pupils' racial characteristics, with the parents more often assigning a slightly higher percentage of black students to a school than shows up in school records. In most instances, parents thought the schools were 40 to 60 percent black, when in fact they were 20 to 40 percent black.

If children of other all-black towns do not have access to schools of better quality, in cognitive terms, than those reviewed here then location in the suburban ring may not provide the educational advantages being sought. It is unlikely that some communities in this set have access to schools as good as those described here, and therefore they are realizing a much smaller return on parental investment. One is surprised that the children of Richmond Heights tend to be developing cognitively at a faster rate than others, but there should be no surprise that the North Fontana situation seems to be less bright.

There is no way to get directly at school tone in these environments, but a principal from one of the eastern communities, in addressing himself to the issue, stated the following:

> "I have been principal here for nine years and I am white. Also, since I will be getting into negative factors I first want to state that ninety-nine percent of the children are friendly, warm, and lovable. They have the same basic needs as all children have but in their community the schools are in the position of filling a larger percentage of these needs than do schools in the typical white suburban community. Naturally I am referring more to nonacademic needs, but even so I guess we also have to fill a larger gap in the academic than in so-called better communities."[47]

This principal then went on to recount some of those life style characteristics of his pupils which he thought influenced the educational outcome:

1. Give the impression they really don't care about academic learning.
2. Quickly resort to fighting as a way of reacting to anything which displeases them.
3. Use socially unacceptable language to each other and to adults.
4. Become very much afraid of threats made by their peers.
5. Are easily upset.
6. Will extort things from others.[48]

This is a partial listing of items this principal feels influence the learning environment. It is obvious that the behavior displayed by these students is not the behavior approved by the schools. To what extent the students respond negatively to the school is unknown; but it is highly probable if the principal views student conduct as nonconforming, that students are also likely to view the school as a hostile environment. It was not possible to secure information on cognitive development on schools in this system, so one cannot begin to evaluate the influence of school tone on academic achievement.

COGNITIVE DEVELOPMENT IN A SELECTED SET OF BLACK SUBURBANIZING COMMUNITIES

Unlike the all-black towns, black suburbanizing communities generally represent places in which blacks have taken up residence during the most recent period. One might be led to believe that their reasons for seeking residence beyond the central city would more nearly conform to those of other suburban movers. If this is the case, these alternative schools or school conditions might constitute a motivating factor. Data describing the cognitive character in the schools in the principal target zones of black suburban movers are extremely difficult to acquire, however.

Those communities which served as the secondary targets of black residential entry during the sixties were less reluctant to provide data on school achievement. Because of the limited data available that describe the congnitive attributes of schools in black suburbanizing communities, the analysis can hardly be viewed as systematic. The communities for which information was available were Carson, Pomona, and Richmond, California, and University City, Missouri. The social class position of blacks in these four communities shows a good deal of variation, with Carson representing the higher status black community and Richmond and Pomona representing lower status black communities. University City is closer in status to Carson than to the latter two communities.

It should be noted that those communities which were earlier described as spillover communities simply represent a physical extension of the inner city ghetto, and thus one might question the significance of the social context on school tone. In this regard, Harold Connolly, describing Carson and Inglewood, stated that they "served as extensions of the Watts-Willowbrook-Compton-South Los Angeles ghetto."[49] Since Carson represents an upper middle class black community, it will be compared with other zones of upper middle income black residence in the central cities of both Los Angeles and Chicago, in order to ascertain the role of tone on cognitive outcome.

The Case of Carson

Carson is the place of residence of the highest status black population in Los Angeles County located outside the central city. The evolving zone of black residence within the city of Carson is essentially confined to the northern sector of the community, which is contiguous to other zones of black residence. In two of the neighborhoods in which blacks have settled, more than 95 percent of the housing was constructed during the sixties. Black students are served principally by three elementary schools, each of which is in close proximity to the areas of black residential concentration (see Fig. 3–2). As should be expected, the neighborhoods which are characterized by the greatest physical isolation are also those in which the racial makeup of the school is more than 80 percent black. The other two schools, in which the lion's share of the remaining black pupils in Carson are enrolled, are located in neighborhoods undergoing racial transition. In 1972, one of these schools showed a black enrollment of 54.5 percent and the other 40.6 percent. These two schools include black residents whose economic status is slightly higher than that of the neighborhood previously described.

In the larger subdivision administered by the Los Angeles Unified School District, which includes Carson, the median level of sixth grade verbal achievement was 5.1 years. This conformed to the California state norm in 1972. Among the schools principally attended by the black students of Carson, verbal achievement in two instances was found to be close to the district norm. In the one school in which the student racial composition was overwhelmingly black, the median verbal achievement level was only 4.4 years. In the other two schools with large black enrollments, the reading achievement level was established as 4.9 and 5.2 years, respectively. But in neither instance did the latter schools' enrollment include more than 55 percent black students. In none of the remaining schools serving the children of the city of Carson does the reading level deviate as far from the subdistrict norm as is true for the one school which is the most severely racially imbalanced.

It is true that the social status of the residents of the latter school is slightly lower than that of the remaining two schools with large black enrollments, but the difference in median family income in this situation is that which separates lower middle class from upper middle class. That this distinction is important cannot be resolved here, although Mayer and others, in their analysis of a southern school system, found that there was no real distinction in verbal achievement between those they described as middle class and upper class.[50] These

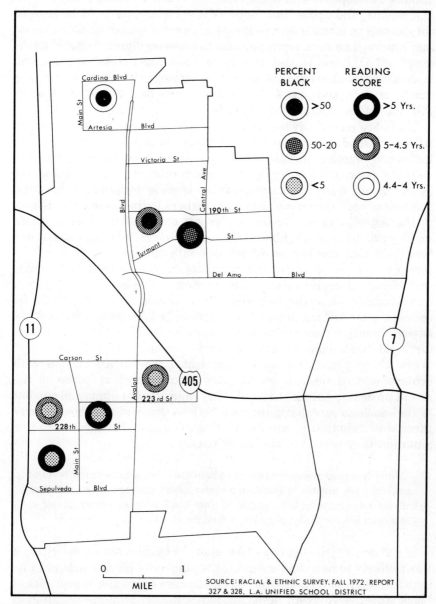

Figure 3–2. School Racial Composition and Cognitive Development in Carson, California

authors developed a four-class typology which included lower, working, middle, and upper, but found that achievement could be seen to vary simply in terms of a two-class typology, lower and middle. That is, they observed no significant differences between their lower and working class backgrounds, and their middle and upper class backgrounds. It should be pointed out that their class typology was based on housing characteristics, and that such a means of evolving a class description will not suffice in many communities.

There are no data available to provide clues to school tone in those schools attended principally by black students in Carson. In Inglewood, another middle income suburb located to the north and west of Carson and a community in which relatively large numbers of blacks moved during the sixties, there is some documentation of the reaction of both the citizenship and teachers to the presence of blacks in the schools. As in Carson, blacks are concentrated only in those schools which serve neighborhoods undergoing racial transition. It has been said that the Inglewood schools with the largest black enrollments in 1967 were at the bottom half of the spectrum in both verbal and nonverbal achievement.[51] Responding to this evidence, Bonacich and Goodman state the following: "This cannot be accounted for by socioeconomic factors, since of the three only Woodworth showed low enough family incomes to receive money under Title I of the Elementary and Secondary Education Act for compensatory programs."[52] While these writers do not discuss school tone in association with achievement, they do point out aspects of teacher response to the recent presence of black students. They indicate that almost 38 percent of the teachers saw discipline as a serious problem in schools where there was a significant number of black students. In response to this situation they described one black parent's view:

> Many teachers are incompetent to deal with black kids at the level of emotions, are unsure of their own motivations, and are very sure that they do not want to have to deal with irate black parents, or challenges to their own authority by escalating student reaction to discipline.[53]

If Carson in 1971–72 was like many suburban school districts, it was unlikely to have had a significant number of black teachers in its school system, as it seems that black teachers follow the appearance of black students. A recent newspaper article describing the situation in the suburbs of Cleveland, Ohio indicates that black teachers are found in a small number in all those communities where black students were found in small number, but that they constituted a major sector of the teaching staff in East Cleveland, a community which had become predominantly black during the previous decade.

A number of schools situated in the city of Los Angeles, but found in a zone that included black middle income populations, were reviewed to determine how well they fared in terms of cognitive development. Here one is simply concerned with how well schools attended by blacks, holding social class constant, fare in a central city versus a suburban environment. It appears that the selected schools in the city of Los Angeles were able to perform a superior job in developing cognitive skills, at least in terms of sixth grade reading achievement (see Table 3–3).

The selection of a limited number of schools does not permit one to generalize to the larger population. One of the more obvious differences among these schools is the higher average IQs in the Los Angeles sample. There is little doubt that measured IQ tends generally to boost performance in cognitive development. Whatever else IQ measures, it does measure previous achievement in cultural learning. Thus the children in the previous sample might have been exposed to middle class symbols for a longer period of time.

As one moves out of the contiguous zone of middle income black residence in Los Angeles and into zones where the black population is described as working class, then reading achievement characteristics of the level prevailing in school A in Carson is encountered. A brief

Table 3–3. A Comparison of Cognitive Achievement in Selected Carson and Los Angeles City Schools

	Sixth Grade Median Reading Level	% Black	IQ	Transiency	Social Class of School Neighborhood
Carson School					
A	4.4	80.7	88	60%	Lower Middle
B	4.9	54.5	96	48%	Upper Middle
C	5.2	40.6	89	34%	Upper Middle
Los Angeles School					
A	6.2	37.7	101	33%	Lower Middle
B	5.4	79.4	95	72%	Lower Middle
C	6.0	91.8	99	37%	Upper Middle

Source: Summary Report, Mandatory State Testing Program, Fall 1973, Research and Evaluation Branch, Report No. 328, Los Angeles Unified School District.

Note: Social Class of School Neighborhood was independently derived. The method employed is described in Chapter Four.

review of the Cincinnati data shows that reading achievement does indeed vary as a function of social class. Among the small number of predominantly black schools in the Cincinnati sample it was found that the median achievement level of schools which are described as lower status is 3.9 years, and of those which might be described as working class is 4.5 years. The schools which might be described as black middle class showed a median achievement of 4.9 years. Thus school A in Carson shows achievement attributes of the Cincinnati working class school, while the other two schools show middle class black achievement levels. Thus in this instance a tripartite social status mechanism does show achievement level differences, although Mayer and others found only dual class difference in a southern community.

It is interesting to note, however, that in the Cincinnati case, teachers did not perceive lower class students to differ in behavior from middle class students, but did indicate the behavior of working class students to be less desirable than either of the other two groups, as measured by pupil characteristics scores. One is not certain what the implications are here, though it would tend to indicate that the most hostile school environments would occur under conditions of black working class students entering previously all white suburban schools. Needless to say, this position is not buttressed by extensive findings, and may well be invalid; but it also may well reflect a conformity/nonconformity school norm dimension that affects pupil-teacher interaction.

In Chicago's South Shore community a similar picture emerges. In the early sixties, Robert Havighurst had described the schools in this community as high status schools, a designation employed to indicate the lack of difficulty in teaching in such schools or the extent to which school norms and student norms are compatible. He described one teacher's response from a high status school in the following way: "We've based our whole course of study on the gifted. It is the same with curriculum guides. As for discipline problems, well, they are practically non-existent."[54]

In 1965 this district was less than 10 percent black; but by 1972 a significant change in racial composition had taken place, although as early as 1965, three of the elementary schools were already predominantly black. The status of the entering black population was lower than that of the resident white population, according to Harvey Molotch.[55] By 1970 the neighborhoods of South Shore were a mixture of working, lower middle, and upper middle income residents. Although blacks had become firmly established as the dominant population in most schools in the district, there was but a single school where reading achievement was associated with working class level previously described (4.5 years). In all other schools in 1969–70, median reading achievement exceeded five years—the level previously described as being associated with middle class black status in Cincinnati. In one school the level of reading achievement was 7.4 years, but blacks constituted less than half the enrollment there.

More recent data on cognitive development in Chicago schools is not available; thus one is unable to indicate how well the schools in this district have continued to serve the entering black population. One noticeable adjustment is evident, though, and that is the presence of majority black teachers in schools having majority black enrollments. To what extent these teachers influence cognitive development and feelings of self confidence is unknown.

Gloria Powell recently demonstrated that self-esteem was on the increase among black students in the schools in her sample in three southern cities.[56] Contrary to previous studies, she showed that black students expressed higher self-esteem than the sample of white students in the same communities.[57] She likewise demonstrated the highest levels of black self-esteem were found among blacks in segregated schools. This issue led Reginald Jones to comment:

> What evidence exists concerning the effects of school integration on intergroup attitudes and intergroup behavior? If we are going to talk about integration as an educational goal, then we must have answers to these questions lest we err in developing cognitively able Black children at the expense of their social and emotional development.[58]

Unfortunately, Powell does not provide data on cognitive development in her study and thus the issue raised by Jones remains unresolved, although one should note that Powell did not find the same high level of esteem among black students in the one northern city that she described elsewhere.[59]

Apparently, if Carson is used as an example, blacks moving into suburban school districts are no more likely to attend schools where the level of cognitive development is high than they would by attending central city schools with a similar social class makeup. In the Los Angeles example it seems the level of cognitive development is higher in the middle income city schools than in those schools attended by blacks in Carson. The Chicago example is more diffuse, with the social class mix in South Shore showing greater variation than in the western Los Angeles area in which observations were drawn. The shortcoming of such comparisons revolves around the use of data on cognitive achievement at a single point. The effect of changes in school tone in a given school district upon cognitive development over an extended period of time are unknown. Thus the more important question becomes whether the more stable and learning-conducive atmosphere develops and is subsequently more readily maintained in the central city or in the suburbs?

At this point it can simply be said that the characteristics of those schools which have come under investigation here do not show a significant advantage accruing to the suburban environment. Of course the evidence describing the recent decline of black student enrollment in the Chicago metropolitan ring[60] might be interpreted to indicate that black parents believe that their children will receive a better education in non-central city schools. But before a final opinion is offered, the cognitive character of the schools in University City, Missouri, another relatively high status community which was a target of select black central city movers during the sixties, should be reviewed.

The University City Schools and Cognitive Development

In 1972, University City operated ten elementary schools, but only six of them utilized a K–6 organizational structure. Five years earlier, only one school in this universe had a majority of black pupils; but by 1972, half the elementary schools in University City had majority black enrollments. University City has traditionally received recognition for having developed a high quality school system. Such a description is supported by data describing the cognitive character of the system's schools. This fact was also recently recognized by a representative of the St. Louis black press, which expressed support on its editorial page for a school bond levy it felt would assist in maintaining the established reputation for educational excellence of the community's schools. This editorial reflects the interest of the black central city press in schools which are beginning to provide education for a growing number of that paper's clients. The editor admitted that it was unusual for it to engage in editorial comment on the school affairs of suburban communities. Unfortunately, the school tax levy issue failed to receive majority support. Whether this failure of the school levy was related to the changing racial composition of the schools cannot be ascertained at this point, but for a system which has developed a reputation of having good schools, it appears that this action was a step backwards.

University City is a composite lower middle class community with individual neighborhoods which range from working class status to upper middle class status. Zones of black residence in the community,

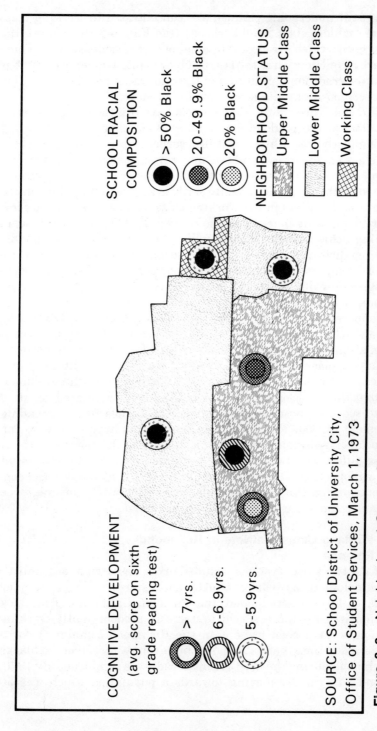

SCHOOL RACIAL
COMPOSITION

⬤ > 50% Black

◉ 20-49.9% Black

◯ 20% Black

NEIGHBORHOOD STATUS

▨ Upper Middle Class

▦ Lower Middle Class

▨ Working Class

COGNITIVE DEVELOPMENT
(avg. score on sixth
grade reading test)

◎ > 7yrs.

◉ 6-6.9yrs.

◯ 5-5.9yrs.

SOURCE: School District of University City,
Office of Student Services, March 1, 1973

Figure 3–3. Neighborhood Status, School Racial Composition, and Cognitive Achievement in University
City, Missouri

which is still undergoing change, are concentrated in working class and lower middle class neighborhoods (see Fig. 3–3). These are the neighborhoods which are closest to zones of black residence in St. Louis and nearby Wellston. Thus the entry of blacks into University City has followed the traditional pattern and the outcome is a staged evolution of racial composition on a school by school basis.

To date, only three of the K–6 schools have run the course of racial change. Two of the predominantly black K–6 schools serve working class neighborhoods, while the third serves a predominantly lower middle class neighborhood and two upper middle class neighborhoods. The level of cognitive development in this cluster of schools is clearly associated with social rank, with sixth grade reading achievement ranging from 5.5 years in the working class schools. The schools serving a predominantly black clientele range from 5.5 years to 6.5 years in reading achievement. Black families in one of the upper middle income neighborhoods are of higher social rank than their white neighbors, while in the other neighborhood of similar status the opposite pattern prevails. It is in the latter two neighborhoods that reading achievement reaches its highest level.

It is apparent that reading achievement in predominantly working class black schools exceeds that which is characteristic of the scores of children attending school in Carson and East Palo Alto. As a matter of fact, working class schools in University City show the kinds of performances that describe lower middle class schools elsewhere. Thus it seems that the black movers to University City have indeed acquired access to schools whose cognitive character as measured by reading achievement exceeds that of schools that blacks have been entering when social class is held constant. It is difficult at this point to account for these differences, but an attempt will be made to determine what set of variables from alternative systems would contribute to the cognitive outcome in this set of schools, and to identify what might be significant components of cognitive development.

The Working Class Districts in Richmond and Pomona

The final two school systems included in our assessment of cognitive outcome include those districts which administer the schools attended by black children in Richmond and Pomona, California. The black population in both these school systems is predominantly working class. Blacks have been present in the Richmond community for a longer period of time than in Pomona; but even so, movement of blacks into Richmond during the most recent decade was significant. By 1970, Richmond was rapidly moving towards a population which was 50 percent black. In contrast, the black population in Pomona represents recent entry and thus constitutes a much smaller part of the total population of that city.

The present Richmond Unified School District underwent a major reorganization in 1964, wherein it was expanded to include a more diverse social class population.[61] This move had the potential of reducing the proportion of black children in the district from 40 percent to 25 percent.[62] In 1968 the Richmond district included 45 elementary schools, but black children, because of the patterns of black residential development, were concentrated in only six schools. Although the Richmond Unified School District contains more than twice the number of schools administered by the Pomona district, black children tend to be clustered in a similar number of schools in both districts. In each community there is also a similar distribution of economic resources within black residential areas, although Richmond shows a somewhat larger percentage of lower middle income families. It seems that longer residence in Richmond might have provided a slight advantage in black family income. This factor has led to the development of at least two neighborhoods in the latter community which are higher in social rank than corresponding neighborhoods in Pomona.

It appears that this difference might have produced some differences in cognitive output, as the school in the higher status neighborhood in Richmond does show slightly higher levels of reading achievement than the lower status schools. Alan Wilson, commenting on the Richmond schools and black academic performance specifically, states that: "Negro students from predominantly Negro elementary schools which have fewer than 50 percent lower-class students do somewhat better than those from schools with more lower class students."[63] The raw scores reported on a school-by-school basis for Richmond in 1968 show a strong relationship to socioeconomic rank as reflected in 1970 census reports by census tract. The lower reading performance levels characteristic of schools attended largely by black pupils were used recently by white parents as argument against attempts at school integration in the Richmond Unified School District.[64] But more important than performance, according to Rubin, was that white parents saw the situation as "threatening to inundate their schools with black children, whose lifestyle and values they abhor."[65]

The record of achievement in predominantly black schools in Pomona shows a narrow range of difference. Among the five schools which serve black residential areas, sixth grade reading achievement ranged from 4.1 years to 4.6 years in 1972–73.[66] This performance level is akin to that which described achievement in the predominantly black elementary schools of East Palo Alto. It should be re-

membered that the residents of East Palo Alto were slightly higher in
status (in social class terms) than those of Pomona; yet both were
identified as working class communities. The schools attended by
blacks in the latter community fell into the lowest quartile on sixth
grade reading performance.

One paradox that emerges from the utilization of crude ecological
data is that two schools serving a lower class black population show
higher performance level than two of the schools serving a working
class population. The fifth school which also serves a working class
population does show a higher level of performance than the others in
this group. Needless to say, neither of the two school districts seem to
show evidence that black children are attending schools that promote a
level of cognitive output differing significantly from that found in
central city schools, when social rank is held constant. It has been
demonstrated elsewhere that the black presence in these two communities has created dissension, as whites show fear of a black
takeover. In Pomona this fear is reflected in the following newspaper
account:

> It is difficult for oldtimers to see the unquestioned dominance they
> have enjoyed for the eighty-three years that Pomona has been a city
> slipping away so quickly, particularly when they prided themselves on
> progressive city administrations which have planned ahead, expected
> growth and moved ahead of time to provide facilities.[67]

The author further shows how this conflict has penetrated the schools.
He indicates that:

> . . . there has been sporadic violence in the schools. For a time, police
> prowled corridors. Black parents complain their children are picked on
> by administrators and white students. White parents insist that violence
> is instigated by blacks and that black students—for the most part new to
> an old, established, pleasant city—are asking too much, too soon.[68]

These comments are indicative of forces that affect school tone. To
date, it appears that there have been very few attempts to measure the
impact of tone on academic performance. Nevertheless, it has become
increasingly evident that it does in some ways influence cognitive
output. At this point, however, the relationship has simply been shown
to be tentative. Thomas Sowell, in describing the conditions at one
Cincinnati elementary school, highlights the essence of school tone. He
states:

> Although Frederick Douglass School did not attain the erstwhile
> academic achievement of Dunbar, it was striking because its ancient
> building stood in the midst of a run down slum, with no fence around it,

no bars on the windows, no graffiti, quiet halls, and an atmosphere of human relations among the staff which would have been a credit to a middle class private school.[69]

He further states that "the point is, certain human relations are essential to the educational process, and when these conditions are met then education can go forward—regardless of methods, educational philosophy, or physical plant."[70] The latter school is one of those previously described in this chapter as showing a positive school tone and a corresponding increase in school performance above that of its social class peers by 0.5 years. If tone can add significantly to the level of cognitive output, every effort should be made to explore the possibility of enhancing tone.

A REAPPRAISAL OF THE SUBURBAN EDUCATIONAL PICTURE: CONSEQUENCES FOR THE BLACK MOVER

The lengthy discussion of the educational consequences of black residential mobility, leading to the establishment of residence in the metropolitan ring, has left unresolved the definition of the kind of education received. This is not by choice, but is a function of an inadequate data base on which to make definitive statements. Nevertheless, an attempt was made to broach a number of recurring issues in the educational arena, and, on the basis of limited data, to place them in the context of black suburbanization. Among the issues touched upon and reviewed were (1) racial segregation, (2) parental expectation, (3) the school environment, and (4) cognitive development. The overriding emphasis has been on the latter factor, as it is thought to be the most important from the perspective of those who assume that a given residential environment can insure educational advantages not found in alternative environments.

Racial Isolation

Movement to the suburban ring seems seldom to have led to a permanent diminution of racial isolation in the schools without intervention in the school assignment process by external factors. Thus, racial isolation in suburban school systems seems not to differ significantly from the pattern characterizing inner city schools districts in the throes of racial transition. It has been said that only voluntary attempts at school desegregation occur in suburban communities with small black middle class ghettos.[71] Only three of the communities identified as black suburbanizing communities were included in Christine Rossell's review of desegregation action in 91 cities. Among those,

Pasadena, California (Pasadena Unified School District includes the schools in the community of Altadena) and Pontiac, Michigan were under court order to desegregate. The other community, East Orange, New Jersey, had taken no action at all.

The racial balance situation in the latter community recently led a journalist to state that Newark could not look to its adjoining suburbs for relief from racial imbalance in the schools because, "The City's suburbs, such as Irvington to the west and East Orange in the north-west, are themselves adding quickly to their black population."[72] The Fleischmann Report shows further that Wyandanch, a community in which our field survey team worked, was the most racially imbalanced (minority) district in the state, with 96.3 percent of its school population described as minority.[73] The only evidence uncovered in this analysis of a community's (among those previously identified as zones of recent black entry) voluntarily attempting to deal directly with the problem of racial isolation in the schools, was Shaker Heights, Ohio. The latter school district has been involved in a programmatic effort to eliminate its one minority imbalanced school over a period of three years. This was done through a two-way busing program. Shaker Heights conforms to Rossell's community type which is likely to show a willingness to alleviate racial imbalance voluntarily.

Southern school districts included in this study have generally reduced racial isolation as a result of court order. Among the communities so affected are those in the Washington and Miami metropolitan rings. More recently Kinloch, Missouri, one of our all-black towns, was ordered to merge with the larger Florrisant-Ferguson District in order to alleviate racial imbalance.

Parental Expectations

It was assumed that parents who recently enrolled their children in suburban schools would expect more from those schools than they did from inner city schools. How this "more" is to be defined is unclear at this point; but one suspects that parents would assume that their children would receive a superior education in the new environment. More often than not it would logically follow that parents would expect an improvement in their children's performance on a standardized battery of tests—at least it is by such measures that professional educators attempt to determine the educational output of individual schools. But we are not at all sure that these are the measures or dimensions of education that are held in highest esteem by this group of parents.

Needless to say, parents from the survey communities expressed a variety of levels of satisfaction with the quality of education they thought their children were receiving. In some instances it was apparent that perceptions of quality were based on an individual school's cognitive output, but in others the educational quality appeared to be related to some other measure of institutional performance. Sternlieb expressed the opinion that black families might be receiving less in the way of improved educational quality than they had been led to expect from such schools. Speaking directly to the situation associated with an increase in Plainfield's black population, he had this to say:

> Even more striking however, has been the response of the students to achievement tests. There has been a decided decline both by year and grade level. Based on Iowa Tests of Basic Skills the performance of Plainfield's students is decidedly under the national norms. There is more a decline in measured performance than in measured potential. The gap indicates the need for even more effort in the school system— and the community cannot afford it. Unless there is outside support for the school system it will have to falter. Given the importance of this input, the newcomer to the "zone of emergence" will find his goal much less rewarding than he had hoped for; the rung in the ladder to upward mobility for his children has been broken.[74]

In an earlier part of this chapter, parental expectation was assumed to be associated with the level of educational attainment of the families themselves. It was expected that the highest levels of parental expectation would be associated with Group I or modernizing families. Unlike the families of the all-black towns, the great majority of families settling in the major entry communities fit this description. Only 7 percent of the communities were in Group II. Among this community category are such places as Plainfield, New Jersey; North Amityville, Freeport, and Spring Valley, New York; Pontiac, Michigan; and Florence-Graham, California. Wellston, Missouri was the single community in this group that could be described as traditional. By and large, then, the movers to new outlying districts should expect a greater return on their investment in the move—as expressed by level of educational quality—than should the residents of the all-black towns.

School Tone
An issue that received rather extensive but somewhat oblique attention in this chapter was that of the school environment. It was posited that since the largest number of black movers to the suburbs were working class, this might result in a conflict in the values between pupils and school personnel. This theme has not received exhaustive treatment, at least from the perspective of an emerging

school tone—a condition emphasized here. The statistical significance of school tone was derived from an analysis of data describing a sample set of schools in the Cincinnati school system. School tone was expressed as the lack of convergence of student-held and teacher-held norms. This measure was derived through an analysis of data describing pupil characteristics and teacher morale.

Teacher morale was found to be positively related to the teacher's perceptions of the norms and values of their students. These evaluations contributed to the explanation of cognitive development. While the contribution of pupil characteristics was considerably less explanatory than IQ or transiency, it is nevertheless a dimension about which greater understanding is needed. Likewise, it was found that pupil characteristics were positively related to transiency, which in turn was negatively associated with reading achievement. There is some evidence of increasing interest in this general topic. Ronald Henderson recently attempted to evaluate what he chose to describe as school climate. His framework is that of "self-other phenomenon (symbolic interaction) in which all participants are affecting and being affected by the other constituency."[75] Henderson, however, was essentially interested in the school climate in uniracial schools. Data from Cincinnati tend to support the notion that school tone or climate was the most negative under conditions of racial transition.

The General Issue of Cognitive Development

The previous discussion can only lead eventually to what is generally thought to represent the most important dimension of the educational system—cognitive development. Somehow it appears that each of three conditions previously discussed is known to influence cognitive development and in turn is influenced by it. The reduction of racial isolation has been thought by some to represent a way of increasing black school achievement, while others have fought to maintain the status quo because they were fearful that black students would interfere with the efforts of their children to attain a good education, as measured by performance on standardized tests. Similarly, it has been shown that parental expectations revolve around cognitive output; likewise, the atmosphere prevailing in a given school setting is thought to bear some relationship to cognitive outcome. So at the base of all the arguments that have been put forth here, cognitive development must be viewed as a focal concern.

The discrepancy in levels of cognitive development between race and class tends to heighten interest in this phenomenon. At the same time it raises other questions, which prompt one to reconsider how important such measures are vis-à-vis others. A few are convinced that cognitive development as measured by performance on standardized tests tends to be overemphasized. Most are now familiar with the lengthy arguments, based on built-in cultural and class biases, which have been employed to debunk the validity of such measures. On the other side of the ledger there is a growing body of literature that tends to support the notion that cognitive output is essentially related to heredity, and thus the gap between blacks and whites on these measures is likely to persist.

But neither the cultural apologist nor the biological determinist has come to grips with the validity of the conceptual issue of the merits of these measures, as labels employed in tracking individuals into a quasi-permanent niche in American society. If these issues cannot be resolved by scholars, it is unlikely that citizens wil be inclined to give less weight to such measures when it comes to determining the most important index of quality of the educational experience. This being the case, one is likely to continue to chase an illusive goal designed to upgrade one's own status, or to permit those with high status to protect their advantage. Given this state of affairs, it is only logical for black parents to expect the educational system to bestow some of these previously denied advantages upon their children, if indeed the educational system is the great leveler it has been hailed to be.

If levels of self-esteem are as important as some contend, is this not a worthy measure of educational quality? However important self-esteem might be, professional educators are likely to view it as an outcome of social and psychological nurturing *outside* the primary purview of the schools. It appears that measures of scholastic achievement will no doubt continue to represent the principal index of educational quality and competitive advantage for some time to come. If black parents assume that the transfer from an inner city environment to an outer city environment will provide a significant improvement in their children's performance on these measures, they are likely to be disappointed.

It is true that occasionally such improvements do show themselves, but they are the result of dedication to the task of reaping such improvements and simply do not flow from environmental transfer. An evaluation of the Shaker Heights experience showed that black sixth grade students who were transferred to other, nonsegregated Shaker Heights schools showed norm-expected gains as a result of the transfer.[76] Thus even in a high status school system such as Shaker Heights, where the social class mix was moderately homogeneous and the norms and values of the population were doubtless quite similar, the results did not exceed those considered average in terms of cognitive gain.

> However, it appears that only in school systems which have a tradition of providing high quality education are there real efforts to maintain the preexisting performance standards once blacks enroll in the system in relatively large numbers. The implication of this practice is to provide educational advantages of the type discussed here only in those communities where the entering blacks possess upper middle class status, or at best lower middle class status. Since black movers are essentially working class, they can no doubt expect educational quality, like all other services, to suffer a decline when they begin to constitute a significant element in the suburban population.

The Pasadena school system, which operates under a court ordered desegregation plan, has recently demonstrated that its school program is undergoing a decline in quality as measured by changes in levels of cognitive output. Black performance during a three-year period on sixth grade reading achievement, already lower than that of other ethnic groups, declined even further, although there was some fluctuation in performance from year to year.[77] To be sure, cognitive performance by each of the evaluated ethnic groups varied as a function of socioeconomic status, but likewise it is also evident that socioeconomic status as measured by median family income is just one variable contributing to performance. The upshot of this whole discussion is that the Board of Education wishes to have the desegregation plan invalidated on the grounds that it has contributed to declining educational quality.

It is unknown at this point how important these measures actually are in influencing a given individual's future status in American life, although there is some evidence that assigns it little importance. But if black parents display the same faith in the educational system as do other Americans, then they are likely to be disappointed if they anticipate major changes in their children's cognitive development to follow a shift in environment. For those black families escaping conditions they deplore in inner cities, however, cognitive performance as an index of school quality may be only minimally important.

❄ *Chapter Four*

Economic and Social Dimensions of the Black Suburban Ring Population: A Black Subcultural Approach

The populations residing beyond the margins of the central city but within metropolitan areas are generally held to possess greater economic resources than the diminishing population left behind in the central city. In the minds of many, non-central city residence is tantamount to acquiring middle class status, within the metropolitan context. While data describing status of individual suburban zones indicate much variation in economic well-being, the myth supporting the prior notion continues to spread. It appears that during the most recent decade the status of suburban residents became even more diverse than formerly, as well paid blue collar workers began their trek to outlying areas in ever larger numbers. Thus suburban residence embraces a variety of socioeconomic groups possessing numerous life styles but with one basic desire—to flee the physical congestion and deterioration, as well as the social decay viewed by some as the modal condition of life, in the nation's larger and older central cities.

The objective of this chapter is to focus attention primarily on the socioeconomic status of those outlying communities which have majority black populations, and secondarily on those which witnessed major change in the size of their black component during the previous decade. It is generally acknowledged that the suburban ring is the preserve of white America, but with the general shift of population from the central city to the suburbs, an increasing number of blacks have been caught up in this movement. Since the communities included in this study are also diverse in terms of their socioeconomic character, the analysis that follows should provide the reader with a cross-

sectional view of the general socioeconomic status of non-central city
black residents.

SUBURBAN RESIDENCE AND
ECONOMIC STATUS

During the early sixties, it was estimated that a minimum median
family income of approximately $6,000 was required to facilitate occu-
pancy of a suburban home.[1] Since this was considerably more than the
median income of the black population at that time, it was presumed
that suburban residence would continue to be out of bounds for most.
Nevertheless, blacks have begun to settle in these communities in
limited numbers. The points of interest here are (1) the economic
status of those communities which have served as the target communities; (2) the status of those communities which have traditionally
served as the place of residence of black metropolitan ring populations;
and how these two compare in successfully providing black populations
with the kinds of life chances sought by most Americans.

Again, our most intensive analysis will focus on those outlying
black communities which are characterized as having a black majority
population. Most of these, though not all, have been predominantly
black since their inception. The author has described the evolution of
the older of these places during the middle sixties.[2] The socioeconomic
status of the remainder of these communities is derived from recent
census reports. The question of who chooses to reside where, within the
constraints of economic circumstances, is one which provokes much
interest. The question of which blacks choose to take up residence in
the suburban ring has generally eluded researchers. The salient characteristics of the black populations which have chosen to settle in the
metropolitan ring will be cast within a social class framework. Since
social class is so interwoven with the myth of suburbia, it appears to
represent a logical point of departure.

A Social Class Approach to
Black Suburbanization

The whole notion of social class as it relates to black America has
received a good deal of attention from scholars representing a variety
of disciplinary as well as polemical points of view through the years. To
date there exists no authoritative definition in this area, and the
likelihood that a configuration will be developed that will have broad
spectrum acceptability seems a bit far-fetched at this point. Part of the
difficulty associated with the development of a meaningful taxonomy
in this area had to do with the duality of the basic components of such a

construct. The duality is reflected in the static status measure of such a device and the implicit behavioral component which is often associated with the former. The problem is further complicated by disagreement as to what represents the most appropriate criteria for deriving status identity.

Income and occupation have frequently been employed as a means of objectively assessing social class in America. The limited differentiation among black Americans, at least on the income measure, until recently led E. F. Frazier to cast doubt on the validity of income as an appropriate measure for deriving social class among blacks.[3] More recently Jessie Bernard, following Frazier's lead, suggested that it was culture and not class that promoted the major cleavages in the black population.[4] Both Frazier and Bernard saw the status of black populations as being basically related to group conduct, growing out of a set of moral dictates that they valued. Indeed, it is the latter aspect of class that holds the greatest interest for most scholars, but it is likewise the most troublesome aspect of the problem. Herbert Gans has simply defined class as a heuristic device,[5] but his typology of class, which is based on focal concerns, has much to recommend it, for it represents more than simply a nominalist approach.[6]

It appears the closest attempt at this type of an approach, as it applies to the black population, was the classic work of Drake and Cayton. The latter work delineated both the objective and subjective dimensions of the social class of Chicago's black population on the eve of World War Two.[7] While Gans's notion of class subcultures revolves around the role of the family in a given life cycle state, Edward Banfield, a more recent commentator on the issue, has based his on temporal orientation.[8] Both Banfield and Bernard seem to support the notion of cultural determinism in their assessment of the behavioral correlates of class. The issue of social class and life style differences among black Americans is far from resolved. Given the unique history of blacks in America, the conflict both between and among scholars both black and white is likely to continue.

If settlement in communities beyond the margins of the central city is induced by the desire of persons to improve their lot, then one would suspect that the current movers to the set of communities included in this study would represent an upwardly mobile population. It is true that such a move could possibly represent a circular one in a status sense, yet at the same time represent a rational choice in terms of identifying a more compatible environment. It is unlikely that the information assembled here will lead to further clarification of the issue on social class among black Americans, but to ignore the issue is not likely to enhance our understanding of how blacks participate in

urban residential markets. Unfortunately, the data used for this purpose is only marginal in terms of delineating the various dimensions of
social class previously mentioned.

How important is black culture as a force in the residential choice
processes and subsequently our behavior within the chosen residential
milieu? Questions of such importance cannot be easily answered on the
information available for this research; thus definitive answers are
difficult at best. It is not difficult to develop a nominal social status
hierarchy for the purpose of community identification, but beyond this
point problems that plague most studies of this general type begin to
appear. The issues of future orientation raised by Banfield and external adaptation promoted by Bernard are, for the most part, constructs
that remain to be tested by others in a more rigorous fashion. Nevertheless, aspects of these dimensions will receive occasional mention
here.

The central issue is whether the current movers to suburban locations differ from that group of black nonmovers in significant ways,
relative to economic status and social and psychological outlook. Do
the communities chosen for residence reflect basically the way the
housing market operates in American urban areas, or a sense of black
belonging that leads to the development of non-central city communities which are ethnically homogeneous? Are the life styles that
prevail within these communities essentially conditioned by their
status compositions, or more importantly by their cultural founda-
tions? Lacking a fully acceptable construct to serve as a model, the
answers that emerge are likely to be tenuous indeed. Nevertheless,
this does not justify a turning away from an issue which, although
volatile, begs investigation.

As a matter of convenience, a nominalist description of the communities under investigation is constructed. As in the previous work
by this investigator, the approach initiated by Joseph Mooney to determine intraurban poverty areas will be employed. Unlike Mooney,
however, our interest here transcends concern with poverty identification, although the manner in which he derived his interest group is
held to be instructive. His method of defining urban poverty areas is
both simple and concise: census tracts with median family incomes less
than two-thirds the level describing the median family income of total
Standard Metropolitan Statistical Area were identified as poverty
areas.[9] Mooney's support for his position is as follows:

> The advantage in using a certain percentage of the SMSA's median
> family income as the poverty cut-off level is that one largely avoids the

problems associated with differences in costs of living among the various metropolitan areas which are inherent if a particular absolute income level is used as the cut-off point.[10]

As our concern largely revolves around the differential price structure prevailing within individual housing markets, a sliding or relative income structure is used to derive social class identities. In a previous work this writer stratified urban black populations into several categories based on whether they possessed median family incomes less than two-thirds and 90 percent; or equal to or greater than 90 percent. The three categorical identities were as follows: lower class, working class, and middle class.[11]

For the purpose of this investigation the third category has been expanded to include groupings described as lower middle class and upper middle class. This was accomplished by including those whose median family incomes exceeded that of the reference unit by fifteen percentage points. This group is labeled upper middle class, while those falling within the range of .90 to 1.14 percent of the median are identified as lower middle class. The reference income in this instance is that describing the income distributions of the population residing in each of the metropolitan rings of interest. It is assumed that housing prices vary from one market area to another; thus this relative income categorization would be appropriate in this context.

Life Style or Class: Is There a Distinction?

With all the weaknesses that such an approach incorporates, it will nevertheless be employed as a framework for attempting to get at other facets of the problem. Some of the other related facets are associated with the indirect or subjective measures of a number of items that undergird aspects of class and culture and subsequently black life style. Many writers have attempted to differentiate life style among blacks, holding social rank constant. Drake and Cayton differentiated their Bronzeville's residents into the "respectables" and the "shadies," based on source of income.[12] Bernard employed a different dichotomy, which she labeled the acculturated and the externally adapted.[13] In both instances it is implied that some force, whether internal or external, acts upon individuals in such a way as to lead to a specific style of life. It is inferred that the chosen style of life's influences upon one's social acceptability is crucial in promoting interaction with others whose life style is predicated upon an alternative value set.

Thinking of this kind has led to the notion that there exists a valid black subculture which is an outgrowth of the black experience in the

142 Black Suburbanization

United States, and that its dimensions can be identified. Implicit in this notion is that racial oppression has prompted individual blacks to respond to that oppression in a variety of ways, and that the most frequently identified coping mechanisms have come to be recognized as elements of the subculture. These subculture coping mechanisms are transmitted from generation to generation, requiring only adaptation to new situations.

It seems that the principal argument at this point between both lay persons and scholars is which of the variety of coping mechanisms are valid and should be accorded acceptance. The works by both Bernard and Banfield suggest that the acceptable dimensions are those in accord with some moral ideology—in this instance, the Protestant Ethic. For those who have found it difficult to comply with this ethic, social status has often been denied. But further, if these individuals do not exhibit guilt feelings as a result of this inability to cope, they are considered to be farther removed from the crucible of American culture and thus still in need of acculturation.

Black culture, it appears, is manifested in a variety of practices and attitudes that have aided black individuals in the process of adaptation in an environment over which they have had little or no control. The changes which have occurred in the nature of economic development during the last generation have imposed burdens upon this adaptive repertoire that could not have been foreseen by its practitioners, and have rendered elements of the repertoire maladaptive from the perspective of some. The question that remains is what kinds of adaptive mechanisms are best designed to permit blacks to function on a level that is least troublesome in terms of their effect on significant others in an urban milieu. In a crude way, we will attempt to sort out some of the characteristics that differentiate by social class those blacks who have opted for residence outside the central city.

It is possible that the conclusions derived from primary information describing that group of communities previously identified as black towns will not strongly resemble life styles prevailing in other black suburbanizing communities possessing similar objective traits. Even this small band of communities possesses a diverse set of characteristics in terms of the age of the settlement, its initial racial character, environmental esthetics, stage of development, and public image. A number of these communities have been the place of residence of black populations for several generations, while others have only recently been occupied by a significant number of blacks. Similarly, a number of these communities evolved in a rural setting and only at a later time found themselves surrounded by newer suburban communities that were all white.

The Social Class Identity of the All-Black Towns

In many ways the structural evolution of some of these communities is reminiscent of Eyre's description of the emergence of the shanty towns of Montego Bay, Jamaica. Eyre states that segments of the flow of population into the shanty towns "consist largely of people who desire to escape from many aspects of life in the inner city (crowding, high rents, crime) and wish to find alternative accommodations."[14] Similarly it appears that Eyre's description of housing patterns and types bears some resemblance to housing in segments of these communities, depending upon their age and the extent to which the community is an impoverished one. Evidence of this is consonant with his statement: "Since shanty towns are essentially the product of personal initiative, construction is highly individualized and incorporates anything ready to hand."[15] The origin of the older of these communities, especially those in highly urbanized settings, might represent a truncated form of shanty town development that was not permitted to proceed because of the difference in the history of metropolitan development in the United States vis-à-vis that in developing nations. But regardless of the theory of structural form, it was the communities in this group, along with a few others, which constituted the only communities of significant black residence in nonsouthern suburban zones (metropolitan ring communities) until the recent period.

Variations in Social Class Identity

The objective description of the black towns (communities) based on median family income shows that the modal class category is working class. The lower class designation is the second most numerous among this group, while only one community was identified as lower middle class and another upper middle class. Similarly, the principal black growth communities during the sixties, described here as suburban, were likewise identified as being principally working class in makeup. In both instances about 60 percent of the communities in the two groups could be described in this way. The principal difference lies in the smaller percentage of lower class communities among the suburbanizing group and the much larger percentage of lower middle class communities among the group. Thus the percentage of analagous community types is quite similar within these two universes. The one commonality universal among both sets of places is intensity of residential segregation on the basis of race.

Among this small group of communities, many of whom have served as pioneer suburban ring residences for small cluster of blacks, there is much variation in the economic composition of their population Relative economic status varies from an upper middle class identity for the Hollydale, Ohio, community to Brooklyn, Illinois, which possesses all the major dimensions of poverty. Regardless of the relative status of those communities identified in an earlier work as all-Negro towns, they each showed some progress during the sixties—if a whitening of collars can be viewed as a superficial measure of economic progress. In each instance there was some reduction in the percentage of blue collar workers in the labor force. Urbancrest, Ohio showed a change of only slightly more than 1 percent, while in Glenarden, Maryland, blue collar composition shifted from 85 percent in 1960 to 37 percent in 1970. The latter community represents a growth community, and the former represents a community undergoing a population decline. Table 4–1 depicts the social class composition of the black towns.

From Table 4–1 it is clear that in all these communities save one, the labor force is predominantly blue collar. One weakness of our classification is apparent at this point. There is an obvious discrepancy in the class status assigned to Hollydale and Glenarden. The former community has been identified as upper middle class, although slightly more than three-fifths of its workers are blue collar. Yet Glenarden is termed lower middle class with fewer than two-fifths of its workers engaged in blue collar occupations. This points up vividly one of the weaknesses of using a single measure to derive class identity.

Table 4–1.   Class Composition of the All-Black Towns In 1970, with General Changes in the Characteristics of the Labor Force

		% Blue Collar Workers	
Town	*Class Position*	*1960*	*1970*
Glenarden, Md.	Lower Middle Class	85	37
E. Chicago Hts., Ill.	Lower Class		83
Robbins, Ill.	Working Class	84	72
Cooper Rd., La.	Lower Class	90	84
Lawnside, N. J.	Working Class	75	67
E. Palo Alto, Cal.	Working Class		68
Brooklyn, Ill.	Lower Class	80	71
Kinloch, Mo.	Lower Class	89	74
Wyandanch, N.Y.	Working Class		69
Roosevelt City, Ala.	Working Class		77
Richmond Hts., Fla.	Working Class	80	70
N. Fontana, Cal.	Lower Class		71
Urbancrest, Ohio	Working Class	86	85
Hollydale, Ohio	Upper Middle Class		61
Lincoln Hts., Ohio	Working Class	86	77

Source: U.S. Bureau of the Census, 1960 & 1970 Census of Population and Housing, appropriate PHC(1) series.

To proceed a step beyond the nominal description based on relative economic status of the population represents an excursion into an uncharted area. An attempt will be made to identify a group of measures that is frequently cited as representing aspects of a black subculture as an expression of social status. The validity of these measures is likely to be somewhat questionable in terms of what they in fact describe. Nevertheless, such a crude attempt is made as a means of deriving dimensions that are thought to be unique to the black experience.

Among the measures employed are those designed to determine if the current residents are found to be living within communities of opportunity or communities of despair. Opportunity in this instance reflects the absence of signs of threat to one's economic and psychological survival. In communities of opportunity one would expect low levels of unemployment (see Table 4–2), low levels of poverty, and low levels of welfare dependence on the economic side; on the psychological side, the absence of fear for one's physical safety, the absence of evidence of family instability, and the ability to influence one's life chances by exerting some control over one's fertility. Communities of despair would evince an opposite set of traits and would be more in keeping with the life chances available to black Americans generally, regardless of place of residence. For those of the Banfield persuasion, communities of despair would serve as evidence that their practitioners engage in a lower class life style and thus their problems are essentially related to their inability to alter current behavioral traits. Yet others would contend that the despair was associated with their inability to cope with an impersonal system, given limited resources with which to undertake this task.

The economic dimension has usually been given greater direct emphasis than others of the social status constellation when attempting to dissect suburban communities. It is generally treated in this way

Table 4–2. The Pattern of Unemployment Prevailing in All-Black Towns in 1970

Low Unemployment		Average Unemployment		High Unemployment	
Glenarden, Md.	2.0	Wyandanch, N.Y.	5.1	Cooper Road, La.	8.9
Richmond Hts., Fla.	2.4	Brooklyn, Ill.	5.5	Roosevelt City, Ala.	10.0
Urbancrest, Ohio	—	Lawnside, N.J.	5.9	N. Fontana, Cal.	12.6
Hollydale, Ohio	2.8	Kinloch, Mo.	6.2	E. Chicago Hts., Ill.	13.8
		E. Palo Alto, Cal.	8.1		
		Robbins, Ill.	8.2		
		Lincoln Hts., Ohio	8.7		

Source: U.S. Bureau of the Census, 1970 Census of Population, appropriate PC(V) series.

because gross information is more readily available, and secondarily, because many of the other population attributes are thought to flow from the former. Here concern is with the nature of economic security as it relates to the position of blacks in urban non-central city locations. Economic security in this instance will be gauged by the extent to which the respective populations are (a) unemployed, (b) living under conditions of poverty, and (c) dependent upon public assistance for financial support. It is generally assumed that the more economically secure populations are involved in the movement from the central city to the suburbs, and, more recently, from older suburbs to newer areas. Mobility is, therefore, a way of adapting to one's circumstances.

Since a status rank has already been assigned to the fifteen black towns, an implicit statement regarding economic security has already been made. Nevertheless, there is need to review how these same communities fare on measures other than relative economic position within the metropolitan ring. This group of communities can be divided into those characterized by population growth during the sixties and those characterized by population declines (see Table 4–3). In this instance, growth basically attributed to net migration might be assumed to be the more relevant indicator of the possession of economic security. On the other hand, those communities which were characterized by net out-movement were communities in which the search for economic security transcended the potential existing within the home community. When the prevailing level of poverty is employed as a measure of economic security, it is found to be almost identical to the grouping that emerged when employment levels were used. The incidence of poverty prevailing in 1969 ranged from 4.3 percent in Glenarden, Maryland to 49.1 percent among the population of Cooper Road, Louisiana.

Table 4–3.   Growth Characteristics of All-Black Towns During the 1960s

Rapid Growth (Greater Than 30%)	Slow to Moderate Growth (Less Than 30%)	Non-Growth (Absolute Population Decline)
Glenarden, Md.	Robbins, Ill.	Kinloch, Mo.
Wyandanch, N.Y.	Lawnside, N.J.	Roosevelt City, Ala.
E. Palo Alto, Cal.	Cooper Road, La.	Lincoln Heights, Ohio
E. Chicago Heights, Ill.	N. Fontana, Cal.	Brooklyn, Ill.
Hollydale, Ohio		Urbancrest, Ohio
Richmond Heights, Fla.		

Source: U.S. Bureau of the Census, 1960 & 1970 Census of Population and Housing, Appropriate PHC(1) series.

Again employing the concepts of economically secure populations and economically insecure populations, it is possible to generalize about the extent to which these populations might be expected to enjoy the higher qualities of life that are assumed to prevail beyond the margins of the central city. Employing the incidence of poverty prevailing in 1969 (see Table 4–4), the only two communities which can be viewed as economically secure are Glenarden, Maryland, and Hollydale, Ohio. In both instances less than 10 percent of the families were living in households described as poverty households. Another six communities might be viewed as marginally secure with levels of poverty lower than that describing the general poverty level of suburban fringe black populations. These include Lawnside, New Jersey; Robbins, Illinois; Wyandanch, New York; East Palo Alto, California; Richmond Heights, Florida; and North Fontana, California. The remaining communities, which constitute almost half the total group, are best described as economically insecure communities, although even among the latter group there exist large variations in the prevailing incidence of poverty. Those described as externally insecure are places where one-third or more of all households live under conditions of poverty as represented by inadequate incomes.

Again, it should be pointed out that reliance on the Social Security Administration's absolute poverty threshold is not without serious drawbacks. Given that the communities which make up this group are geographically diverse and that regional income differences do exist, the levels of poverty reported here are distorted by regional variation in income and the variations in the level of living associated with these

Table 4–4. Economic Security Characteristics of the All-Black Towns as Measured by the Incidence of Poverty, 1969

Economically Secure	*Marginally Secure*
Glenarden, Md.	Lawnside, N.J.
Hollydale, Ohio	Wyandanch, N.Y.
	Robbins, Ill.
	E. Palo Alto, Cal.
	Richmond Heights, Fla.
	N. Fontana, Cal.
Moderately Insecure	*Extremely Insecure*
E. Chicago Heights, Ill.	Brooklyn, Ill.
Urbancrest, Ohio	Kinloch, Missouri
Lincoln Heights, Ohio	Roosevelt City, Ala.
	Cooper Road, La.

differences. Earlier it was reported that the class schema employed here was partially patterned after the practice adopted to identify urban poverty areas. Thus the lower class income categories developed for this study are congruent with those Mooney would have identified as poverty levels.

The gap between the poverty level followed here and that derived employing the Mooney threshold is wide ranging. The ratio between these two thresholds varies from 0.92 in the case of Cooper Road to .43 in the case of Glenarden. This would seem to imply that the real incidence of poverty in those communities previously described as secure or marginally secure is higher than reported when utilizing the Social Security definition. One suspects that a more valid approach to deriving an incidence of level of poverty commensurate with the pattern of income distribution characteristic of a given metropolitan ring is to develop a set of weights that take into consideration these differences and then apply these to the levels reported by the Census Bureau. While this would generally result in an increase in the incidence of poverty, it would leave the poverty rank of these communities intact.

Four of the communities among this group have half of all families located within the lowest one-third of the income range. These communities by the definition employed here are lower class communities, but would constitute poverty communities if one employed the terminology of Mooney. The communities which fit into this category are East Chicago Heights, Cooper Road, Brooklyn, Kinloch, and North Fontana. It is apparent that at least one-third of the communities in this set of suburban fringe communities are economically insecure and thus can hardly be thought of as communities whose image fits the myth of suburbia.

The results of a field survey undertaken during the summer of 1972 should lend additional insight into the characteristics of the residents in selected places possessing poverty level incomes. There is some discrepancy between Census Bureau estimates and field survey estimates of the incidence of poverty prevailing in these communities. As was mentioned earlier, some of the discrepancy is associated with small sampling ratios in some communities, while additional differences could be attributed to changes in the general economic environment over the three years separating the collection of information. First, attention is focused upon those communities in which the sampling ratios are of the order to 10 percent. In two of these communities there is evidence of improvement, while in the other two further deterioration is evident. The change in the two lower class communities were in the opposite direction, but the change was not

Table 4–5. Changes in the Incidence of Poverty in Selected Communities, 1969–1972

	Class Status	1969 (percent)	1972 (percent)	Difference
Glenarden, Md.	Lower Middle	4.3	10.5	+6.2%
Richmond Hts., Fla.	Working	13.2	8.8	−4.4%
Kinloch, Mo.	Lower	32.8	35.6	+2.8%
Cooper Road, La.	Lower	49.1	46.0	−3.1%

Sources: Census of Population and Housing: 1970 Census Tracts, Final Report PHC (1)—Individual SMSA's, and 1972 All-Black Towns Field Survey Report.

sufficient to alter their status as extremely economically insecure communities (see Table 4–5). Glenarden, on the other hand, was moving toward the marginally secure status, while Richmond Heights was moving into the secure category.

Factors Contributing to the Prevailing Incidence of Poverty

A review of the characteristics of the households whose family income, based on the Social Security Administration definition, would place them in a state of poverty reveals a number of conditions that contribute to low family income. The combination of precipitating conditions vary from community to community. Richmond Heights and Glenarden, both of which were major growth communities during the previous decade, and both found among the more economically secure communities within the group, might be expected to possess similar poverty producing conditions. In both communities, poverty was indeed most frequently associated with the same factors of low educational attainment and female-headed households. The effect of female heads is more pervasive in Glenarden than in Richmond Heights. Almost 90 percent of the lower income households in Glenarden are headed by females, almost half of whom are in the labor force.

The condition of this segment of the population is aggravated by their low levels of educational attainment. In this instance the modal level of educational attainment is nine to twelve years. In Richmond Heights the level of educational attainment appears to be of greater importance than the sex of the household heads in leading to poverty level incomes. The modal level of educational attainment among the inadequate income group in the latter community is less than eight years, a condition which is equally distributed among the sexes. Paradoxically, there are persons whose level of educational attainment exceeds high school in Richmond Heights, but for whom poverty is still a prevalent condition. Poverty would be expected to produce greater hardships in Richmond Heights because of the large family size of the poor households.

In the two poverty communities of Kinloch and Cooper Road, the same conditions seen in the above communities show themselves, but additional conditions are also present that further aggravate economic security. In Kinloch the age structure of the population itself works against the maintenance of economic security. Length of residence in this community would set most of the poverty residents off as old timers. More than 60 percent of this population has resided within the community for twenty or more years. More than 35 percent of all of the poor are elderly poor, with some still in the work force. Given the existing age structure, one would expect that a low level of educational attainment could be anticipated. More than half of the total (but in this instance the majority of female heads) are elderly women with small families.

It seems from the existing data that Kinloch is in fact a residential community largely made up of persons from another era who have arrived at a decision to spend their waning years in an environment in which they have spent much of their prior lifetime. Thus this population has attempted to cope with the environment in which they find themselves by simply accepting their lot as fate. There are a number of similarities between Cooper Road and Kinloch, with the one major difference related to the percentage of the elderly among the poor. Nevertheless, most of the poor have resided in Cooper Road long enough not to be thought of as newcomers. Low level of educational attainment with more than two-thirds of the household heads having completed fewer than eight years of formal education is characteristic. Among the female headed households, only about one-fifth are elderly. Fewer than half the females heading households who are in the labor force participating ages are actually in the labor force. This is probably indicative of the absence of opportunity for black women with limited formal education in the Shreveport metropolitan area. The vast out-movement of blacks from this labor market during the previous decade lends support to this position.

The reported conditions, which are common to the poor in this select set of outlying communities, are assumed to be poverty inducing. To what extent they actually explain the prevalence of poverty is a matter that cannot be answered resolutely. There has been no attempt to specify the needs of the labor market in which these individuals are participants or potential participants. But it is rather obvious that persons with limited skills are only minimally rewarded in these labor markets, and the market can only absorb a certain number of persons with the previously identified attributes. In the case of Kinloch there is little that can be done to minimize the incidence of poverty given the community's residual status, although the qualities of life of those possessing this status could be enhanced. In the latter case, the residential environment in Kinloch would have to be made attractive to persons with little potential for poverty in order to improve or deflate the incidence of poverty. But tactics such as these do not necessarily alter the lot of the resident population. In some instances these outlying communities simply represent pockets of economic wastelands possessing noncentral locations.

One's view of himself and his community can be assumed to be partially derived from his assessment of neighboring communities. The relative well-being of these communities vis-à-vis their nearest neighbor, employing median family income as a measure of well-being, is illustrated in Table 4–6. In only three instances are the all-black towns better off in terms of current income than are their nearest neighbors. Glenarden, Hollydale, and Richmond Heights are the only communities with a median family income exceeding that of their closest neighbor, and in each instance the nearest neighbor community is one which also possesses a black majority in its population. The other extreme is represented by the relationship of Kinloch to Berkeley. Here, the latter community is characterized by a median family income almost double that of the black community abutting its eastern flank.

In several instances the central city black community also appears to be more economically secure than these suburban outliers. Brook-

Table 4–6. The Economic Well-Being of All-Black Towns Expressed as the Ratio of Median Family Income to That of Their Nearest Neighbor Community

Black Town	Ratio of Well-Being	Nearest Neighbor
Glenarden, Md.	0.83	Palmer Park, Md.
Hollydale, Ohio	0.87	Woodlawn, Ohio
Lawnside, N.J.	1.19	Magnolia, N.J.
Robbins, Ill.	1.26	Midlothian, Ill.
Wyandanch, N.Y.	1.33	Deer Park, N.Y.
E. Palo Alto, Cal.	1.51	Menlo Park, Cal.
Richmond Heights, Fla.	0.91	Perrine, Fla.
N. Fontana, Cal.	1.57	Fontana, Cal.
E. Chicago Heights, Ill.	1.37	Chicago Heights, Ill.
Urbancrest, Ohio	1.57	Grove City, Ohio
Lincoln Heights, Ohio	1.51	Woodlawn, Ohio
Brooklyn, Ill.	1.38	Venice, Ill.
Kinloch, Mo.	1.89	Berkely, Missouri
Roosevelt City, Ala.	1.21	Bersenner, Ala.

lyn, Kinloch, Urbancrest and Cooper Road are all economically less secure than the aggregate central city black community in their respective metropolitan areas. Even so, it might yet be easier to cope with poverty at least in terms of effectiveness, in these outlying environments, although there are some who view the problem in the following way:

> ... in some ways, however, the poor in suburbia are worse off than those in the city. Since poverty is in part a relative problem and they live in a considerably more affluent environment, they are considerably worse off by comparison with the large majority of suburban residents.[19]

Whatever happens to be the prevailing point of view, poverty is not a stranger to a sizeable share of the residents of the all-black towns. Among these, only Glenarden and Hollydale seem to be significantly free from the vagaries of poverty. On the other hand poverty is endemic in Kinloch, Brooklyn, Roosevelt City, and Cooper Road.

Welfare Dependency as a Measure of Economic Security

A final measure of economic security which will be touched upon here is welfare dependency. Unlike the prior two security measures the latter is a peripheral measure, but one which has recently been viewed as an outcome of an aspect of a set of unique black life styles. Welfare dependency is largely associated with one of the four categorical support programs jointly financed by the federal and individual state governments. That categorical program which critics most frequently associate with aspects of black culture is the Aid to Families with Dependent Children (AFDC) component. During the mid sixties, Daniel Moynihan raised the specter of black family deterioration as leading to a condition of welfare dependency unprecedented in American life. In support of this position Moynihan remarked that "Among Negro and other races, 48 percent of first births were out of wedlock, which would suggest that fully half the female population began childbearing in circumstances predisposed to dependency."[20] Statements of this sort have frequently come under attack by those who question the validity of the latter author's thesis. But Moynihan steadfastly holds to this position, as his more recent statements attest. Among such statements are the following: "It is now about a decade since my policy paper and its analysis. As forecasting goes, it would seem to have held up. There has been a pronounced 'up and down' experience among urban blacks."[21]

Others agree with Moynihan that welfare dependency is indeed becoming a very serious problem, but that its increase as reflected by the increase in the numbers of families receiving financial support under the auspices of AFDC is associated with other phenomena. Piven and Cloward attribute the accelerated increase in welfare dependency during the sixties to government's response to the urban disorders of the period.[22] To whatever one attributes these causes, the phenomenon is one that exists and provides a tenuous and sometimes stigmatizing source of financial support. The issue here is whether the factors that lead to this necessity are as pervasive in these outlying communities as within the central city.

If welfare dependency tends to undermine one's sense of self-respect, and denigrate the value of work and correspondingly one's sense of inner control, then one could expect it to promote ill consequences for those who are forced to seek it as a form of permanent refuge. It has been reported, though, that very little research has been focused upon this topic.[23] Those who are supportive of the family deterioration thesis obviously see this as a negative force leading to a state where the children in such households can look forward to a nonrewarding future, in terms of the traditional reward structure.

In 1970, almost half the black families described as being poor, were dependent upon public assistance. In those instances where such families were headed by females, the dependency level reached 63 percent. Since most black families are now located in the nation's larger central cities, it will be assumed that the level of dependency rises above the 48 percent level for the nation as a whole. This latter conclusion is based on the condition of greater family instability in larger urban environments and the greater ease of securing support in the latter places. A dependency level of 50 percent, based on those families who have been described as poor, will be employed as a benchmark in distinguishing between the central city condition and the non-central city condition. Indirectly, this should permit one to distinguish between a set of forces prevailing within these two sets of environments.

Welfare dependency in the all-black towns runs the gamut from no dependency in the case of Hollydale, to more than half of the poverty population receiving public assistance in East Palo Alto. The latter community is the only one in the group whose dependency on public welfare closely resembles that of central city populations. An examination of the welfare dependency syndrome in the central city of the metropolitan area in which these communities are located reveals that five of the central cities are characterized by welfare dependency levels greater than 40 but less than 50 percent. In general, those central cities in which welfare dependency exceeded 50 percent were those in which black migration during the previous decade had been unduly large.

DeJong and Donelly, who were concerned with the impact of AFDC payments on black migration during the fifties, found a significant association among these variables for larger northern and western cities.[24] These writers are careful, however, to point out that AFDC is not a primary cause of migration.[25] There is no clear-cut association between migration and welfare dependency among this set of communities. High levels of dependency are to be found in both communities of limited entry during the decade as well as those with relatively high entry levels. The level of welfare dependency is generally lower in the all-black town than in central cities in general. In only three communities was the level of dependency comparable to the central city level. The communities possessing central citylike welfare rates were East Palo Alto, Brooklyn, and Lincoln Heights. Six communities were found to be only slightly less dependent on public assistance, whereas five communities showed signs of only limited dependence on welfare. The latter group included Hollydale, Glenarden, Robbins, Lawnside, Richmond Heights, and Urbancrest. Thus, public assistance payments do not contribute significantly to the maintenance of economic security in one-third of these communities, although dependency is high to moderate in the other two-thirds.

There appear to be no easy answers explaining why dependency varies greatly from one community to another among families whose incomes are below the poverty threshold. Both individual attitudes and public policy condition the extent of dependency. Sav Levitan and others state that "the stigma of welfare has certainly deterred many eligible persons from applying for assistance."[26] They then go on to say, "Where government handouts are allocated to giant corporations in financial straits and to millionaire farmers, a poor mother with children is not likely to feel less worthy of aid nor more reticent in seeking it."[27] Thus it appears that public policy can elicit an attitudinal change on the part of a potential user of the system. The latter statements by Levitan and others refer only to the AFDC component of the public assistance program, but it is this segment that represents the growth component of public assistance and the one upon which most blacks are dependent for support.

It is the increasing number of persons who secure support in order to provide for children where the father is absent that has created a stir and has raised the issue of the community's responsibility for providing support to the nondeserving poor. AFDC recipients are often viewed in the latter light by members of the urban working class. Local policy in terms of eligibility requirements sometimes reflects these attitudes as well. Walker and Tweeten, in attempting to statistically assess those variables influencing participation rates in AFDC programs, found that a set of local specifications did produce negative coefficients reflecting a deterrent effect.[28] The specific variables included mandatory school attendance and suitable home requirements. These same writers showed that 84 percent of the increase in participation rates was associated with increases in illegitimacy rates.[29]

Those states and communities introducing policy constraints are no doubt partially motivated by the desire to curb the burden imposed on the taxpayers by those viewed by them as the undeserving poor. On the issue of attitudes it is not certain if a person harbors a fixed set of attitudes regarding welfare dependency or simply evaluates his or her options on the basis of rational economic choice. One writer states:

> Indeed, for many mothers with low earning power, welfare is a perfect substitute for work, if income alone is the criterion. Such a woman would have to have a strong aversion and/or a strong desire to work not to seek welfare in these circumstances.[30]

Age structure and previous work experience probably conditions attitudes toward welfare. Among the communities under investigation, if the previous assumptions are valid, one should expect the highest level of participation in assistance programs to be associated with the incidence of young females with limited work experience, and those whose educational characteristics dictate access only to low wage rate jobs. Unfortunately it is not possible to test this notion with the information available, since the number of women under 30 either not in the labor force or receiving assistance is small.

However, our field survey results will allow for generalization in some instances. Young female household heads (under 30 years old) constituted a very small segment of the population in all but five of these communities. In most instances the number of employed and unemployed female heads is about the same. The only factor that appears to be related to the decision not to seek employment is size of family. For those women who are older and whose marital dissolution occurred during residence in the community, the wife chose to remain in the community because she thought it a good place to bring up children. Whether or not a woman was in the labor market in the latter instance seems to be largely related to the opportunity structure in the market and the educational characteristics of the head. In a male dominant labor market such as North Fontana, women who assume the role of household heads are prone to seek public assistance. On the other hand, most female heads in Glenarden are employed in those clerical and service occupations that are commonplace in the metropolitan area of which they are a part. It is generally apparent that the residents of these communities are not overly dependent, although there are circumstances in which dependency represents the only rational option available given one's circumstances. Seldom do dependency rates approach those that are characteristic of the central city, although in one or two cases it would be difficult to distinguish individual communities from their central city counterparts.

A Composite Index of Economic Security

The variations in levels of unemployment, the incidence of poverty, and the incidence of dependency allow one to generalize regarding the condition of economic security generally prevailing among the residents of these communities. A composite score reflecting the extent to which these various indexes of economic well-being are present among residents is employed as a means of describing these communities along a continuum of economic security (see Table 4–7). The greatest weight was assigned to the employment measure and the lowest to the dependency measure. Those communities which were categorized as economically insecure failed to qualify for points on either index if they were characterized by high levels of unemployment, poverty, and dependency. Only four communities (less than 5 percent) were awarded points on the basis of low levels of unemployment, while three others received points for lack of dependency. The latter group included communities in which fewer than 15 percent of those described as poor were dependent upon public assistance.

The latter measure is the most bothersome. It implies that a small minority of the poverty population will choose public assistance as a source of support in most instances. Under the circumstances, this decision is likely to represent a rational one from the perspective of the individual household head. One suspects family instability and/or dis-

Table 4–7. The Economic Security Characteristics of the All-Black Towns

Secure	Score	Relatively Secure	Score
Glenarden	63	Richmond Heights	39
Hollydale	56	Urbancrest	30

Marginally Secure	Score	Insecure	Score
Robbins	19	Kinloch	0
East Palo Alto	14	Roosevelt City	0
Wyandanch	14	Lincoln Heights	0
Lawnside	7	Brooklyn	0
North Fontana	7	Cooper Road	0

solution and illegitimacy are the principal pressures provoking one to choose this option in the face of adversity. The condition of dependency is partially influenced by how well the individual participants are able to ward off family instability and illegitimacy. The largest number of communities receiving points did so because they had only a small percentage of their households characterized by poverty, relative to the prevailing national level for blacks. Needless to say, communities of opportunity within this universe is small, and the modal community category is that of despair (see Table 4–7).

Economic Security in Black Suburbanizing Communities

Before proceeding to an assessment of the level of psychological security prevailing within these communities, the notion of economic security developed here will be applied to a larger set of places that represent black metropolitan growth poles. In most instances, these growth poles represent communities of recent black entry and are thus in some ways black suburban prototypes possessing a variety of social class attributes. Among this alternate set of communities, only East Palo Alto and Wyandanch are procedurally similar in terms of the process which undergirds the prevailing pattern of temporal-spatial evolution. Thus it is possible to compare the newly emerging set of black communities with those which evolved during an earlier period and, in some instances, under very different sets of circumstances.

The communities included among those described as black suburbanizing communities were those which were the principal targets of black entrance during the previous decade. Therefore, these communities simply represent growth zones largely based on movement from the outside. A number of suburbanizing communities which had previously attracted blacks in relatively large numbers proved to be relatively less attractive during the sixties.[31] In many ways these communities tend to differ from the all-black towns. Many of them are larger, representing industrial satellites either at the margins of the central city or more remotely located. They are often communities which have become unattractive environments for mobile whites.

Where the communities have tended to be larger, their populations have tended to be more diverse. The larger number of these communities exceed 40,000 in population size, with the black percentage ranging from just over 6 percent in Silver Spring, Maryland and Hayward, California to almost three-quarters of the total in Compton, California. The size of the community, though, is not the principal regulator of the rate of change in racial composition. Variable rates of change characterize communities in each size category. Of course, it is obvious that if all the ingredients that foster racial turnover are present, change will occur most rapidly in the smaller communities. Wellston, Missouri, with fewer than 10,000 persons, is a case in point: in 1960, Wellston was less than 9 percent black, but by 1970 had become almost 70 percent black. Seat Pleasant, Maryland provides an even more exaggerated example. Table 4–8 shows that there is considerable range in the percent black, but the smallest percentages tend to be found in the larger places.

Table 4–8. Size Categories of Black Suburbanizing Communities and Percent Black in 1970

Small ≥5,000 <20,000	% *Black*
Wellston, Missouri	69.0
Takoma Park, Maryland	14.0
Seat Pleasant, Maryland	77.4
Warrensville Hts., Ohio	22.4
Spring Valley, N.Y.	23.4
Roosevelt, N.Y.	68.5
Markham, Ill.	50.3
Browardale, Fla.	90.7
Intermediate ≥20,000 <40,000	% *Black*
Carol City, Florida	14.0
E. Cleveland, Ohio	59.8
Shaker Hts., Ohio	14.9
Hempstead, N.Y.	36.8
Harvey, Ill.	31.5
Westmont, Cal.	80.5
Willowbrook, Cal.	82.3
Florence Graham, Cal.	56.0
Brownsville, Florida	91.0
Large ≥40,000	% *Black*
Silver Spring, Md.	6.1
E. Orange, N.J.	54.1
Plainfield, N.J.	40.0
Hayward, Cal.	6.2
Richmond, Cal.	40.1
Daly City, Cal.	13.3
Freeport, N.Y.	19.2
Pontiac, Mich.	27.5
Carson, Cal.	12.2
Pomona, Cal.	14.2
Altadena, Cal.	31.3
University City, Mo.	21.2

Source: U.S. Bureau of the Census, 1970 Census of Population, appropriate PC(V) series.

The Social Class Structure in Black
Suburbanizing Communities

Among the suburbanizing communities there is also a more diverse class structure than characteristic of the all-black towns. While the working class designation predominates among each group, about one-fifth of these communities are middle class compared to only 2 percent of the latter. Another fifth of the suburbanizing communities are lower class. Among the all-black towns, almost two-fifths of the communities had been designated lower class. As a group of communities, there is little question that the suburbanizing community group is more economically secure than the former group, but the question remains, how much more secure?

Five communities have been included among this group which could possibly distort the general picture. These communities represent a set of relatively large, predominantly black, unincorporated zones lying on the margins of the central city in Los Angeles, Miami, and Ft. Lauderdale. These zones were assigned a formal identity by the Census Bureau for the first time in 1970. Prior to that date, data was not available that would permit one to measure changes taking place during the decade. This phenomenon was also observed in 1960. The Census Bureau assigned a formal identity to a number of black peripheral clusters, when they in fact were simply physical appendages of the larger black community located within the principal town. During the earlier period, such places were simply identified as psuedo towns by this writer.[32] In this instance, the decision regarding the treatment of such places is made more difficult by not having longitudinal data on changes taking place within them, in addition to the fact that a different set of research objectives are at the core of the study.

Among the pseudo communities, two are lower class communities, while three show up as working class communities. Two of the working class communities—Westmont, California and Browardale, Florida— appear to be communities of recent entry, while the others appear to have undergone little change. Thus, in the case of Willowbrook and Florence-Graham, California and Brownsville, Florida, there seems to be little evidence that they were major targets of black entry during the decade.

The black suburbanizing communities show greater strength than do the all-black towns in the critical area of economic security, as reflected in their employment rate. Almost two-fifths of the communities in this universe are characterized by low rates of unemployment. Both the class composition of these communities as well as the general labor market conditions in individual metropolitan areas are contributors to this condition. In none of the middle class communities is there evidence of high levels of unemployment. However, in the Los Angeles metropolitan area none of the identified communities could be described as a low unemployment rate community, regardless of its social class makeup. This, no doubt, reflects the general labor market situation in Los Angeles. Poverty is less intense among the suburbanizing group of communities. Only Florence-Graham, California and Wellston, Missouri possessed levels of poverty typical of those of the most economically insecure of the all-black towns.

Welfare dependency is quite widespread among the poor in the black suburbanizing communities; but seldom does it approach the levels commonplace among central city communities. The level of dependency was in the intermediate range in most communities in the latter group. Dependency within this universe, besides being associated with poverty, is associated with the presence of the aged (.277) female headed households (.338), median family income ($-.468$), median educational attainment ($-.278$), and fertility index (.227). When considering only the all-black towns, the correlations between dependency and these variables is elevated. Aside from poverty and income, the variable exerting the greatest influence is sex ratio ($-.697$), age 65 and over (.453), female headed households (.361), and fertility index (.317).

The statistical associations are higher among the all-black towns. It is apparent that dependency is more difficult to explain among the black suburbanizing communities. There may exist either attitudinal differences, or different eligibility requirements facilitating ease of qualifications among communities in the larger group. But considering the fact that the all-black towns and the black suburbanizing communities with only a few exceptions are nested within the same metropolitan rings, this seems to minimize the latter possibility. The one noticeable difference is the greater association between age and dependency among the all-black towns, and female heads and dependency among the suburbanizing communities.

The same measuring technique as employed earlier to evaluate economic security among the all-black towns was employed in grouping the suburbanizing communities along the same continuum. Most of the economically secure communities posted higher scores than their all-black town counterparts. Glenarden, the most secure of the black towns, would rank fifth if placed in the universe of suburbanizing communities, and Hollydale would rank seventh. There is greater similarity among the relatively secure communities in the two groups than is the case with those which were economically secure. The marginally secure group embraces the largest group among the suburbanizing communities. The latter concentration strongly indicates that the suburbanizing communities, as a group, are a good deal more economically secure than are the all-black towns. The most severely deprived communities are Wellston, Missouri; and Pomona, Richmond, Willowbrook, and Florence-Graham, California among the suburbanizing communities; and Kinloch, Missouri; Roosevelt City, Alabama; Lincoln Heights, Ohio; Brooklyn, Illinois; East Chicago Heights, Illinois; and Cooper Road, Louisiana among the all-black towns.

The social class designation derived using median family income as the single class-determining variable, while often exhibiting some relationship to the derived economic security identities, likewise turn up cases that deviate from this pattern. The greatest discrepancies between economic security and class status are found in Carson, California; Takoma Park, Maryland; and Spring Valley, New York. Carson, the single suburbanizing community to be identified as upper middle class, was defined as being only marginally secure economically. It seems only fair to assume that this community would have emerged as secure or at least relatively secure. On the other hand, Spring Valley, New York, a working class community, showed up in the column with the economically secure communities (see Table 4–9); and Takoma Park, Maryland, which was identified as a lower class

Table 4–9. The Economic Security Characteristics of Black Suburbanizing Communities

Secure	Score		Relatively Secure	Score
Warrensville Hts.	83		Hayward	46
Takoma Park	76		Roosevelt	34
Shaker Heights	68		University City	31
Silver Spring	66		Markham	31
Suitland	58			
Carol City	51			
Spring Valley	51			
Marginally Secure	Score		Insecure	Score
Carson	28		Wellston	0
E. Orange	24		Pomona	0
Maywood	24		Richmond	0
Hempstead	24		Willowbrook	0
Daly City	24		Florence-Graham	0
Browardale	25			
Harvey	17			
Altadena	14			
Plainfield	14			
E. Cleveland	14			
Brownsville	10			
Compton	7			
Pontiac	7			
Westmont	7			

community, ranked number two among all the communities in economic security. The latter community, more than any of the others, illustrates the weakness of a single index in measuring social rank. Takoma Park, while designated lower class when median family income was employed as the sole discriminating variable, was assigned the highest rank of all the communities when an alternate ranking procedure was employed. The measures of economic security developed here seem to produce a grouping that is more compatible with the alternate multivariate procedure than that based simply on median family income.

Social Rank Employing an Alternate Procedure

The results of the factor model on factor 1, labelled Socioeconomic Status, shows that it is those communities which blacks entered in relatively large numbers for the first time during the sixties that possessed the highest economic status. The factor score break points employed by Rees were followed in this instance to distinguish among communities possessing a given rank (see Table 4–10).[33] The factor structure does not permit a class labelling, as was engaged in earlier, but does provide a metric that measures the distance between communities on a common dimension.

The high status communities were those in which blacks were generally found in small number, constituted less than one-fifth of the total population, contained few persons over 65, where unemployment was low, female heads few, and blue collar workers relatively few. These were the entry communities where rents were high and home values were also high. Only one of the all-black towns showed up among the high status communities and that was Glenarden, Maryland. The variables that had the highest positive association with this factor were: Percent Who Lived Elsewhere in 1965 (.992), Ratio of Median Family Income to That of Nearest Neighbor (.891), Female Clerical Workers (.908), Professionals (.836), High School Graduates (.758), College Graduates (.627), Fertility Index (.719), and Percent Aged 20 to 44 (.721).

The variables which were status depressing were Percent Blue Collar Workers (−.844), Percent Less Than High School (−.777), Population Size (−.687), Percent 65 and Older (−.655), Percent Nonwhite (−.603) and Percent Unemployed (−.543). Similar variables have been employed to define social status in other factor ecological studies. Occupation and education tend to be more important than income (.618) in influencing social rank in this universe. This has led to a changed identity for several communities which had been identified earlier as working or lower class communities based on income. Thus,

Table 4–10. Socioeconomic Status of Black Metropolitan Ring Communities (Factor 1)

(Factor Score)

High Status *(>0.66)*	*High Middle Status* *(0 to 0.66)*
Silver Spring	Westmont
Suitland	Altadena
Carson	Seat Pleasant
Takoma Park	East Cleveland
Hayward	Harvey
Warrensville Heights	East Orange
Carol City	Freeport
Glenarden	Roosevelt
Daly City	Hempstead
Shaker Heights	Maywood
Spring Valley	Hollydale
University City	East Palo Alto
Pomona	Wyandanch
	Markham

Low Middle Status *(−0.66 to 0)*	*Low Status* *(<0.66)*
Plainfield	Urbancrest
Richmond	Roosevelt City
Browardale	Cooper Road
Richmond Heights	Kinloch
Pontiac	Lincoln Heights
Willowbrook	Wellston
	North Fontana
	Lawnside
	Robbins
	Brooklyn
	East Chicago Heights

a community with a youthful age structure, high median level of educational attainment, and high percent white collar employees is likely to generate a higher factor score than a community with a higher median family income, older age structure, lower median educational attainment, and larger percent blue collar workers. All the low status communities (with the exception of Wellston, Missouri) are from the group described as all-black towns.

There is often observed a negative correlation between percent black and community status—that is, higher percent black is generally associated with decreasing status. Meyer previously noted that:

. . . although the socioeconomic status of blacks is inversely related to their relative proportion in the total population, this does not imply that there necessarily is a causal relationship between the two. That is, one cannot infer that black Americans will have greater opportunities for attaining a higher economic status if they are a relatively smaller proportion of the total population.[34]

It should be noted, however, that a number of communities with simple black majorities were identified as high middle status communities. It seems that the factors that lead to low social status also lead to a more intense concentration of blacks within a single community. This is partially related to the fact that the lower status communities as a rule are residual communities, whereas the higher status communities are those characterized by initial group entry. There are, however, exceptions to this generalization within this universe. The extent to which the intensity of racial concentration is associated with socioeconomic status is not fully understood, as most studies simply mirror the covariation of these variables at a single point.

The internal pattern of black concentration within individual community varies. But more often than not, the black concentration at the block level is significantly higher than is reflected by the percentage of blacks in the community at large. Among the high status communities only Silver Spring, Maryland and Carol City, Florida showed any discernible variation in the pattern of black occupancy characteristic of that prevailing in the nation's major central cities. In the latter community blacks represent the majority population in a minority of the blocks in which they are found. In Silver Spring, Maryland, not only do blacks represent the minority population in most blocks, but the blocks showing a black presence tend generally to be dispersed (see Figure 4–1).

There is one possible hitch to this pattern. Since more than 75 percent of the Silver Spring black population are renters, there is a possibility that racial segregation manifests itself in the form of racial imbalance at the level of the multiunit apartment structure rather than at the level of the block. Carol City, on the other hand, is a community of single family structures and is thus, at this point, simply less intensely segregated at the block level than is characteristic of this group of communities. Whether this represents a turnabout in individual and institutional behavior is unknown. But it is apparent that an elevation in the status of the black population does little to deter the development of black residential enclaves in the community of entry.

Carson, California, is a good case in point as it is the third ranking community in terms of socioeconomic status in this universe, and it is more intensely segregated than the communities in this category in general. It appears that a developer produced new single family housing specifically for a black clientele in two separate zones within the community. In a third zone there is evidence of racial turnover. In some respects Carson differs little from Glenarden, Maryland, which has been labelled an all-black town, in terms of housing market de-

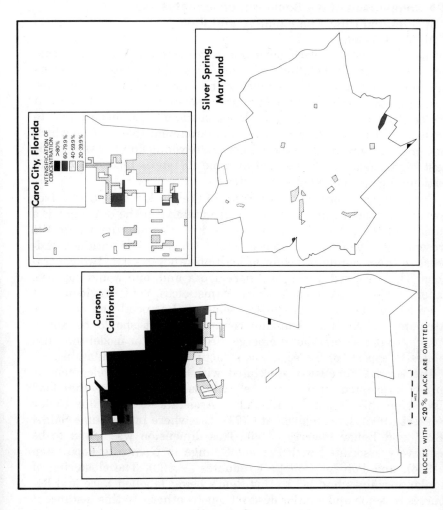

Figure 4–1. Black Residential Concentration in Three Suburban Communities, by Block

velopment. They are likewise similar in social status, but, because the city of Carson is larger and blacks constitute only 12 percent of the total population, the population is viewed as less segregated in terms of the factor structure.

A Comparison of the Socioeconomic Status
of Suburbanizing Communities and the
All-black Towns

The status of the black suburbanizing communities is as a rule higher than that of the all-black towns. This higher status can generally be attributed to the selectivity of the suburbanizing populations. In most instances they represent migrant populations from the central city or elsewhere, who have, no doubt, made a conscious attempt to locate a more satisfactory residential environment than that in which they previously resided. These are generally young families who are at least high school graduates and in some instances include a disproportionate share of college graduates.

For instance, more than 30 percent of the black residents of Silver Spring, Maryland represent college graduates. On the other hand, a number of the all-black towns are residual communities where the present black population represents one which has maintained residence in these communities for at least one and, in some, two generations. They evolved during a different era and, one would suppose, under a different set of motivating circumstances. Yet it is evident that a few of the black towns possess some of the social and economic attributes of the suburbanizing communities. It should be noted, though, that a second factor emerged from the factor model that also relates to aspects of the economic structure of these populations.

The second dimension associated with economic development is largely associated with poverty conditions. The variables that load highest on this dimension are Public Assistance (.906), Blue Collar Workers (.905), Unemployment (.771), Elsewhere in the Same SMSA (.828), and Below Poverty (.636). This dimension was found to be negatively associated with Percent Change in Nonwhite Population (−.954), and Percent College Graduates (−.820). The clustering of similar variables had led to this item's being labelled Race and Resources by some and similar descriptions by others. In this instance it seems appropriate to label this dimension Jobs and Resources (see Table 4–11).

Communities scoring highly positive on this dimension are those communities where economic conditions are most precarious, while those with high negative scores are most secure. Given the interpretation of this dimension, there are a few surprises regarding how certain

Table 4–11. Jobs and Resources of Black Metropolitan Ring Populations (Factor 2)

	(Factor Score)		
Scarce Resources (0.66)	Low-Scarce Resources (0 to 0.66)	Low-Developing Resources (−0.66 to 0)	Developing Resources (−0.66)
Brooklyn	Florence-Graham	Markham	Hollydale
Wyandanch	Westmont	Hempstead	Warrensville Hts.
Cooper Road	Wellston	Carson	Urbancrest
	E. Chicago Hts.	Roosevelt City	Silver Spring
	Browardale	Plainfield	Willowbrook
	Pomona	Carol City	Richmond Hts.
	Pontiac	Harvey	Lawnside
	Freeport	Glenarden	
	Richmond	Daly City	
	N. Fontana	Robbins	
	E. Orange	University	
	Hayward	Roosevelt	
	Compton	Altadena	
	E. Cleveland	Seat Pleasant	

communities line up. In most instances the individual communities are distributed along this dimension in the expected way. Brooklyn, Illinois turns out to be the most precarious community in terms of jobs and resources, while Warrensville Heights, Ohio turns out to be the most secure. The occupational structure is associated with both the socioeconomic status factor and the Jobs and Resources factor. Because of the importance of occupational structure on the well-being of the universe of communities, it is dealt with in greater detail in a later chapter.

INDICATORS OF PSYCHOLOGICAL SECURITY

Now that the economic well-being of these residential communities has been assesssed, attention is turned to the psychological dimension. The problem of attempting to assess the latter is far more difficult than the former. The variables selected as crude indicators of psychological security simply represent a set of measures for which data are available and thus can in no way be thought to represent ideal measures for such an undertaking. This leads to the necessity to state that an assessment of psychological security is incipient at best, but it is expected, nevertheless, that some insight into this aspect of well-being might be gained from the data at hand.

The Quality of Environmental Safety

Among the variables identified earlier as those that might be related to psychological security, safety has been accorded the greatest
emphasis as a cause for people leaving one environment in favor of
another. The moving behavior of many urban populations is thought to
be triggered by fear for their personal safety and/or for their physical
possessions. Since it is generally acknowledged that crime rates are
higher in the nation's central cities than in outlying suburban zones,
the question arises, how safe are the environments occupied by blacks
in outlying locations? It is possible to assess the safety dimension of the
environment of the all-black towns. Unfortunately, it is not possible to
extend this assessment directly to the black suburbanizing communities. It is possible, however, to generalize from a set of known
conditions that tend to foster safety or a lack thereof to environments
for which there is an absence of survey data.

Most of the residents of the all-black towns viewed their communities as being at least moderately safe. The safe communities
tended to be those which were small and contained a small percentage
of youth. None of the respondents in the Hollydale sample viewed their
community as unsafe, but the highest percentages of respondents
viewing their community as very safe were found in North Fontana,
Brooklyn, and Urbancrest. In none of these communities did the population exceed 2,000. The greatest fear for their safety was expressed by
residents of several of the growth communities, where more than 25
percent of the sample population perceived their communities as unsafe. Almost two-fifths of the residents of Robbins and Wyandanch and
about three-tenths of the sample in East Palo Alto and Kinloch saw
their communities as unsafe. The two variables that appear to be most
highly associated with safety are community size and age structure. In
those communities hovering near 10,000 persons which were the
targets of intraurban movers during the decade, there tended to be a
heightened sense of the lack of safety. To what extent this simply
reflects the entrance of an alien group as opposed to an increase in the
incidence of crime is unknown.

Fertility Behavior and
Psychological Security

The question of psychological security growing out of the ability of a
group to exert control over its fertility behavior is a complex one and
an issue difficult to address. National black fertility levels are higher
than those of the white population by as much as 40 percent, but this is
to be expected given the differential distribution of those attributes
that impinge upon fertility behavior. The general trend in black fertil-

ity behavior has paralleled that of white behavior during most of the recent period, with the fertility gap remaining rather stable, although Farley points out that the differences in the fertility behavior of black and white women in the sixties have not always followed a rational pattern.[35] For some years prior to 1940, black women in cities exhibited lower fertility levels, as expressed by the child-woman ratio, than white women in cities.[36] Since World War Two a reversal of this pattern has ensued, the causes of which are no doubt associated with a number of complex changes both in terms of personal decisions and public policy.

The critical issue is whether current levels of fertility reflect conditions that promote stress in the mother. If current levels of fertility result in the development of families of the desired size, then the necessary kind of control over fertility has been achieved. On the other hand, if fertility behavior leads to a condition of dissatisfaction, then it is apparent that the desired control is absent. Two things must be kept in mind: the distinction between an unwanted pregnancy and an unwanted child, and the fertility goals established by the parents as opposed to some external agency. The black response to the establishment of family planning centers in black neighborhoods is somewhat mixed, as the following statement by Charles V. Willie, a leading black sociologist, illustrates: "First, I must state categorically that many people in the black community are deeply suspicious of any family planning program initiated by whites."[37]

Much of the increased concern regarding black growth and the potential for genocide within the black community emanates from statements attributed to public officials and the work of the Commission on Population Growth and the American Future. A black member of that Commission, Eleanor Holmes Norton, who admitted to some skepticisms about its task, states the Commission's position as follows: "that people should be able to have only as many children as they choose and recommends a policy to reduce unwanted fertility, and improve the outcome of pregnancy."[38] She further comments:

> The real issue for black people and other minorities is how to improve the quality of their lives, in other words, getting better education, jobs and social services. We must demand the right to access to better contraceptives and to family planning services so that we can be free to have children when we want them.[39]

The General Pattern of Black Fertility

During the sixties there emerged a pattern of fertility decline within the black population offsetting the trend begun during the forties. The black child-woman ratio in 1970 was 490, or approximately 30 per cent lower than it had been ten years earlier. The impact of continued urbanization on fertility levels showed itself with a child-woman ratio of 465 for the nation's central cities, while the rural level stood at 570. The child-woman ratio will be employed to assess the fertility picture among blacks in outlying metropolitan communities. Since the child-woman ratio simply measures surviving children and women in the childbearing ages, it deviates from true fertility levels to the extent that there are variations in mortality levels affecting these two segments of the population.

Thus the general fertility level, which is an expression of births occurring during the interval of a single year per 1,000 women of childbearing age, would, if multiplied by five, coincide with the child-woman ratio if the appropriate mortality statistics were applied. Of course, for these two indexes to be congruent there could be no significant variation in this fertility behavior over the five-year interval. Given the existing ratio between these indexes, it seems that a child-woman ratio of approximately 400 would show a general convergence of black and white fertility differences at the more recent date. Likewise, if the pattern of black movement to the suburbs coincides with that of whites in terms of stage in the life cycle, then suburban fertility levels could exceed those prevailing among blacks in the central city.

The general situation of fertility differences within the black population as a function of place of residence can be gleaned from Tables 4–12 and 4–13, below. Black movers to the rings in Washington, St. Louis, and Cincinnati show fertility levels that are very much higher than those characterizing the central city black population. This could mean that in these communities large scale movement to the central city from the rural South had been dampened and thus some curbing of central city fertility levels has occurred. If this is the case, the central city black population in these communities will begin to age, while the reproductive potential in an outlying area will increase. A reversal of this pattern prevails in Cleveland and Detroit, the implications of which are not clear. The black population in Cleveland has a lower fertility rate than the white population,[40] a situation which is somewhat unique. Among the metropolitan areas in Pendelton's sample, only Cleveland showed signs of fertility convergence between blacks and whites in both the central city and the suburbs.[41]

Fertility Levels in the All-Black Towns
The prevailing fertility levels in the all-black towns have a tendency to be higher than the mean levels for both central cities and other nonrural locations (see Table 4–12). Within five of these communities the 1970 fertility levels exceeded those which described the

Table 4–12. Fertility Differences in the All-Black Towns

Place	Fertility Level	
East Chicago Heights, Ill.	717	)
Kinloch, Missouri	591	)
Wyandanch, New York	590	)
North Fontana, California	589	) High Fertility
Brooklyn, Illinois	579	)
Cooper Road, Louisiana	546	)
Lincoln Heights, Ohio	535	)
Glenarden, Maryland	530	)
East Palo Alto, California	500	) Declining Fertility
Robbins, Illinois	500	)
Richmond Heights, Florida	415	) Incipiently
Hollydale, Ohio	415	) Low Fertility
Roosevelt City, Alabama	363	)
Lawnside, New Jersey	324	) Low Fertility
Urbancrest, Ohio	214	)

Source: Derived from appropriate Census Bureau reports.

mean black fertility rate. These unusually high fertility communities included E. Chicago Heights, Illinois (717), Wyandanch, New York (590) North Fontana, California (589), Brooklyn, Illinois (579), and Kinloch, Missouri (591). The unusually high fertility rates in these communities are obviously associated with their low economic status, origin of inmovers, and educational attainment. For this group of communities in general, fertility was found to be positively correlated with previous fertility, population size (.547), residence in central cities in 1965 (.496) elsewhere in this SMSA in 1965 (.488), and negatively associated with owner occupancy (−.421).

Even the moderate fertility communities among this group exhibit relatively high fertility levels, as can be seen in the case of Cooper Road, Louisiana (546), Lincoln Heights, Ohio (533), and Robbins, Illinois (500). Hollydale, Ohio (415) and Richmond Heights, Florida (415) are the only two communities which demonstrate fertility behavior that is more nearly typical of that of urban fringe communities in general. Roosevelt City, Alabama (363); Lawnside, New Jersey (324); and Urbancrest, Ohio (214), all low fertility communities, have fertility levels that are seriously constrained by their older age structures.

Fertility Levels in Black
Suburbanizing Communities

Even among the black suburbanizing communities fertility is generally high. In many ways the two sets of communities parallel one

Table 4–13. Fertility Differences Among Black Suburbanizing Communities

High Fertility	Level	Moderately High Fertility	Level
Wellston, Mo.	763	Florence-Graham, Cal.	519
Carol City, Flor.	595	Roosevelt, N. Y.	517
Pontiac, Mich.	577	Hayward, Cal.	515
Spring Valley, N.Y.	574	Brownsville, Fla.	503
Freeport, N.Y.	572	Plainfield, N.J.	492
Westmont, Cal.	566	Compton, Cal.	486
Suitland, Md.	546	Seat Pleasant, Md.	485
Browardale, Fla.	542	Richmond, Cal.	485
Harvey, Ill.	533		
Moderately Low Fertility		Low Fertility	Level
Markham, Ill.	447	E. Orange, N.J.	369
Willowbrook, Cal.	447	Daly City, Cal.	344
Hempstead, N.Y.	437	Pomona, Cal.	340
University City, Mo.	434	Silver Spring, Md.	319
Maywood, Ill.	433	Takoma Park, Md.	315
Altadena, Cal.	427	Shaker Hts., Ohio	285
Warrensville Hts., Ohio	418		
Carson, Cal.	416		
East Cleveland, Ohio	409		

Source: Derived from appropriate Census Bureau reports.

another in fertility behavior if fertility-influencing variables are held constant. Wellston, Missouri (763) and Shaker Heights, Ohio (285) represent the two ends of the fertility spectrum, but they likewise represent opposite ends of the social status spectrum and are far removed from one another along the life cycle continuum. These two status conditions show their influence on fertility behavior generally among all communities in the universe (see Table 4–13). The variations in fertility behavior among these communities are considerable, but less than one-fifth of the total were characterized by levels which might be described as low.

THE GAP BETWEEN DESIRED FAMILY SIZE AND CURRENT FERTILITY BEHAVIOR

Given the variations which have been observed in fertility behavior among the two universes of black residence, the issue of what represents reasonable fertility behavior, considering the social class and life cycle stage of the individual communities, is yet to be broached. One is hesitant to extend oneself into the never-never land of optimum fertility as it relates to specific groups. This fear is based on the nature of the measure employed, the lack of detailed understanding of group specific fertility goals, and the manner in which any assessment of this sort is likely to be interpreted by others. Nevertheless, if psychological security is in any way associated with one's ability to exert control over one's fertility, then an attempt must be made, however crude, to come to grips with this issue.

Unwanted Pregnancy or Unwanted Births?

There is little direct evidence that would permit assessment of current fertility performance in terms of the desired fertility experience of black families in the United States. The results of recent research indicate that the level of unwanted fertility is undoubtedly higher than most would suspect. In 1970 it was estimated that 15 percent of all births occurring to never-married women during 1966– 70 were unwanted, while 44 percent were unplanned.[42] This finding highlights the distinction between unwanted pregnancy and unwanted births. It appears that approximately one-third of the unwanted pregnancies are translated to mean unwanted births. This issue has created some problems among demographers because of its subjective implications. The question raised by Professor Hauser in response to the Westoff and Ryder paper on this topic is instructive. Hauser seems to doubt the validity of the approach employed by Westoff and Ryder in determining the level of unwanted births. In reply to their findings, Hauser stated: "A woman is telling you four years after the event when that child might be raising hell, and she is not talking with the interviewer with ease."[43] He further states, in relationship to the use of the survey method in acquiring information of this type, that "there is going to be a differential in the extent to which sexual relations are preceded by the intent to have or not to have a child."[44]

Hauser's argument revolves around the distinction between an unwanted pregnancy and unwanted child—two different situations sometimes treated as homogeneous concepts. It seems, though, that the Westoff-Ryder study did make this distinction, as the following statement by them appears to illustrate: "Thus, among ever-pregnant women who intend to have no more children, 52 percent of blacks compared with 30 percent of whites report their last pregnancies as unwanted."[45] The point to be emphasized here is that blacks have been able to exert only limited control over their fertility and thus are characterized by excessive fertility.

Excessive fertility is an expression of the ratio of the desired family size to actual family size. The National Fertility Study of 1970 shows that 27 percent of all black pregnancies are unwanted.[46] Levels of unwanted pregnancies tend to vary with income and education. A more recent study focusing on the fertility behavior of low income black and white women shows that 57 percent of the black women had one or more unwanted births after the desired number of children had been attained, in comparison to 34 percent for the white women in their sample.[47] An attempt is made here to make operational the concept of excess fertility by deflating community child-woman ratios by a factor representing strength of control as a function of social status. Such a measure, while instructive, leaves much to be desired and is likely to generate sharp criticism.

There is growing evidence that the percentage of unwanted pregnancies among ever-married black women can be specified with some precision. Both the Bauman and Udry Study and the National Fertility Study show that the incidence of unwanted pregnancies is highly correlated with the level of educational attainment of women exposed to the risk of pregnancy. For those who have completed high school, only about one-fifth of the pregnancies are undesired, while those with less than a high school education show a range from 30 percent to as many as 55 percent of their pregnancies unwanted. Only among those black women with four or more years of college are unwanted pregnancies negligible. These findings provide input for deflating child-woman ratios to levels that would represent the desired level if the couples involved had effective control over their fertility behavior.

An Evaluation of the Level of Excess Fertility

In 1970 the national child-woman ratio for blacks was 490. This level exceeded the average for blacks in central cities by about 7 percent. Since it is customary to find suburban fertility in excess of central city levels, the national average will be employed as a surrogate for blacks suburban fertility levels. The national level was deflated by 20 percent (a conservative estimate of the level of unwanted pregnancies given the available information) to yield a child-woman ratio of 392. The latter level is considered the desired level of black fertility if the evidence previously reviewed can be considered valid.

The fertility level of each individual community within the two universes under investigation was subsequently deflated by a factor representing its social rank as derived from the factor model (see Table 4–10 above). The actual fertility level prevailing in the higher status communities was deflated by 10 percent; in the high middle status communities by 20 percent; in the low middle status communities by 25 percent; and in the low status communities by 40 percent. Each deflation level is a conservative modification based on the findings of the studies previously mentioned. If the deflationary values depress fertility levels of the individual places equal to or below that of the deflated national level, then status factors are considered to represent the sole contributors to existing high levels of fertility, and these could be overcome by increased access to more effective contraceptive techniques.

In those instances where the deflation does not bring fertility down to the hypothesized desired level, one might attribute the higher levels to other factors. Does a unique black culture explain the levels in those communities which remain high after a conservative deflation factor has been applied? There can be no reliable answer to that question at this point. With such a crude device only extraordinary deviations from the hypothesized norm might raise suspicion that cultural differentials exist.

Approximately 20 percent of the black suburbanizing communities maintained levels of fertility lower than the hypothesized norm without deflation. Five of the six were communities previously described as high status communities, and the sixth was a high middle status community. This possibly represents a fertility convergence that is catalyzed by social status. In all other instances it was necessary to deflate in order to have fertility levels at or below the hypothesized norm. Among the all-black towns most high fertility communities would have fertility levels below the hypothesized norm after being deflated by the appropriate factor. The exceptions are Glenarden, Maryland; East Palo Alto, California; Wyandanch, New York; and East Chicago Heights, Illinois. Only East Chicago Heights falls into the low status category. In each of the other communities the appropriate status deflation measure was insufficient to reduce the existing fertility levels to the hypothesized norm. This suggests that there exists a lag between the attainment of a defined status level and fertility behavior.

Thus it appears that the recent improvement in socioeconomic status has not led to fertility levels commensurate with that status. Just what factors contribute to this lag is not well understood. One possibility is that living in another suburb in 1965 is the clue to this phenomenon, as another suburb in this instance might well have represented a semirural community. Westoff and Ryder, in their evaluation of contraceptive practices employed by urban blacks, found that central city blacks employed more effective contraceptive behavior than their suburban counterparts. They went on to say, "The suburban black, on the other hand, is much closer in many characteristics to his rural than his urban cousin."[48] It should be remembered here that most black suburban movement did not get underway until the second half of the decade of the sixties, and most of the movers originated in central cities, where the black population was already showing increased contraceptive sophistication.

Those communities among the black suburbanizing group which continued to exhibit high fertility after deflation included two high status communities: Suitland-Silver Hill, Maryland, and Carol City, Florida. Four high middle status communities—Westmont, California, Harvey, Illinois, Freeport and Roosevelt, New York—were earlier referred to as working class communities. Only Pontiac, Michigan and Wellston, Missouri were found on the lower end of the status spectrum, and status alone did not explain their existing levels of fertility. Part of the discrepancy between the depressed fertility level and the hypothesized norm might be related to the broad range of factor scores defining status groups. The range of scores may simply be too broad and thus do not permit the application of the most appropriate deflationary factor in a given instance. Clearly, this is an initial excursion into a complex arena and is characterized by a variety of weaknesses.

Eleven communities stand out as deviant in their fertility behavior as related to their social status. They vary in their deviation scores from Carol City, Florida, with a high of 133, to East Palo Alto, California, with a low of 8.[49] The three ranking deviations are all associated with communities possessing a southern location. It is thought that region of origin has some impact on the lowering of fertility rates. Neal Ritchey recently showed that blacks with no southern rural experience had the lowest fertility among the three black residential groups in the sample employed by him, and that blacks with southern rural experience but no longer living in the South possessed fertility levels that were intermediate in this universe.[50]

It is not certain whether persons of southern rural origin desire larger families or simply continue to employ ineffective contraceptive techniques as a matter of custom. Westoff and Ryder reported blacks under thirty residing in rural environments in 1965 reported the condom and the douche to be the most frequently used contraceptive practices.[51] This population was shown to employ less effective measures than their counterparts in large cities, where the pill had become the modal technique. Likewise, a larger percentage of the former group failed to use any contraceptive techniques. This seems to imply that the risk of pregnancy is not viewed with the same alarm that it is among blacks in larger cities, or conversely, that rural black families generally desire larger families than their urban counterparts. By 1970, more than half of all the low income urban black women in the Bauman and Udry sample were using physician administered contraceptives that included the pill, the IUD, and sterilization techniques. These are acknowledged to be the most effective.[52] The extent to which black suburban women employ these techniques is likely to reflect social status as it relates to the education of the woman and the extent to which a tradition of employing the less effective techniques is an entrenched one.

If the recently reported findings on unwanted pregnancies among black women are accurate, then it appears that suburbanizing black populations have not been very successful in exerting control over their fertility behavior. Fertility control appears to exist only in Silver Spring and Takoma Park, Maryland; Daly City and Pomona, California; Shaker Heights, Ohio; and East Orange, New Jersey. Among these communities the convergence of fertility in terms of social status and life cycle stage tends to conform to the expected level as a function of desired level of fertility. In most other instances the gap between the hypothesized norm and actual fertility level is explained by the operation of the above two factors. This probably indicates a lag between status change and shifts to more reliable contraceptive practices.

Even when more effective practices are employed there seems a need to provide effective instruction in the use of these techniques, as the high failure rate among users of these techniques among black women residing in low income neighborhoods attests.[53] Lack of fertility control is apparent in most black outlying communities, assuming that lower fertility is indeed an expressed desire of these populations. Only two of the all-black towns were seen to be effecting a convergence toward the hypothesized norm—Hollydale, Ohio and Richmond Heights, Florida. But for most others the current high levels of fertility indicate either an inability to exert control over this area or the persistence of cultural patterns and values that support existing fertility behavior. If the premise assumed here is correct and the technique developed to measure the gap between actual and desired fertility is not overly faulty, then it is obvious that a form of psychological insecurity growing out of inability to exert control over fertility prevails in the great majority of non-central city black communities located within a metropolitan context.

MARITAL STABILITY AND PSYCHOLOGICAL SECURITY

The final dimension of psychological security, marital stability, is, like its predecessor, somewhat troublesome. The premise one wishes to investigate is the role of the external environment on marital stability, especially whether there are variations in environmental attributes that tend to foster or hamper stability. If Paul Glick's data showing variations in the level of stability as a function of size of place are acceptable, then one is led to conclude that the more complex the environment the higher is the probability of marital dissolution. Glick showed that size of place explained twice the amount of a variance undergirding black separation ratios as did region of residence.[54] Not only does Glick believe size of place to play a role in marital disruption, he likewise contends that migration also enters the picture.[55] His latter conclusion tends to rest on the fact that interregional movers in particular are breaking with tradition and this can be expected to have some impact on marital stability.[56]

Marital Disruption and Environment of Residence

A casual review of marital disruption rates prevailing in selected central cities in 1970 shows them to be universally high. The highest rate was observed in Newark, but Los Angeles showed a similar rate of marital disruptions. It is not clear if these unusually high rates are associated with high levels of migration during the decade or not. However, New York, a target for unusually large numbers of black migrants, was characterized by a level closer to the average for blacks in large cities.

The level of marital disruption among black families seems to have changed little since 1965, and in 1970 about one-fifth of those disruptions were attributable to separation and divorce. At the national level the combined effect of the latter slightly exceeds the role of widowhood in promoting female-headed families. While the data on female rates of disruption have been employed in this instance, the objective is not to attempt to explain the incidence of female-headed households. The female rate was employed because children of broken unions tend to remain with the mother, and thus it is contended by some social scientists that the life of the mother and child are prone to become more stress ridden than in those instances where marriages remain intact. Thus the issue at hand is whether the environments in which black enclaves have developed beyond the margins of the central city are more or less prone to promote marital instability than are other external environments.

Data illustrating the level of marital stability at the local level (census tract) for blacks are diluted by the inclusion of data describing the total population in all instances where the total population and the black population are not synonymous. In most instances the data from communities identified as all-black towns are essentially uncontaminated, although there are some exceptions. Among the black suburbanizing communities there is seldom a case in which racial isolation is so intense that the total population and black population represent one and the same. Thus it was only possible to examine rates of marital dissolution in 14 of the 35 suburbanizing communities included in this universe. The black percentage of the total population varied from a low of 55 percent in Carson neighborhoods to a high of approximately 90 percent in Richmond, California neighborhoods.

In most instances where the black population exceeded some critical level, the black percentage of the census tract level exceeded 80 percent. In those instances black marital dissolution rates were simply representative of conditions in those environments where blacks were clearly the majority population. In comparing the two black population groups on this index, it should be kept in mind that in some instances the dissolution rates would probably run slightly higher in black suburbanizing communities if it were not for the fact that these rates were probably depressed by the presence of other elements.

Only four of the thirteen all-black towns for which there is information have a higher proportion of nonintact marriages resulting from separation or divorce than those recently reported by Paul Glick. Based on the Glick findings during the sixties, a break point of 16 percent was employed to distinguish between those levels that were more representative of central city environments than non-central city environments. The mean rate of black marital dissolution among the central cities which constitute a part of the metropolitan universe employed here was approximately 25 percent. The lowest central city rate prevailed in Birmingham in 1970, with 18.6 percent; the highest rate prevailed in Newark. During the previous decade, Birmingham experienced an absolute loss in its black population, while Newark was a major destination for blacks migrating from the South Atlantic region. The contrasting migratory experience of these two places should possibly be reflected in their incidence of family stability. Families remaining in Birmingham tended to be almost twice as stable as those who were residents of Newark. In only a few instances did marital dissolution rates in the outlying communities approach those prevailing within the central cities.

In none of the all-black towns did nonintact marriages, excluding those associated with widowhood, reach one-fifth of the total marriages, although Brooklyn, East Palo Alto and Lincoln Heights came very close to that limit. Nine of the thirteen communities for which there are data show marital dissolution rates lower than the threshold established to distinguish between the central city condition and the non-central city condition. Both Glenarden and Lawnside are characterized by dissolution rates of less than 10 percent. A brief review of the data on social rank shows that the lowest rates of marital dissolution in the all-black towns are associated generally with the communities which have the highest status, and the highest rates are generally to be found among the lower status communities. Some exceptions to this generalization are apparent, as one finds Roosevelt City among the stable communities and East Palo Alto among the unstable communities.

Marital instability tends to be higher among the black suburbanizing communities than among the all-black towns. Of the fourteen communities for which only minimally distorted data were available, only six were characterized by rates of less than 16 percent. Again the lower rates were generally associated with higher status communities. Carson, with an index of 7.5 percent, was lowest for all communities, regardless of category. The Carson rate was probably partially depressed by the greater presence of nonblacks in the unit of analysis; nevertheless, the social rank of Carson's black population should lead to relatively low levels of marital instability. The crude approximation between social rank and marital stability would lead one to speculate that in communities such as Warrensville Heights, Shaker Heights, Silver Springs, Takoma Park, and University City, the level of marital stability should be relatively low.

The higher rates of marital instability among the working class population in satellite cities, industrial suburbs, and large unincorporated areas suggest the operation of a set of factors bearing a strong similarity to those operating in central cities. This implies that a unique life style is practiced by black marriage partners which is promoted by a combined set of external and internal forces. It has been stated that the key causal factor promoting divorce is indeed the style of life.[57] At this point, marriage dissolution among blacks is still associated with nonlegal breaks, or separation. Divorce exceeds separation only in Altadena, Carson, and East Cleveland of the suburbanizing communities, and only in East Palo Alto of the all-black towns. In several other communities, divorce and separation appear to be in balance. Blood has shown that this phenomenon is not entirely related to income, since black men in the same income category as white men are much more likely to be separated from their wives.[58] The question then is, does a change in one's residential ambience influence stability when other critical factors are held constant? It does appear that instability is partially minimized, but other factors impinging upon the marital relationship are not completely inoperative simply as a result of shifts in the residential environment.

Marital instability continues to plague black families, and marital disruptions are stress producing—divorce and separation ranking second only to the death of spouse in terms of emotional impact.[59] Given the psychological impact of marital disruption, those communities in which marital stability is highest can be said to represent the more psychologically secure environments. Psychological security growing out of marital stability is thought to be directly linked to other aspects of psychological well-being.

Marital disruption is frequently viewed by one or both parties as individual failure, prompting a chain reaction of self-doubt of his or her ability to play by the rules established by the larger society. Obviously, this is just one of many factors which might have been investigated as indirect evidence of the psychological well-being of non-central city black residents. It does provide some indications of family stability in alternative environments when other threatening economic and social forces are at a minimum.

BLACK CULTURE AND GROUP SECURITY

Two dimensions of community well-being prevailing in the black territorial communities beyond the margins of a selected set of central cities have been viewed in some breadth. This brings us once again to the notion of the existence of a black culture and the ways that that culture has shaped the evolution of these communities. There is a widespread consensus that a constellation of traits exists that implies the existence of, if not a black culture, at least a black subculture. The generally accepted notion is that blacks, like most other Americans, have adopted a basic set of values that translates into a national culture, but because of the group's position in American society it has developed a number of traits or patterns of behavior and values that deviate, at least minimally, from those of other subgroups in the population.

Social Science Views of Black Culture

The extent to which the various social sciences have addressed themselves to this topic, as well as the orientation and emphasis employed, varies greatly among the individual disciplines. Cultural geography, a highly developed phase of the discipline of geography, ranks low among the social sciences in past contributions to knowledge of this topic. The traditional approach of geography to the subject of culture, in terms of landscape features, which are supposed to reflect a group's impact upon its environment, has hampered its contribution to an understanding of black culture—although Wilbur Zelinsky acknowledges that black culture has left its mark upon several major urban areas. He avers, "In such places as Harlem and Atlanta, an Afro-American culture has come into being unlike any that existed

earlier in the nation."[60] One is uncertain what it is Zelinsky is refer-
ring to, but at least his is an admission by a representative of the
discipline of geography that a legitimate black culture does exist.

Much of the work that treats black culture has tended to focus on
aspects of lower class behavior, sometimes identified as lower class
culture or subculture. It is this constellation of traits that has been
singled out for treatment by a number of social scientists during the
past decade. In some ways it is understandable that white researchers
view the behavior of large segments of the black population as deviant,
productive of problems that doom its members to a perpetual state of
poverty and dependence. It is true that the initial state of the black
man in America was that of a servant without either significant status
or power, and thus the evolution of the black man in America and his
associated culture must essentially start from this base. This was
pointed out by Bryce-LaPorte when he stated, "Whether the shift from
past to present, rural to urban, or plantation to ghetto has serious
consequences for the life chances, the institutional and political economic development, and the life style and culture of black people, is a
question deserving serious sociological study."[61] Obviously what the
black man is in America is a reflection of his ability to adapt to the
impact of a set of institutions designed to promote the welfare of
the white population at his expense.

The Emergence of Black Culture

The necessary adaptive mechanisms have had a variety of effects on
the individual black psyche, effects often singled out to illustrate their
impact upon an evolving black culture. No better illustration probably
exists of the variations among individuals in a single city than that
recently developed by Robert Coles.[62] The generational differences
between parents and children and their responses to a universally
recognized set of institutional restraints are anecdotally developed by
the writer. Implicit in their responses is the emergence of new attitudes and values likely to affect an emerging and continuously
changing black culture. A statement by one youngster interviewed by
Coles (admittedly taken out of context) sums up this emerging situation: "I'm not religious like my grandmother, and I'm not scared like
my parents are."[63] This statement does much to describe the backdrop
out of which black culture has emerged in the United States.

The literature is replete with examples which show how blacks have
historically been prepared for their roles as Americans who differ from
other identifiable racial, social, and cultural groups. Coles quotes one
black grandmother as saying, "It takes a lot of preparing before you

can let a child loose in a white world. If you're black in Louisiana it's like cloudy weather; you just don't see the sun much."[64] The same theme is reiterated by the noted black psychiatrist team of Grier and Cobbs when they state, "The worlds of blacks and whites are different and blacks need special armor to wage wars."[65] The previous statements were developed to simply state that the emergence of a black culture, however defined, cannot be readily understood unless one starts with how the individual black personality has been historically subjected to the impact of a social system designed to promote a sense of positive identification in persons of European origin, and, either by intention or simply as a feedback process, a sense of negative identity among blacks. As the social system has been modified over time, the process of black cultural development has taken on different dimensions.

It was indicated early in this chapter that researchers interested in the notion of black culture have generally dichotomized practitioners of the culture into the "respectables" and "nonrespectables." This tends to conform to the notion that some blacks have been able to internalize the basic values promoted and developed by persons of European origin, while others simply have not, and thus their behavior is viewed as disrespectable. This theme was recently elaborated upon by Lee Rainwater in an analytical attempt to come to grips with the conceptual issue as an epilog following a detailed description of black life styles in a specific federal housing project. Rainwater describes one kind of adaptive behavior, which appears somewhat characteristic of a sizeable number of youthful ghetto residents, and which tends to be viewed negatively by some researchers and local residents as well. The practitioners of an expressive life style no doubt correspond to the group that Drake has dubbed nonrespectables and Barnard has identified as the externally adapted. Rainwater describes the "expressive adaptations as constructive efforts of young lowerclass Negroes to fashion a gratifying way of being."[66]

This underlying basis for the development of the expressive self is thought to be related to the absence of mechanisms which would permit one to develop a positive self-identity through normal channels. The closing off of normal channels leads to what Rainwater chooses to describe as alternative games, in which the objective of play is the exploitation of accessible others. The motivations for the behavior observed is often a response to the opportunity structure prevailing within one's functional environment. The notion presented by Rainwater and others that the various threads of black culture evolve out of the black individual's interaction with a social structure that traditionally has been restrictive, makes black cultural development easier to trace, both through space and time; both elements have played a major role in the evolutionary process of black becoming.

The constellation of traits associated with an expressive life style has been emerging over a period of several generations and has flourished more readily in one kind of environment rather than another. Some aspects of the adaptive behavior that Rainwater describes as expressive were attributed to blacks a generation earlier by Gunnar Myrdal. Although Myrdal was careful to note that blacks in general were no more aggressive than whites, he did admit that a higher level of aggression was associated with what he identified as "the sullen criminal youths found mainly in northern cities."[67] Mrydal likewise pointed out that emphasis on pleasure seeking by some blacks was associated with the harshness of the life they were forced to endure. Thus it appears that these traits have been both emerging over a long period of time and finding heightened development in an urban environment.

The point of this discussion is to attempt to place black cultural development in a context that will permit it to be described as a process phenomenon, wherein certain kinds of outcomes can be identified as a function of how various elements of the black population have been able to negotiate a social system that is itself in constant flux. If successful, one could then identify a number of adaptive styles in which blacks have engaged, and as a means of more fully addressing the question where there simply exists a single overarching black culture, which is often identified as a lower class black subculture or a cultural continuum reflecting the differential experiences of members of the group.

The Continuum of Black
Cultural Development

In the four generations since the abolition of slavery, black Americans have shifted from a predominantly rural environment dominated by an economy vitally dependent upon their presence, to an urban environment dominated by an impersonal economy in which black people are frequently superfluous. Over this entire period changes have modified the cultural equipment that the black man possessed as he emerged from slavery. One would speculate that modifications during the first and second generation were relatively minor. Blacks continued to be confined to the cultural hearth, and the social controls associated with slavery had only gradually given way to a quasi-state of dependency wherein much of the old social etiquette was still enforced.

Blacks adapted to this modified state of affairs through an extensive involvement with the church. This religious involvement enabled the group to seek other-world rewards, while at the same time making a viable adaptation to the circumstances in which they found themselves. Obviously such an adaptation had a variety of impacts upon the black personality, such that it is thought to have influenced intragroup as well as intergroup interaction patterns.

Writers who view patterns of black behavior in terms of the dichotomous respectable/nonrespectable dimension are frequently implicitly acknowledging the failure of the effective operation of the principal internal social control—religion. The external control associated with white punishment was ever present but was of limited effectiveness in intragroup relations. Employing a nomenclature of the type developed by Rainwater, one might describe the modal black subculture during this period as adaptive-suppressive, but with aspects of the maladaptive-aggressive evolving out of those external experiences that resulted in the rejection of the rules of racial etiquette which had been established following slavery. One would project that those blacks who migrated from the South prior to the large scale demands for black labor in the North probably represented persons who found great difficulty adapting to those external forces over which they had no control.

The previous statements are in line with Marc Fried's comment that "cultural patterns are themselves the result of economic, political, and social realities in the past and present."[68] He likewise takes up the issue of the stability of cultural forces in stating that "cultures can be drastically modified by changes in the environment while maintaining the symbols and appearances of continuity."[69] It is not known for certain what role the maladaptive-aggressive personalities played in developing variant cultural patterns in the urban North; they might simply have become adaptive-assertive in their new environment.

Associated with a move from the rural South to the urban North was a lessening in the intensity of spiritual forces which had previously played an important role in guiding patterns of intragroup interaction. At the same time, there was a reduced need for blacks to demean themselves in their relations with nonblacks. Thus there emerged in the North a new black personality which found alternative ways to adapt to an alien environment. Both external and internal social controls were being modified such that a ghetto personality and its associated cultural repertoire were beginning to emerge. The emphasis here is on the continuum of adaptive practices that blacks have had to make as they moved from one environment to another under conditions of changing secular and spiritual forces. Obviously the changes occurred at different rates and persons in the new urban milieu found themselves at different points on the adaptive continuum.

One point that seems clear is that although white attitudes in the North differed somewhat from those prevailing in the South, the magnitude of those differences was probably less than had been imagined. The absence of a system of codification specifying the nature of expected black behavior did much to create a vacuum and left the question of expected behavior ambiguous. This has no doubt led recent migrants from the South to fare as well in the northern environment as long time black residents. The adaptive-suppressive behavior of segments of the latter group is likely to have been advantageous in assisting these groups in negotiating a system that in reality was undergirded by only weakly modified racial attitudes.

The manner in which blacks have adapted to a system over which they have had virtually no control largely dictates where segments of that population stand on the economic and psychological security dimensions previously described. It appears the adaptive suppressive individuals, by emphasizing one set of values, were able to gain a foothold in a society which was willing to minimally reward black conformity to a set of ideals held in esteem by the supporters of the Protestant ethic. These comprised the parents of those that Proctor has described as individuals whose habits are low risk, such that they have emerged as the new black middle class.[70]

Those blacks who have made few gains in terms of the ideals held up by white America would probably be described by those scholars (who would hold them entirely accountable for their plight) as maladaptive-expressive. Thus, on the index of economic security employed in this study, individual communities might be thought to be practitioners of modalities that are self-defeating. It is out of this context that Kenneth Clark arrived at this description of the ghetto as pathological. This is expressed in the following statement:

> Because the larger society has clearly rejected him, he rejects—or appears to reject—the values, the aspirations, and techniques of that society. His conscious or unconscious argument is that he cannot hope to win meaningful self-esteem through the avenues ordinarily available to more privileged individuals. These avenues have been blocked to him through inadequate education, through job discrimination, and through a system of social and political power which is not responsible to his needs.[71]

Out of the latter context it is easy to observe the evolution of human interactional responses, which have been previously described as expressive. It has been said that "A man defines himself in part by the web of his relations with others, in part by his relation to the place where he lives and works, in part by his relation to his subculture and culture."[72] Max Lerner's position on how man defines himself simply states that a given set of interactional patterns are conditioned by the significant contacts of the actors as they are filtered back against a subcultural screen that provides the appropriate signals leading to both an external and internal response.

In a setting that fosters social isolation and simultaneously provides few material resources, then the kind of exploitive interpersonal relations described by Rainwater are likely to occur, provided external intervention is limited. In such situations there are quite likely heightened tensions between family and peer group which grow out of generational conflict over what represents an appropriate set of behaviors. The maladaptive-expressive syndrome is likely to emerge out of this context. The prototypic environment for this style of behavior would be the poverty zones in large northern cities. When life style and cultural repertoire are translated in spatial terms, easy generalization leads to confusion, for few zones have a totality of their actors engaged in a common set of practices. David Sopher, in attempting to come to grips with this categorical problem, states the following:

> Their location on the map of culture is not fixed; except in their common use of symbolic markers, ethnic groups need not be culturally uniform nor need people having such common culture belong to a common ethos.[73]

What is at issue here is the strength of the geographer's approach to the study of culture, with primary emphasis being placed on the culture area and secondary emphasis on culture group. The former emphasis leads to a search for landscape markers associated with a group's presence and will thus minimize the role of individual interaction, both in terms of internal and external patterns. Because blacks have traditionally played a somewhat passive role in national development, landscape markers have not always been easy to identify, such that they might be expected to reflect aspects of black culture. The crumbling shack in the cottonfield, just like the crumbling tenement in some forlorn ghetto neighborhood, represents features introduced by others, but with which the black occupant had to devise an adaptive strategy. This then leads to the next question of how meritorious are the concepts of core, domain, and periphery in describing the territorial units that are occupied by blacks in varying intensity.

It would seem that if the above territorial unit designations are to have any merit in identifying black culture areas, they will have to be deployed in association with the distinctive orientation of various segments of the black population. In only one instance is there evidence of this cultural territorial grouping schema's having been employed in association with black Americans. G. M. Lewis used this device as a spatial frame of reference for describing changes in the black population distribution in 1960.[74] Implicit in the Lewis article is that there is a single constellation of black cultural traits, which is practiced with varying intensity as the black population in a given area decreases as a porportion of the total. While there is some merit in this assumption, it has not been sufficiently well developed to serve as the basis for highlighting a total black cultural system.

It should be pointed out that Lewis did expand this schema (which was initially developed by Meinig in association with the Mormon culture)[75] to include noncontiguous microcosms that he identified as enclaves.[76] Instead of discussing a common core, domain, and periphery that are universal in their application to zones of black culture, there might exist, let us say, a core location for each of the major adaptive mechanisms that blacks have developed in different time and place contexts. The contention here is that there have emerged at least four basic patterns of black adaptation over time, and others are obviously in the process of coming into being. The adaptive-suppressive mode might be thought to represent the core culture of the rural South, and within this same context there evolved a maladaptive-aggressive style that might be thought of as a peripheral form of black culture. A maladaptive-aggressive stance in the rural or small town South might have led to an adaptive-assertive style in the urban North.

Two styles constitute patterns that were born in the urban North, but now have a national distribution—the maladaptive-expressive and adaptive-expansive. The former is associated with limited resources and limited transactions beyond the margins of one's defended neighborhood. The latter is associated with expanding resources, obtained through legitimate channels, and an ever increasing range of transactions which broaden one's horizons and simultaneously expand his cultural repertoire. Both of these are no doubt peripheral to the adaptive-assertive stance that for two generations has represented the core culture of the urban North.

In some instances those socialized in the latter context may adopt one or the other of the former styles depending on the set of circumstances influencing their life chances. The core culture in both the urban North and rural South led to the value model described by Rainwater as the goal of the good American life.[77] But the idiosyncracies associated with having to adapt to a hostile environment has led to alternative mechanisms that would produce immediate rewards, even if one's life chances were reduced as a result. Working class white ethnics, who encountered less hostility in American cities and who were not afflicted by a perverse form of racism, have no doubt been more successful in dealing with their external environment and, consequently, in the pursuit of the good life.

The adaptive-expansive mode is a fairly recent development and is associated with the weakening of racist attitudes, or at least a recognition that the overt practice of those attitudes is not in the national self interest. It no doubt has the smallest number of practitioners at this time. This constitutes the new periphery of black culture, and like the periphery of Mormon culture described by Meinig: "We are dealing here not with an expansion of Zion but with a dispersion into Babylon."[78] This, simply stated, means that blacks add to their cultural repertoire those elements that enable them to find a satisfactory adjustment to the world in which they move without denying their blackness, and openly practice elements of learned tradition which have grown out of their existence in the United States.

The constellation of traits that constitutes the black subculture varies as a function of experience, which includes region of birth, generation in which one reaches adulthood, and the resources available to the individual. To think of a single black culture which describes all blacks is unrealistic. Yet many white writers, and lay persons as well, tend to think in terms of a given set of traits that would permit the development of easy and universal stereotypes. Among that intrinsic set of cultural components described by Zelinsky as artifacts, sociofacts, and mentifacts,[79] geographers have traditionally emphasized artifacts because they are more easily mapped. In this discussion much of the emphasis has been on mentifacts and sociofacts, as artifacts tend to derive from the latter. No attempt has been made in this chapter to specify the intensity of artifactual practices or makers that tend to characterize the communities in the universe under observation. What will be attempted is a specification of the cultural mode that is dominant as function of the evidence of economic and psychological security prevailing in those communities. It should be further noted that the terminology employed here is only appropriate in the context of development of black Americans against a backdrop of externally imposed constraints associated with a system of pervasive racism.

The Identity of Individual Communities on the Cultural Continuum

Now that a black subcultural continuum has been posited and described, the job is to identify the universe of communities under investigation in terms of the described pattern of subcultural development. This is a hazardous task, but it should be remembered that the terminology employed is ecological and does not describe the behavior of any single individual. Likewise, the identifying terminology reflects the modal condition of subcultural development. Communities described as being economically insecure (but psychologically more secure in terms of the dimensions previously described) are thought to represent adaptive-suppressive orientations. Such communities would be more commonplace in the South and are likely to be characterized by the presence of an older population (median age 40). Many of the all-black towns fall in this category. Brooklyn, Illinois; Kinloch, Missouri; Roosevelt City, Alabama; and Cooper Road, Louisiana represent core communities while East Chicago Heights, Illinois; Urbancrest, Ohio; and Lincoln Heights, Ohio might be described as peripherally adaptive-suppressive. An issue highly important in this connection is what subcultural mode characterized the offspring of the older residents of their communities. It would appear that if the resources and rewards available to the developing young in these communities were not overtaxed, the youth might develop an adaptive-assertive mode. On the other hand, one would conjecture that an adaptive-suppressive older generation, in an environment where resources and rewards were restricted as a result of an intensive internal competition of the sort characteristic of central city ghettos, would lead to a disproportionate shift to the maladaptive-expressive mode.

The adaptive-assertive mode seems to have taken hold in East Palo Alto, California; Robbins, Illinois; Wyandanch, New York; Lawnside, New Jersey; Richmond Heights, Florida; and North Fontana, California. Greater economic security prevails in these communities than in those previously identified, although psychological security is generally of somewhat lower order. Of the latter group, East Palo Alto, Wyandanch, and Robbins are thought to be peripherally adaptive-assertive. The largest single group of adaptive-assertive communities appear to be found among the black suburbanizing communities: almost half the communities in the latter group can be considered adaptive-assertive.

Among the all-black towns the adaptive-expansive identity can only be extended to two communities—Glenarden, Maryland and Hollydale, Ohio. It is conjectured that the adaptive-expansive mode is associated largely with the presence of third generation families of southern origin and second generation families of northern origin practicing the adaptive-assertive subcultural mode. The adaptive-expansive community is essentially made up of persons whose interpersonal transactions extend beyond the realm of their internal ethnic world and whose children have access to greater economic and psychological resources. This results in reduced need to engage in excessive intragroup exploitation. Even in these communities the full subcultural continuum is present, but the dominant expression is associated with the adaptive-expansive mode. It is in these communities that the middle class status might be applied, but socioeconomic status and subcultural mode are not perfectly congruent.

This situation was recently highlighted by Kronus, who states that for middle income blacks,

> It is evident that interracial contact or desegregation, has predominantly been achieved in the area of work and work only. . . . It may be that individuals interact quite intensively on the job, but contact can also exist of a few brief polite words exchanged in passing.[80]

Nevertheless, even these superficial interaction patterns should lead to reciprocal exchanges and the adoption of selective subcultural traits among the interacting individuals. The nature of the interaction pattern and the economic and psychological resources and rewards growing out of this pattern will affect the extent to which old and new practices will be emphasized or deemphasized. Five of the black suburbanizing communities seem to fall in the latter category: Warrensville Heights, Ohio; Shaker Heights, Ohio; Silver Spring, Maryland; and Suitland, Maryland.

A REVIEW

The previous lengthy discussion of the socioeconomic status of metropolitan but non-central city black communities has been undertaken to ascertain if the environment of residence enhances one's opportunity to live an economically and psychologically secure life. The conclusions reached are mixed in that it is difficult to determine the impact of physical environment on one's life condition. Various subcultural modes that impinge upon the probability of security occur from place to place. It is not certain that the selection of a specific environmental niche reflects a seeking of a more satisfactory living environment in terms of the physical qualities of the environment or the social and psychological attributes of the environment. Out of necessity, adaptive-suppressive groups have least access to externally pleasing esthetic environments. In some inner city adaptive-suppressive neighborhoods, the offspring of mature families become maladaptive-expressive under conditions of continued restriction of available economic resources, engaging in behavior that further minimizes the esthetic appeal of these environments.

The quality of the physical environment in adaptive-assertive neighborhoods is probably conditioned by the juxtaposition of adaptive-suppressive zones with adaptive-assertive zones, and the extent to which the practice of acceptable subcultural traits is rewarded by the gate keepers of the larger society. It seems that the maladaptive-expressive mode is heightened in a second generation by economic denial in adaptive-suppressive zones and psychological denial in adaptive-assertive zones. Needless to say, the restrictions imposed by the larger society fosters internal conflict within zones of black residence. Black youngsters who have been able to escape the trauma of this conflict and oppression emerge in a subsequent generation to be transmitters of the adaptive-expansive mode.

In the final analysis, subcultural variations reflect the access provided black Americans to the national opportunity structure. A superficial view will lead one to assume that the system is more open than in fact it is. This is the view held by many politicians, and their supporters, who see expanding black opportunity encroaching upon the gains made by working class whites, who have only recently acquired a modicum of security themselves. But continued restriction of both economic and psychological security leads to a state of intensified intragroup exploitation, to which the white population can deny claim out of a distorted perception of how the real world operates. The scale of the maladaptive-expressive population is a function of restricted opportunity and an increase in nonmeaningful transactions, both within the internal ethnic world of most black Americans as well as in the external nonethnic world.

Environments that promote the maladaptive-expressive mode serve as the basis for a new form of slavery—the incarceration of those who must choose to seek rewards via nonlegitimate mechanisms. Drug abuse and other heightened forms of maladaptive behavior (which in the context of the practitioner is adaptive) lead to enslavement, physically and mentally. The stigma attached to the new slaves is much like that associated with those released from bondage more than a century ago. Black suburbanization is no doubt an attempt to secure economic and psychological security within the confines of some acceptable subcultural mode. Cole's phrase, "It is the same, but it's different," permeates black being in America, and consequently has promoted the development of a continuum of subcultural stages among black Americans.

An expressive style probably characterizes a large share of the black population, but it is only when such expressiveness is distorted by the absence of adequate economic and psychological resources that the modal subcultural patterns that evolve might be considered another penalty for being a participant in a racist—albeit institutional—system of social and economic development.

✳ *Chapter 5*

Black Ring Residence and the World of Work

> The world of work represents a significant force in American life for it not only influences how well one and his family will fare in an exchange economy, it also provides participants in the work force a measure of status that is not entirely related to the pecuniary rewards associated with the work activity. In the previous chapter the focus was on the current economic status of black metropolitan populations residing outside the central city in selected locations, and the subsequent interaction of the economic and psychological dimensions that lead to the evolution of a continuum of subcultural stages. In this instance attention will be focused on employment structure, employment accessibility, and the position of the communities under investigation along the continuum of the national pattern of labor force development. As in the previous chapters, the information utilized in describing the all-black towns is more fully developed than that describing the black suburbanizing communities. But several all-black towns are prototypic of selected suburbanizing communities and thus tend to permit a degree of generalization. By the same token, there are major differences to be found in the two universes that will sometimes preclude easy generalization.

THE CHANGING EMPLOYMENT STRUCTURE

The literature treating the changing employment structure within metropolitan areas frequently details the structural differences in employment opportunity between the central city and its suburbs.

195

During the previous generation, most new jobs have sprung up in an emerging suburban environment, and these largely include those job categories that in a previous generation had been anchored in the central city. Low income populations (and minority populations in particular) have been cut off from these emerging job opportunities by both economic and social barriers to the acquisition of housing in reasonable proximity to employment sources. Some jobs have been expanding in the central city, but they have been principally concentrated in the categories of professional and managerial jobs.[1] Given this evolving pattern, an attempt will be made to determine if the black worker located outside the central city is advantaged by his location in the suburban ring in terms of his access to emerging employment opportunities.

A number of items have appeared recently in the literature that describe the general progress that blacks made in the economy during the decade of the sixties. The position taken on this issue as a rule reflects the perspective of the writer. Ben Wattenberg and Richard Scammon, whose paper on black economic progress touched off a debate between them and several black scholars and groups, reported that during the decade blacks increased their share of the good jobs from 40 to 64 percent of all the jobs held by blacks.[2] It is true that there were some significant shifts in the black occupational structure, but the Wattenberg and Scammon paper tends to overplay that progress in their loose definition of good jobs. Andrew Brimmer, too, noted major occupational advances for blacks during the decade but was careful to point out that these gains tended to be concentrated in selected areas.[3] Brimmer showed that progress essentially occurred in the black share of openings in the category of professionals, clerical, and crafts, while operatives and service workers constituted in the aggregate a larger share of the total jobs than they had in 1960. His statement regarding this phenomenon is instructive: "Their occupational center of gravity remained anchored in those positions requiring little skill and offering few opportunities for further advancement."[4] This being the case, it appears that the Wattenberg and Scammon position is one designed to invalidate the accusation of benign neglect advanced by some black critics by operationally defining good jobs in such a way as to be misleading.

If those writers had not included operatives in the good job category, at least in the sense that these jobs permitted shifts from one class category to another, their statement in this regard could be viewed without suspicion. Jack Nelson contends that many of the additional jobs acquired by blacks in the inner city occurred as a result of vacancies created by white movement to the suburbs.[5] But if jobs are moving to the suburbs, it would appear logical that blacks shifting their place of residence to the metropolitan ring would share in the allocation of those jobs and thus become involved in an improved occupational distribution. While this notion possesses some validity, it is not equally applicable to the two sets of black communities in the universe under investigation. The all-black towns, which in several instances reflect residual communities characterized by net out-migration, would not represent appropriate units for the purpose of such an investigation. On the other hand, those communities described as black suburbanizing communities should generally reflect a sharing in a more diversified employment environment such as that emerging in the metropolitan ring.

The All-Black Towns and
Occupational Status

Among the all-black towns, three communities possessed occupational structures similar to that characteristic of the national black occupational structure ten years earlier, with blue collar and service workers accounting for more than four-fifths of all employed individuals. In Urbancrest, Ohio; Cooper Road, Louisiana; and East Chicago Heights, Illinois, the more traditional black occupational structure remained intact. Minor variations distinguish seven other communities from the previous three, which were described as possessing a more nearly traditional occupational structure. These minor variations appear to be related to average age of the work force, regional traditions, and the character of the local economy. For instance, Brooklyn, Illinois; Richmond Heights, Florida; and North Fontana, California differ most from the previously described communities in the percentage of their work force engaged in professional jobs. In each of the latter cases professional workers exceeded the national average by more than 3 percent, whereas the previous communities had only nominal professional representation averaging 5 percentage points below the national average of approximately 9 percent.

In both Richmond Heights and North Fontana black women are overrepresented in private household employment. This is related to a long standing tradition among southern cities and the age of the female work force. Cooper Road, Louisiana, another deep South community, is almost congruent with Richmond Heights on this measure. The explanation of finding more than one-third of the women in North Fontana in the private household sector is not as readily arrived at. But the fact that the black residents of North Fontana are generally of southern origin, added to the general opportunity structure in this isolated area, no doubt does much to account for this phenomenon. Roosevelt City,

Kinloch, and Lincoln Heights tend to be well above the average in male operatives, as more than two-fifths of all male workers in this group are so employed. The occupational structure predominating in these communities goes a long way in accounting for the prevailing economic marginality, although improvements are beginning to appear in some.

Five of the all-black towns can be said to be in the process of developing a modernizing occupational structure. Thse communities include Glenarden, Maryland; Hollydale, Ohio; Lawnside, New Jersey; East Palo Alto, California; and Wyandanch, New York. The principal distinguishing feature of the occupational structure of this cluster of communities is the growing strength of the professional category and female clericals. While it is true that male operatives constitute the largest single segment of the work force, they are less often a disproportionate share of the work force. There is, yet, however, considerable variability in the share of operatives in the occupational structure within this group. Glenarden's share of operatives is only 15 percent while that of Lawnside is 35 percent. Thus, there is roughly a 10 percent deviation in each direction from the national average for blacks among these communities.

The major distinguishing feature among these communities is the general level of female clericals in the labor force. While it does not exceed the general level in all communities in every instance, more often than not the mean of 22 percent is exceeded. Almost 44 percent of the female labor force of Glenarden were employed as clericals, while only 21 percent of those in Lawnside were working in this job category. The average age of women in the latter community is higher than that in Glenarden, a factor that helps explain the major difference in the extent to which the two groups participate in a given segment of the occupationl structure. But likewise one would have to also consider the general employment opportunity structure in the metropolitan areas in which the additional communities are located.

The modernizing all-black towns are taking on some of the work force characteristics common to other working and lower middle class suburban communities. Many residential communities which are emerging beyond the margins of the central city fail to coincide with the myth often associated with suburban living. Unfortunately, a number of the all-black towns possess occupational structures that will make it difficult for their residents to do more than eke out a marginal subsistence. The fact that a few communities have been able to maintain themselves in this context is commendable. That both Richmond Heights and Urbancrest, possessing a more nearly traditional occupational structure, have managed to remain beyond the margin of the extremely economically insecure communities is no doubt partially related to the impact of their respective local social milieu.

On the other hand, economic marginality should be expected in those communities where the prevailing occupational structures play a constraining role, guaranteeing the persistence of economic marginality. Even so, it should be remembered that suburban residence, simply defined, encompasses a broad spectrum of income types, and the black poor in this environment are seldom found outside the South. Needless to say, one is concerned here with the strength of suburban location in altering the economic well-being of black residents in a positive direction.

The Black Suburbanizing Communities and Occupational Status

The black suburbanizing communities tend to possess an occupational structure that bears many similarities to that which characterized the all-black towns. Some improvements are obvious, however, when eight communities are removed from the group of 35 communities identified as suburbanizing communities.[6] None of the suburbanizing communities are strongly traditional in their occupational structure, as were the most traditional all-black towns. The private household worker category exceeds the national average in only one community—Freeport, New York—although this category accounted for more than 10 percent of the total employment in nine other communities. But only in Plainfield, New Jersey; Pontiac, Michigan; Shaker Heights, Ohio; Takoma Park, Maryland; and Hempstead, New York did these levels rise to heights that tended to be unusual for this universe.

The higher percentage of domestic workers in some of the more affluent colonies and in locations accessible to higher income white communities possibly represents remnants of black colonies which Connolly has described as primarily "domestic service groups."[7] Thus the variety of community types ranges from the economically secure group to the economically insecure group. Although a relative high percentage of persons are found in domestic service in about a third of the suburbanizing communities, the levels are generally below the national average and often less than half the level associated with such places as Brownsville and Browardale, Florida, which were previously removed from this universe. The communities which tend to be more nearly traditional in their occupational structure are Wellston, Missouri; Maywood, Illinois; Freeport, New York; Plainfield, New Jersey; and Pontiac, Michigan.

A third of the communities straddle a precarious balance between the traditional and the modernizing communities. These include Roosevelt, Spring Valley, and Hempstead, New York; Harvey and Markham, Illinois; Compton, Daly City, and Richmond, California; and East Cleveland, Ohio. In most of these communities, the percentage of black professionals is at or below the national level in this job category; yet, generally, black females have readily entered the clerical group in those communities which are viewed as modernizing. The lack of a significant share of the male population in more remunerative occupations would have a tendency to depress family income in these communities.

The largest number of black suburbanizing communities might be thought of as developing a modernizing occupational structure. Most of the communities in this group have at least 5 percentage points above the national average in this category. Female clericals reach the extreme in these communities, unless the totals are depressed by having a large number of black females in the professions. The latter condition distinguishes Takoma Park from Silver Spring. In Takoma Park more than half of the black females are employed as clericals while professionals account for slightly fewer than 20 percent of all workers. Silver Spring, on the other hand, has 35.9 percent of its black work force in the professions, while 37.9 percent of its female employees are found among the clerical group. Both of these communities are situated in the Washington, D.C. suburban zone.

Male operatives are generally found to constitute less than the national percentage in this category, and often the percentage of operatives is akin to the percentage of professionals in those communities possessing a traditional or a transitional occupational structure. Only University City, Missouri is above the average in the category of male operatives while Carson, California is just below the average for this category. The other communities which make up the modernizing group are Suitland and Seat Pleasant, Maryland; Shaker Heights and Warrensville Heights, Ohio; and Carson, Altadena, Hayward, and Pomona, California. In seven of these communities white collar workers represent the majority of workers. More than 70 percent of the black labor force in Suitland is found in this occupational category, which constitutes the high for this universe of communities.

But it should be remembered that an emerging white collar dominance in a few communities is essentially related to the opening up of clerical opportunities to black women. The extent to which changes in the occupational structure (largely favoring black women) have assisted in making it possible for black families to settle in the metropolitan ring cannot be stated with precision, but it appears that the labor force participation rate of black women in general, and of black married women in particular, has resulted in raising the median family income of segments of this population. While black suburban males do not possess the occupational status of operatives at the rate of the national black population, that status continues to dominate the occupational structure even in this environment.

Seldom do black craftsmen exceed the national average within these communities, but when one considers the low participation rate in this occupational category ten years earlier, increased representation might have aided a segment of this population to abandon central city locations. While the black suburbanizing communities show that blacks are generally making some progress in improving their position in the occupational structure, seldom are these improvements of sufficient import to lead to predomiately white collar communities where whites and blacks are both found in relatively large numbers. The white labor force participants are more often found in white collar jobs than are their black "neighbors."[8] The exception to this observation is found in Carson, California, where black workers are engaged in white collar employment more often than whites. The ratio of black to white, white collar workers would be even lower were it not for the fact that black women are more often found in the labor force than are white women, and consequently were the recent beneficiaries of declining job barriers in the clerical field.

In the previous description of the occupational structure in the communities of interest, emphasis was placed on selected occupations only rather than the entire nine-group classification employed by the Census Bureau. Those occupations selected for initial emphasis were employed in the factor model and were the variables that loaded high on the dimension identified as Jobs and Resources. Major emphasis was placed on those occupational categories into which blacks were beginning to move in larger numbers. Nevertheless, the occupational categories chosen for special attention were those that would permit one to observe the extent to which communities were developing a modernizing occupational structure or remaining traditional in their occupational status.

In the previous discussion, craftsmen and service workers were not given special attention but were lumped under the heading "other blue collar workers." The latter two categories, along with operatives and laborers, constitute the bulk of all black blue collar workers. Fortunately for the black worker, there was a reduction in the extent to which members of the group were found in low paying jobs in the laborer category during the decade, and an increase in the group's participation in both crafts and service work. This condition represents both a general change in the nature of the national economy and renewed efforts to increase black participation in the crafts. The crafts have tended to be more restrictive in facilitating black entry into that segment of the labor force. In order to gain more insight into the occupational situation of the black worker in the suburban ring, some attention will be devoted to the latter job categories in selected all-black towns and selected black suburbanizing communities.

THE BLUE COLLAR WORKER IN THE SUBURBAN RING

Among those neglected job categories, only that of craftsman provides strong financial support and at the same time a measure of job protection associated with widespread unionization. The other two categories are generally associated with limited financial renumeration and high level job turnover. It is true, however, that service employment, while providing only limited financial rewards, is often a more stable source of employment than some of the better paying job categories into which black workers have entered. The extent to which service employment shows itself as a major source of work opportunity is largely associated with the nature of the local economy in a given metropolitan area. In 1970, more than 8 percent of all blacks in the labor force were employed as craftsmen, an increase in this job category by more than 2 percent during the decade.

Of the thirteen communities selected for closer investigation, more than half show a level of craft employment that exceeds the national average. Both East Palo Alto and Richmond, California show employment in the trades exceeding 10 percent, but in no instance is the blue collar segment of the work force in these communities heavily weighted toward the trades. It is obvious that the semi-skilled operative job category has been far more important in contributing to the pattern of black settlement outside the central city than has the former job category. In 1969, slightly more than 6 percent of all jobs in the crafts category were held by blacks, whereas 21.6 percent of those classified as service workers were blacks.[9] The movement of the former jobs to the suburbs does not seem to have greatly benefitted those blacks found in the suburban ring, as their share of the jobs in this area continues to remain modest.

Thirteen communities were drawn from a universe of 50 for the purpose of further disaggregating the structure of the blue collar labor force. The communities drawn from the larger population include ten suburbanizing communities and three all-black towns. Examples are drawn from across the spectrum of economic security. The communities utilized for this purpose include Takoma Park and Glenarden, Maryland; University City, Wellston, and Kinloch, Missouri; Carson and Pomona, California; Warrensville Heights and East Cleveland, Ohio; and East Palo Alto and Richmond, California. In each instance two or more communities were selected from a common metropolitan area.

The Craft Worker

Blacks residing in non-central city locations generally held a higher percentage of craft positions than was true of their central city counterparts, but seldom was the margin of difference great: the greatest margin being 2 percent, scored by East Palo Alto. An inverse of this relationship exists between Newark and its suburban extensions of Plainfield and East Orange, both of which have a smaller percentage of their work force engaged in the crafts. Other communities whose share of craft workers was lower than that for their respective central cities were Glenarden, Pomona, East Cleveland, and Wellston. In most instances, though, the level of craft employment more nearly approached that of a given central city than the national level. The central city with the lowest level of black employment in the crafts was St. Louis with only 6.5 percent, while Oakland with 10.4 percent in this job category was highest. The central city descriptions in this instance refer only to those associated with the thirteen communities drawn from the larger universe.

The Service Worker

The service worker category is one in which the black work force has a long tradition of association. Historically, the black service worker was found disproportionately in private household employment—the major source of employment for black women in southern towns and cities during an earlier period. When the service category is dichotomized in order to distinguish between the private household category and other service workers, it is found to be the employer of the single largest number of black workers in 1970. There was a slight increase in the percentage of workers in this category during the decade of the sixties. Brimmer has pointed out that these jobs require little skill. With the rapid expansion of the tertiary sector of the American economy, these jobs represent an expanding sector—and often the only one available to new entrants to the labor force who are without skills.

Service jobs have been disaggregated into five categories by the Census Bureau. These categories are instructive in that they describe the general service areas in which employment occurs. The categories include: (1) cleaning service workers, (2) food service workers, (3) health service workers, (4) personal service workers, and (5) protective service workers.[10] Both black male and female workers are concentrated in the first three categories. Cleaning services are the principal male employer and health services the principal employer of females. However, the variation in importance among the first three categories is smaller for females than for males. Daniel Price, in discussing the participation of black males in category five but with special emphasis on firemen, concluded that the social relationships which existed between firemen during their off duty hours probably impeded the hiring of blacks.[11] Jobs in all these categories except the last are congruent with what Bennett Harrison describes as the periphery of the economy.[12] These are jobs that are characterized by low wages, job instability, an absence of job protection, and low job satisfaction.

Among the central cities associated with the outlying black communities, most have a higher percentage of blacks in the service area than is characteristic of individual non-central city locations. This would generally tend to imply that the economic restraints imposed by the low wage service economy would especially hinder the movement of blacks from the central city to the ring. The mean percentage of service workers in the seven central cities is 21.1. Only three communities show any noticeable variation around the mean; they are St. Louis (+5.0 percent), San Francisco (+2.9 percent), and Newark, (−6.0 percent). In most instances the outlying black communities possess a smaller percentage of service workers than is found in the central city. The exceptions to this situation are Wellston and Kinloch, Missouri; and Pomona, California. Pomona exceeds the Los Angeles average by almost 3 percent, whereas the Missouri community of Wellston exceeds the city average by almost 6 percent. Kinloch is only slightly higher in the service category than St. Louis.

The higher status communities of Glenarden and Warrensville Heights have a service worker force that is only approximately one-half that of the central city average. Most of the remaining communities have levels that are 5 to 10 percentage points lower than that of their respective central cities. Thus the growing service sector of the economy, as it is reflected by the formal job category service worker, has not enabled a significant segment of that population to move beyond the limits of the central city. The level of remuneration and the location of these jobs frequently work against out-movement from the central city.

The Laborer
The decline in the number of black workers performing jobs described as laborer reflects the decline in the absolute number of jobs in

this category, as well as the growing unattractiveness of these jobs to blacks entering the labor force for the first time. One might conjecture that changes in the nature of the economy have simply resulted in a shift in the relative preponderance of service jobs, which now serve as a surrogate for the laborer category, in an economy that is moving beyond goods production to the provision of services. This being the case, one would expect the percentage of the work force in the latter category to be generally lower in the suburban enclaves than in the central city.

Among the central cities in the smaller sample, the percentage of blacks employed as laborers is lower than the national average in this category. Oakland is the only exception and its share of laborers is roughly congruent with the national level of 10.3 percent. Only Richmond, California with 11.4 percent of its black labor force in this category exceeds either the national average or the level prevailing in its respective central city. In Carson, Glenarden, Takoma Park, and Warrensville Heights the percentage of the work force in this occupational category is less than one-half the national average. In all other communities except Wellston and Kinloch the level of laborers is below that of its respective central city.

The additional blue collar categories have not contributed substantially to black settlement in areas beyond the central city. As should be expected, service workers are found most often in these environments, but are less important than operatives in establishing non-central city residence. This probably reflects the operatives' association with a more stable and protective sector of the economy, since the largest number of black operatives are found in the manufacturing sector. Excessive involvement in the service and laborer occupational categories is generally associated with communities previously described as economically marginal. The crafts have not permitted the development of blue collar black suburbs in the same way as they have provided blue collar whites with the opportunity to escape the core city.

A more detailed analysis of the occupational structure is available for other all-black towns than for the black suburbanizing group. A 1972 survey of these communities showed that their occupational characteristics were similar to those reported by the Census Bureau in 1970, at least in broad outline (see Table 5–1). The field survey results showed blue collar workers to be more heavily represented than was to be expected on the basis of the census data. In almost half these communities the margin of error exceeded 10 percent, with the greatest discrepancies showing up in North Fontana, California; Wyandanch, New York; and Brooklyn, Illinois. Part of this error may reflect differences in the sampling fraction. Smaller sampling fractions

Table 5–1. All-Black Towns Occupational Structure, 1972

Occupational Group	Lawnside, N.J. %	Wyandanch, N.Y. %	Brooklyn, Ill. %	E. Chicago, Ill. %	Hollydale, Ohio %	Kinloch, Mo. %	Lincoln Heights, Ohio %	Robbins, Ill. %	Urbancrest, Ohio %	Cooper Road, La. %	Glenarden, Md. %	Richmond Heights, Fla. %	Roosevelt City, Ala. %	E. Palo Alto, Cal. %	North Fontana, Cal. %
Professionals	18	2	—	—	6	7	4	9	11	5	27	9	4	3	—
Managers	5	—	9	—	6	2	4	9	—	—	8	3	4	2	—
Clerical workers	8	—	—	19	12	11	13	23	—	3	23	6	13	15	—
Sales workers	5	5	—	5	—	—	—	—	—	2	—	—	—	—	—
Craftsmen	18	21	18	24	24	13	17	9	22	21	12	14	17	10	—
Operatives	26	32	45	24	12	28	25	14	11	23	12	13	22	33	63
Private household workers	2	—	—	—	—	4	8	5	—	6	—	6	9	2	5
Service workers	10	32	18	19	18	24	13	14	—	24	16	34	17	30	11
Laborers	8	8	9	10	24	11	17	18	33	18	2	13	13	5	16

Source: Field survey data.

were employed in the survey data than in that employed by the Census Bureau. Even though a larger margin of error affects the field survey outcome, these results do provide detail which is unavailable from census tabulations.

The field survey results show the blue collar labor force to be dominated by operatives and service workers, although laborers appear more frequently than are shown in the census reports. In most communities the difference in the percentage of service workers and operatives does not exceed 5 percent. Service worker clearly tends to be the more important occupational category in Richmond Heights, Florida, while operatives represent the dominant blue collar category in North Fontana, California; Urbancrest and Lincoln Heights, Ohio; Brooklyn, Illinois and Lawnside, New Jersey. Hollydale, Ohio possessed the unique position of being predominantly craftsman-laborer in its occupational structure. The major value of the survey data is the information provided describing the journey to work and place of employment. But before proceeding to observe the pattern of work place locations, the contribution of women to the economic well being of family unit will be investigated both in the larger context and in the more restricted environment of the all-black towns.

The Working Wife in the Suburban Ring

Black women have historically played a significant role in contributing to the economic well-being of the black household. Low wages and uncertain employment of black men, coupled with a desire on the part of economically secure white families to live a life of leisure, created opportunity for black women to enter easily into the arena of private household employment, basically in the South.

The ease with which the female segment of the black population could obtain and maintain employment has, according to some analysts, contributed toward the development of subcultural patterns that are viewed as uniquely black. One such assumed pattern that generates much heated debate is the validity of the concept of the matriarchy. Another sometimes postulated development growing out of the recent historic work role of the black woman is her intense familiarity with middle class white culture. Philip Hauser, in viewing this phenomenon, asserts the following: "Furthermore, the tendency for Negro mothers to raise their children according to standards acquired in their contacts with white households has introduced tensions into relationships of father and child as well as husband and wife."[13] Whatever the various impacts have been on the black household, the black woman has historically been a more active labor force participant than her white counterpart.

During the previous decade there was some evidence of decline in black female labor force participation rates. Black female participation rates are declining at the same time white female rates are increasing. Even though the traditional pattern has been altered, how important are the contributions of black women to the economic support of the black household? In the discussion that follows, the importance of the black woman's contribution to the economic well-being of the household relates only to husband/wife households, since the woman may assume the total role of provider when she is household head. Thus the objective is to determine the influence of the woman's contribution on the household's current economic status. Previous note has been made of Harold Connolly's work on black suburbanization which comments on fifteen of 35 suburbanizing communities employed in our factor model. The latter writer was struck by the extent to which married women with husbands present were labor force participants (see Table 5–2).

The number of wives participating in the labor force reaches a peak in the suburbanizing communities, which show a level significantly higher than that of the all-black towns as a group of communities. At least three-fifths of the wives are in the labor force in most of the former communities, while this level is reached in only three of the all-black towns. The intensity of wives' participation in the labor force is positively associated with a community's economic status. Connolly noted that in his suburban universe, participation ran extremely high in those communities where the median family income exceeded

Table 5–2.   Labor Force Participation Rate for Working Wives in Selected Black Suburbanizing Communities

Community	Per Cent Participation
Shaker Heights	62.5
Carson	66.9
Warrensville Heights	65.4
Markham	59.6
Roosevelt	52.3
Maywood	42.9
University City	70.5
Harvey	53.5
Altadena	61.1
East Cleveland	61.7
Spring Valley	60.8
East Orange	61.9
Freeport	56.3
Takoma Park	65.9
Pomona	51.1

Source: Harold X. Connolly, *op. cit.*, p. 103. See Note 14.

$12,000 in 1969.[14] He likewise pointed out that the participation level prevailing among black wives averaged one-third higher than white wives in the same communities.[15] The participation rates of wives in the all-black towns was similar to those of white wives in those communities reviewed by Connolly. Generally, the less intense the level of labor force participation of wives in the all-black towns, the lower the economic rank of those communities. An exception to this is represented by East Palo Alto, California, which managed a working class designation with only slightly more than a third of its wives in the labor force. The lowest participation level occurred in North Fontana where in 1972 only 12 percent of the wives were in the labor force.

This gives rise to the question of what the forces are that promote or restrict wives from actively participating in the labor force. The level of participation most generally seems to be related to the educational level of wives, age of wives, and the general nature of the job market in the labor shed in which an individual community is located. Among the all-black towns the data permits one to ascertain what percentage of the household income is derived from the contributions of one or more employed members in a household. In those communities where wives are not extensively involved in the labor force, the family's income is essentially derived from the income of a single worker; this condition holds in North Fontana, East Chicago Heights, Robbins, and East Palo Alto. The extreme situation is reached in North Fontana, where one person contributes more than 95 percent to the household's total income. In four communities the contributions of two or more household members account for a significant share of the family's income. This group includes Lawnside, Hollydale, Glenarden, and Richmond Heights. In large measure it appears that the higher status of the latter communities is related to the employment of two or more members of a household. Where employment opportunity is unavailable to wives in the all-black towns, the income earned by the husband alone is seldom adequate to lift such communities far beyond the margins of poverty.

A more detailed look at a selected set of communities from the universe of all-black towns will permit a better understanding of the opportunities and constraints influencing the extent to which black wives participate in the labor force. It has already been noted that participation among this set of communities is highly variable and seldom reached the level of participation characterizing most of the black suburbanizing communities. Richmond Heights, Florida and Glenarden, Maryland, with approximately three-fifths of all married women in the labor force, rank high on this variable. Among the working wives who showed up in the Richmond Heights survey data, most were engaged in providing low order services. The nature of the jobs engaged in by most women suggests that there yet remain external constraints that circumscribe the job market in the Miami metropolitan area. Almost one-third of all working wives were employed as domestics in this labor market, with another 14 percent concentrated in health services and food services. It should be noted, however, that 12 percent of these wives were teachers, but less than 10 percent had been able to penetrate the lower level of the hierarchy (clerical workers) in the white collar field.

The low level of participation in this sector of the economy might be partially explained by some of the attributes of the women themselves. One outstanding characteristic is the high concentration of women in the 35–44 age category. Thus, even though the median level of educational attainment is high school graduation, at the time many of these women entered the labor force, opportunity was largely constrained to a much smaller number of occupational openings. So the Richmond Heights working wife reflects the residual of limited prior opportunity principally associated with the time of initial labor force entry, as well as actual and perceived skills, which serve as a limiting factor.

Glenarden, Maryland, a second community where wives are extensively employed, likewise shows signs of both external and internal forces that serve to promote the observed outcome. In this case, a much greater range of opportunity appears to be available to Glenarden wives, for almost 70 percent of them are engaged in white collar (government and industrial employment) jobs, with clerical workers and teachers contributing almost equally. This would seem to indicate the presence of fewer constraints in the Washington labor market than in the Miami market. What is also evident here is the demand for certain kinds of employment, which is somewhat unique to this individual labor market.

It should be pointed out that although there is a larger percentage of women between the ages of 20–29 in Glenarden than in Richmond Heights, the single highest concentration of women in Glenarden is in the 35–39 age category. It is also true that two-fifths of the Glenarden population has had some college education. The most obvious factor associated with households where there were working wives in Glenarden was the extent to which these households produced incomes which exceeded the community average. Almost 70 percent of the households with working wives had incomes in excess of $15,000 a year in 1972, compared to the community median of $12–14,999. Social rank in Glenarden is essentially tied to the presence of working wives.

Lawnside, with a somewhat older population, has a smaller percentage of wives in the labor force, but still ranks high among those all-black towns with a relatively high level of participation of working wives. The female work force is more diverse than in the two previous examples and no doubt reflects the broader spread of women through a larger number of age categories. This in part reflects the length of time blacks have been present in Lawnside. Domestics, teachers, and clerical workers are all present in roughly equal numbers, and no doubt represent generational differences in labor force entry. Like Glenarden, the population of Lawnside is characterized by a median level of educational attainment which exceeds high school.

Lower levels of labor force participation are characteristic of wives in Wyandanch, New York and East Palo Alto and North Fontana, California. Although Wyandanch shows greater similarity to Lawnside than the other two communities, it also reflects some unique differences—the most obvious being associated with the presence of a rather narrow range of employment opportunities for black women in the primary labor shed. Opportunities in the health service area are apparent, as this tends to attract the largest share of female employees. As was true in Glenarden, those Wyandanch households with working wives generally have family earnings that exceed the community average. In the present case the contributions of wives take the earnings level of these households two increments above the median level for the community. This tends to imply that the earnings potential of wives frequently approaches that of husbands.

East Palo Alto, with only slightly more than one-third of its married women in the labor force, is more difficult to explain, other than on grounds that the employment opportunity in the labor shed tends simply to favor the black male worker. Two-thirds of the working wives have found their way into the health service field, the majority of these in the least remunerative jobs in that sector. Since the census data show that almost 30 percent of black females residing in this community are clerical workers, it appears that these are single women who are just entering the labor force.

The most extreme example of limited employment opportunity for working wives among these communities is found in North Fontana, California. Although the strength of this generalization must be tempered by small sample size, there were other communities in which similar sized samples were drawn and for which no similar pattern emerged. Survey data show that 95.2 percent of the household income was secured from the earnings of a single member of that household, the male. No other community in the sample approaches that level of male income dominance, although a 70 percent level was recorded in both East Palo Alto, California and Robbins, Illinois. The extent to which wives participate in the labor force in North Fontana appears to be related to the educational characteristics of wives and the nature of the opportunities available to women possessing these characteristics.

It was previously noted that the level of private household employment engaged in by black women from the North Fontana community was unduly high (34.5 percent), exceeding the level in Cooper Road, Louisiana (32.6 percent), Richmond Heights, Florida (24.8 percent), and Roosevelt City, Alabama (15.3 percent), all southern communities. This factor, coupled with the fact that husbands tend to be concentrated in the more protected manufacturing sector of the labor force, might possibly deter wives from extensive labor force involvement. It should be pointed out that almost half the black working women in this community hail from households in which they are primary individuals, rather than wives or female heads of households. These women are no doubt younger and better educated, and in a few instances have been able to transcend the lower level of the job hierarchy. Among the female heads in our sample there appeared to be almost a complete withdrawal from the labor force in favor of welfare support. Given the opportunities which are available to women with limited skills in this labor market, the decision to withdraw probably represents an economically rational decision in the minds of the potential participant.

The contribution of working wives to husband/wife households has been shown to vary widely among the all-black towns, although the range of variation among a selected number of black suburbanizing communities tends to be smaller. In the all-black towns, the extent to which wives are active in the labor force tends to reflect the nature of the employment opportunity in the labor shed and the age and educational status of wives. Since the average age of wives in the all-black towns is older than that of wives in the selected suburbanizing communities, one would expect this factor to be associated with lower median levels of educational attainment and, consequently, restrictions on the nature of the employment opportunity available to this potential employment pool.

It is postulated that the nature of the wives' work role will influence the subcultural mode described in the previous chapter. Studies that relate specifically to this problem are few, although many writers who have tended to view the black family as matrifocal have obviously implied the existence of such a relationship. The outlook of these researchers was essentially limited to viewing the strength of the contribution of the black mother. Because of her greater employability and employment stability it was thought that she was able to assume the pivotal position of power in the household.

OCCUPATIONAL STATUS AND THE SUBCULTURE CONTINUUM

In this section, concern is primarily focused on the nature of the job performed vis-à-vis adaptive styles, and how this might be reflected in the practices and frequency of traits associated with a given stage along the subcultural continuum. Recently Jan Dizard attempted to relate occupational status to black identity.[16] While he indicated the variation in the intensity of black identity by major occupational groups, Dizard was careful to point out that age was the strongest single variable in its influence on identity.[17] It was noted that the weakest association with a black identity tended to be with managers, craftsmen, and service workers.[18] Since the work force in the all-black towns is comprised of such a small percentage of the first two occupational categories, it is the latter category that is of principal concern.

Religion and the Subculture Schema

It is assumed that among those households in which black women are largely engaged in service employment, the adaptive-suppressive subculture will most often express itself in higher levels of church affiliation. Religion, which was stated earlier to have provided a source of strength in aiding black Americans to accept their lot in American society without showing extreme aggressive tendencies, was an important social control mechanism for two or three generations. Thus one would be led to believe that religion would continue to play an important role in those communities whose occupational structure tended to be traditional.

Dizard, addressing himself to the relationship of service worker category to black identity, stated the following:

> By contrast, service workers generally have been involved in a much more paternalistic relationship with their usually white employer (hospital workers being a major exception in this occupational grouping), a relationship that historically has not been especially conducive to the formation of group consciousness.[19]

If Dizard's scale for determining the strength of black identity possesses a measure of validity, then there should occur a positive association between the extent of religious affiliation and the extent to which black women are found in service occupations, especially private household employment. The decision to use the female occupational structure only as a means of addressing this relationship grows out of the more extensive involvement of black women with the church.

The respondents in the all-black towns were asked if they belonged to church and, if so, to specify their denominational affiliation. The extent to which respondents indicated that they belonged to church varied from all respondents (100 percent) in Hollydale, Ohio to 54.4 percent in East Palo Alto, California. The mean incidence of affiliation is 76 percent. The second question, which sought information indicating denominational identity, not only provided the information sought but brought to light the extent to which persons who had previously acknowledged church membership did not identify with any specific denominational group. This information seems in part to distinguish between those who might be thought of as formal identifiers with religion as opposed to nonformal. The nonformal identifiers might be assumed to possess a more secular orientation, and thus the role of religion as a social control mechanism would be weaker.

The communities possessing the highest levels of religious identity were Hollydale, Ohio; Richmond Heights, Florida; Roosevelt City, Alabama, and Cooper Road, Louisiana. With the exception of Hollydale, religious identity is strongest among the southern communities. The lowest levels of religious identity occur in East Palo Alto, California; Wyandanch, New York; and Glenarden, Maryland. These latter communities all possess modernizing occupational structures. When the communities are ranked, after deflating the original incidence of religious identity by the percentage who fail to indicate a denominational association, some interesting alterations occur. However, the communities which tended to be most secular in the original ranking generally retained a similar rank. The communities with the strongest spiritual identity on the second ranking were Kinloch, Missouri; Lincoln Heights, Ohio; Robbins, Illinois; and Cooper Road, Louisiana.

When female service workers are ranked against formal religious identities a high positive correlation is shown to exist. The position of East Palo Alto probably should be altered if one accepts as correct Dizard's position that hospital service workers tend to differ from other service workers in terms of black identity. These rankings do indeed show a positive relationship between female service employment and formal religious affiliation. This association provides added strength to the validity of the emergence of adaptive-suppressive and adaptive-assertive subcultural modes under a different set of environmental conditions.

Denominational identities of these households show that blacks in these outlying communities, like blacks nationally, tend to be predominantly Baptist. The extent to which this denomination is dominant varies from place to place, and in one community the Baptists represent a secondary rather than the primary affiliation. It has been said that the black denominations provided blacks an opportunity to achieve emotional release in an environment that sanctioned a wide variety of emotional expression. Often those blacks who have moved up the ladder of social status have switched denominations, frequently affiliating with those denominations where overt emotional release is frowned upon and greater internal control is a hallmark. This has led blacks with limited economic resources to identify with the former, and those with greater resources to affiliate with those denominations whose code of conduct tends to hold in disfavor forms of overt emotional release.

The Black Church and Black Culture

There are some who contend that the expressive black life style probably has its origins in the black Baptist church. Likewise the black Baptist church has been accused of being overly concerned with other-worldliness, almost to the point of excluding the problems of this world. Dr. Joseph Jackson, the head of the National Baptist Convention, the largest black church organization in this country, speaking to this issue a few years ago, said the following:

> There is a danger that we may become so anxious to win an immediate victory for the race that we make secondary the winning of spiritual victory for the nation and for the advancement of the kingdom of God among the children of men.[20]

It appears that the Baptist church has provided a sanctuary for those who were oriented toward the adaptive-suppressive subcultural mode; this is not to imply that others did not also encourage this mode nor that this was not a rational mode in terms of its practitioner's perception of his or her world.

The Black Muslims, with their small following, stand in contrast to the Baptist group in promoting self-assertion within the context of this world. Charles Keil points out that men have been more attracted to the Muslim movement than have women.[21] This is a reversal of the traditional strength of religious attraction as a function of sex identification. It has been stated that men are more attracted to worldly churches than to those possessing an other-worldly orientation.[22] William McCord and others also show that church persons with an other-worldly orientation (whom they describe as religious stoics) are characterized by low levels of educational attainment, higher median age (45), and tend to be concentrated in the lower status occupations.[23] Thus the strength of the Baptist church in the all-black towns, although showing some significant variations, is believed to be supportive of the adaptive-suppressive subcultural mode in those communities where this mode was described in the previous chapter as the modal subcultural orientation.

The Methodist church ranked second among five of the all-black towns, but generally far behind the Baptist leader. In Lawnside, New Jersey, which has been described as adaptive-assertive, the Methodist church was only slightly less significant than the Baptist church in its attractiveness to residents of the community. In each of the non-adaptive-suppressive communities, save two, the Baptist denomination is less strong. The two adaptive-assertive communities in which the Baptist denomination is strong are Richmond Heights, Florida and North Fontana, California. In the case of the latter community, field survey results would place it in the adaptive-suppressive class, although census data would indicate an adaptive-assertive status.

Wyandanch, New York, a peripherally adaptive-assertive community, shows the Lutheran faith to be the predominant one, with the Baptist faith secondary. A closer analysis of the individual household response in the latter community shows religious orientation to be associated largely with region of birth. Those respondents who were identified as being of southern origin were more likely to be adherents to the Baptist faith, while those of northern origin often identified themeslves as members of the Lutheran faith. Usually the Church of God (or Church of God in Christ) ranks third among the religious preferences of the all-black towns. In eight communities the latter faith averaged 10 percent of those persons indicating church membership. In East Chicago Heights and North Fontana approximately one-fifth of the respondents indicated that they were members of these church bodies. Like the Baptists, the latter religious group tends most often to be associated with adaptive-suppressive communities. Catholicism shows up as the secondary faith in a single community, Glenarden. Other communities in which Catholicism has acquired a foothold were Robbins, East Palo Alto, Lawnside, and Lincoln Heights. The Catholic percentage in these communities resembles that of the Church of God in other communities.

East Palo Alto, which serves as the deviant case in terms of religious affiliation, is the single community to have households who identify as Muslims. It is obvious that expressed religious preferences in these communities show an identifiable association with aspects of the subcultural continuum developed in the previous chapter. But even more obvious is the association of the female occupational structure and aspects of the subcultural continuum. One is led to agree generally with Dizard's position that service employment, in particular, and black identity bear striking relationships, as these are expressed through denominational preference. It appears the extent to which households express an identification with religion is associated with median age. In those communities characterized by aging populations, formal religious identity is high; but in those communities where the median age tends to be more youthful, there is a diminution in the strength of religious identification.

Charles Johnson, in a study conducted more than a generation ago, showed a weakening of the religious role of the church among southern rural black youths.[24] Although membership continued to be high among this youthful population, the church was viewed as being more valuable as an institution which provided social outlets rather than emotional release. If this trend prevailed in subsequent generations and in alternate environments, then the trend observed among the all-black town should be expected. This, likewise, should be expected to have some impact on the development of the subcultural continuum.

WORK PLACE LOCATION AND SUBURBAN RING RESIDENCE

Blacks living outside central cities but within metropolitan areas constitute a diverse group, although they are somewhat better off in income terms than their central city counterparts. Given the evidence that major shifts are resulting in suburban locations becoming the new employment fields, to what extent do the non-central city black residents participate in suburban job opportunity? This is a very difficult question to answer, since it is not always obvious how important job location was in influencing one's decision to settle in the suburbs. But since most blacks have settled in the older suburbs, Neil Gold states that they are still removed from the exurban enclaves which are the relocation target of many headquarters firms which were previously located in the central city.[25]

The work place locations of the non-central city black work force are diverse. Seldom is it found that workers from a single community overwhelmingly work in a central city environment or a suburban environment. Mixed work place locations are the rule (see Figs. 5–1 and 5–2), although the work place locations of the residents of the all-black towns more often show a pattern of suburban dominance than is true of the black suburbanizing community group. Among the all-

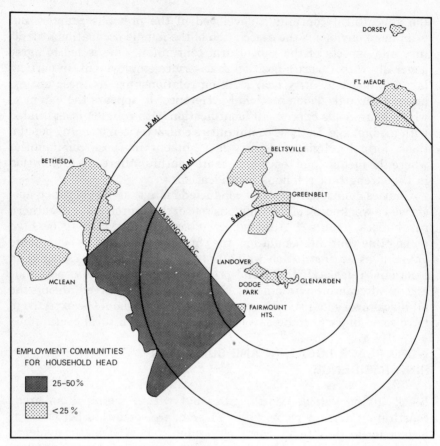

Figure 5–1.   Work Place Locations of Glenarden Work Force

black towns, residents in six communities (40 percent) are principally employed elsewhere in the metropolitan ring, whereas only eight (22.8 percent) of the black suburbanizing communities reflect this pattern. In this instance the dominant job location field is one in which 50 percent or more of the residents are employed in either the central city or the suburban ring.

The emerging pattern is one that appears to be related to (1) distance from the central city, (2) the size of the residential community, and (3) the social class identity of the community. Among the all-black towns and black suburbanizing communities as well, those located contiguous to the central city showed a strong disposition to send their workers to the central city. Urbancrest, Ohio and Cooper Road, Louisiana represent all-black towns whose work forces are basically

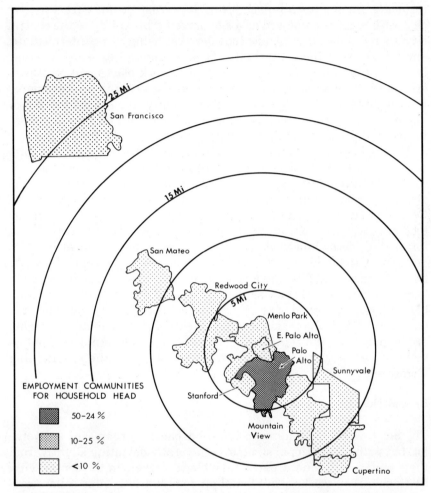

Figure 5–2. Work Place Locations of East Palo Alto Work Force

central city oriented, while the black suburbanites of Daly City, California; East Cleveland, Shaker Heights, and Warrensville Heights, Ohio; and Westmont, California also follow this pattern. In some instances it is possible to specify which employment field provides the most economically secure employment opportunity.

The information secured through the field survey on place of employment for workers from the all-black towns is rich in detail. Since these communities vary both in terms of their relative location within the metropolitan ring and their socioeconomic rank, it is possible to determine how these attributes affect the work place locations of their residents. Among the all-black towns, if average distance from central city work place is employed as a surrogate for proximity to the central city, then communities can be considered as being close, intermediate, and far vis-à-vis the central city. Those communities which average less than ten miles from their central city work places will be considered near; those greater than ten but less than twenty are considered intermediate; and those greater than twenty are considered far or distant. Among the fifteen communities, seven are located in the intermediate distance band, with four each in the near and far bands.

Those communities most distant from the central city tend to represent communities of early black settlement. The close-in communities contain both communities which are aging and those which are undergoing a period of maximum growth. Both Glenarden, Maryland and Cooper Road, Louisiana are examples of the latter type. The intermediate locations contain communities that are highly variable in terms of socioeconomic rank. Needless to say, economic well-being does not appear to be directly related to distance from the central city, as there are marginally secure and economically insecure communities in each distance band. Likewise there is no straightforward relationship between distance band of residence and central city employment. It is true that most of the residents (73 percent) of Cooper Road, Louisiana are employed in the central city, but the lack of alternative employment opportunity rather than distance tends to be the conditioning factor here.

SUMMING UP

The black workers residing in the suburban ring represent a diverse lot, but with occupational structures generally deviating slightly from their central city counterparts. Like black workers in the central city, black suburban workers are found predominantly in blue collar occupations, although a few of the suburbanizing communities are dominated by white collar workers. Somewhat paradoxically, the community with the highest percentage of white collar workers is one of the all-black towns—Glenarden, Maryland. The higher status workers as a rule tend to be found more often in the spillover communities than in the colonies, although there are some exceptions to this rule as well.

The role of the working wife in these communities does much to alter the socioeconomic status of individual communities. The reasons for variations in the labor force participation rates for wives were not always clear; but it does appear that available work opportunity and the education and age of wives are critical variables. Clearly this is a topic that requires more in-depth investigation. Likewise, our attempt to relate the role of religion and occupation to the emergence of the previously identified subcultural continuum must be considered highly tentative. The evidence presented cannot simply be ignored, but it still remains conjectural at this point.

On the question of impact of residential location on employment accessibility we have shed little additional insight. The general question is perhaps too broad for the kinds of data available. Thus it appears that this question is unlikely to be answered in a straightforward way, until such time that studies are designed with this question occupying a central position. Nevertheless, from the information reviewed here, it is obvious that those persons seeking to significantly upgrade their housing environment will be less concerned with employment accessibility. The extent to which the worker tends to be employed in the central city or the suburban ring is directly related to distance of residence from the central city. Thus residents of black colonies which are somewhat remote from the central city more often find employment in nearby communities, while those residents of spillover communities tend most often to be employed in the central city.

Both distance and community status are variables influencing the job location of the black resident in the suburban ring. While this is true, it fails to address the issue of the movement of jobs from the central city to the suburbs. If Charles Christian's assessment of the suburbanization of jobs in Chicago is akin to the national pattern, then there is considerable incongruity between the suburban spatial pattern of job relocation and the spatial pattern of black suburbanization.[26] It is this latter issue that has prompted some social scientists to investigate the possibility of relocating a segment of the black population in the suburban ring.

This investigation, however, has essentially focused on what may be thought of as voluntary moves, constrained only by the individual's awareness space and the manner in which housing is allocated to blacks within the framework of the market process. To overcome the disadvantages associated with this outcome there is need to provide greater information and financial support to those who wish to overcome the friction of distance associated with industrial relocation decisions.

Chapter 6

Selected Services and the Quality of Life Among Suburban Ring Communities

An assessment of the resources, previously described, that are available to blacks in non-central city environments shows that they vary substantially from place to place. These variations reflect the character of individual communities in terms of population size, social class makeup, social or racial origins, and recent changes in social status. The resources that received the lion's share of attention were housing, education, and employment opportunity. These are the resources generally conceded to be basic in attempts to measure the relative well-being of communities in terms of how well they provide access to the American opportunity structure. Not only does the quality of these resources influence the current well-being of families, but the life chances of those who represent future generations as well. While these resources constitute the core of items thought to impinge upon both individual and community well-being, numerous other items are also employed by residents in assessing environment quality.

QUALITY OF LIFE MEASURES AND TERRITORIAL SCALE

The list of items employed by social analysts in attempting to assess the quality of life prevailing at individual places is likely to vary as a function of the scale on which one chooses to make the evaluation, as well as the disciplinary affiliation of the evaluator. The whole notion of quality of life measures and/or social indicators is still in a stage of

223

infancy. Thus reports that pretend to evaluate the quality of life are likely to reflect the stage of development of the art. Michael Flax, who was concerned with evaluating and monitoring the quality of life at the metropolitan area scale, employed ten classes of indicators made up of fourteen variables. The ten indicator categories employed by Flax were unemployment, poverty, health, mental health, public order, social disintegration, racial equality, citizen participation, educational attainment, and air quality.[1] Ben Chieh-Liu, on the other hand, who was concerned with evaluating the quality of life at the scale of the state, employed only nine indicators, but used more than 100 variables in association with these indicators.[2] There seems to be some general agreement among analysts regarding what constitutes an appropriate set of indicators, but the variables employed to evaluate performance on these criteria are seldom uniform. This lack of uniformity is partially associated with the scale at which the desired information is collected.

Selected Services as Dimensions of the Quality of Life

Since attention has already been directed toward the basic dimensions of environmental quality and/or quality of life, attention now focuses on a general category of services sometimes employed as a measure of how well a community responds to the needs of its residents. Unfortunately, it is not possible to secure information at the scale of the individual ring communities which match those that others have employed at a larger scale. Thus one is unable to replicate the work of Flax and others at this scale. Information secured through field interviews allows us to evaluate some aspects of satisfaction with the community service environment within the all-black towns.

Respondents were asked to evaluate the quality of services provided by the local community, or alternative providers when these services were not locally produced. The service areas under investigation are as follows: (1) Police, (2) Recreation, (3) Fire Protection, (4) Retail Services, (5) Health Care, (6) Garbage Collection, and (7) Public Transportation. While these items do not measure directly the quality of life in the same way as those employed by Flax and others, they do provide an estimate of satisfaction with the experiential environment. The following statement by Lowdon Wingo regarding the quality of life is one we find enlightening: "The quality of life, I propose, can be considered to consist of the consumption of the services of the experiential environment, which [has] both physical and social dimensions."[3] He states further that experiential environments are like clubs and one can join a club for a price, as a means of acquiring access to the collective goods of the club.[4]

The Wingo framework seems to be an appropriate one for the kinds of questions we have asked. Unfortunately, this same analogy cannot be applied outside the context of the all-black towns. But special emphasis will be given three of the communities in the group which were essentially entry communities during the sixties, and possess more in common with some of the suburbanizing communities than other all-black towns. Where possible, some comment will be directed to selected suburbanizing communities on at least one of these dimensions.

Size differences and political status constrain the number of services provided by the individual communities in this universe. The larger communities provide a greater range of services regardless of political status, whereas the small unincorporated places seldom provide any services, public or private, with the exception of one or more convenience stores. Thus places like Hollydale, Urbancrest, and North Fontana, with fewer than 2,000 residents, must depend on other communities to provide basic services. These communities often express greater satisfaction with services received than is expressed by communities which provide some or all of these services. The greatest range of services is provided by the communities of Wyandanch and Lawnside. The former community is one of the larger among this group, but is unincorporated, while the latter is a medium sized but incorporated entity. The level of satisfaction with services tends to be higher in the latter community than in the former.

In most of these communities both public and private services are secured in other communities. Whether this is an expression of dissatisfaction with local services or simply reflects the limited range of goods available is unknown. It is apparent, though, that in the case of retail services many communities are only able to provide low order convenience goods, and thus higher order convenience goods and shopping goods must be secured elsewhere. The size of many of these communities, therefore, imposes limits on the range of goods and services which are locally available. The poverty of some of the communities places them in the position of having to depend on surrounding communities or the county to provide such public services as police services, fire protection, garbage collection, and recreational services, even though they are politically independent. In several instances where communities previously had operated their own schools, this function had been totally or partially absorbed by other school districts.

THE COMMUNITIES RESPOND TO PUBLIC
SECTOR SERVICES

Among the services on which residents were queried the largest share falls within the realm of the public domain. This service category includes public safety, fire protection, public transportation, recreation, and garbage collection. While it is true that these services do not fall exclusively in the realm of the public sector, it is this sector which normally assumes responsibility for their provision. Likewise these services find different expressions of importance from place to place. Public safety tends to concern the largest number of individuals in our sample, yet in those communities of extreme poverty the availability of public transportation becomes a critical issue. On the other hand, in growth communities, where youth constitute a significant element, concern is frequently expressed regarding the adequacy of recreational resources. Thus the value placed on an individual service may well influence how that service is ranked in terms of satisfaction.

The General Response of Blacks to
Public Service

Black residents of central cities are generally known to express relatively high levels of dissatisfaction with city services. In almost all cases blacks show greater dissatisfaction than do whites. Aberbach and Walker, reporting on the responses of a sample of black and white respondents in rating selected city services, showed that the highest level of white dissatisfaction on a single service was 33 percent (parks), while blacks showed a high level of 48 percent (teen centers).[5] If blacks residing in metropolitan ring locations are assumed to enjoy a higher quality of life than central city residents, one would suppose that service dissatisfaction would not exceed the 33 percent high that characterized the white response.

The Black Towns Response

Thirteen of the fourteen communities for which data were analyzed showed a level of dissatisfaction in excess of that established as the appropriate threshold on at least one item. North Fontana was the only community in which fewer than 33 percent of the respondents expressed dissatisfaction with a single service. The services with which there was the greatest dissatisfaction were recreation and public transportation. In both instances eight communities showed levels of dissatisfaction that exceeded the threshold.

The second highest level of dissatisfaction expressed was with police services. Six communities showed disenchantment with police ser-

vices: Lincoln Heights, Kinloch, Wyandanch, East Palo Alto, Urbancrest, and Robbins. The highest level of dissatisfaction occurred in East
Palo Alto (52 percent), followed by Robbins (42 percent). The communities showing dissatisfaction with police services represent a diverse lot, containing both traditional outlying black communities with
a history of political independence and the larger unincorporated
communities of recent black entry. Lawnside, New Jersey, stands in
contrast to these communities, as here more than 25 percent of the
respondents viewed police services as highly satisfactory. Perhaps the
human interest story on Lawnside which appeared in the *Philadelphia
Magazine*, was accurate when it stated:

> Philadelphia citizens have put Supercop in City Hall and remain afraid
> to walk their streets. They have put extra locks on their doors and still
> tremble behind them at night. But Lawnside's crime rate is "practically
> nill," according to Police Chief Floard Catlett, and has been for the past
> five years.[6]

Fire protection and garbage collection services were lowly regarded
in four communities. And four communities (Lincoln Heights,
Lawnside, Roosevelt City, and Glenarden) expressed a high level of
satisfaction with at least one of the five public services identified.
Lawnside showed a high level of satisfaction on three items (police, fire
protection, and public transportation); Roosevelt City on two (recreation and garbage collection); and Lincoln Heights on one (garbage
collection). Satisfaction on the largest number of items appears to bear
some relationship to community rank, but high level of satisfaction
was also expressed by communities whose economic resources are
meager.

THE SERVICE RESPONSE AMONG THE
GROWTH COMMUNITIES

In order to more fully understand the response of the residents in their
evaluation of public services, a more detailed description of these
responses will be given for Wyandanch, New York; East Palo Alto,
California; Glenarden, Maryland; and Richmond Heights, Florida. As
stated earlier, these communities represent examples of both the
southern and northern models of black community growth. In the
southern communities settlement is taking place within an environment designed for black occupancy from its inception. In both Glenarden and Richmond Heights, new homes were constructed during the
previous twenty-year period to appeal to that segment of the black
population who wished to reside outside the central city in a suburban

type of environment. Over the years these developments have grown, and the housing design has changed from that typical of the immediate postwar period (small, pastel colored stucco "boxes") to expanded ranch and other more spacious and appealing designs. These were the environments that attracted upwardly mobile blacks who had been socialized in the formal world of racial segregation. The problems expressed with the availability and quality of selected services among these two communities bear some resemblance, but there are obvious differences that reflect dissimilarities in political status, social class mix, and stage in the life cycle.

The Richmond Heights Response

In 1970, approximately one-third of the population in Richmond Heights was between ten and nineteen years old. The age structure of the total population shows that youth, which includes the under-ten segment of the population, constitute the overwhelming majority of all community residents. The most prevalent service deficiency expressed by community residents is directly related to both the age structure of the population and the political status of the community. When this population was asked to cite the most critical problem in the community growing out of the inadequacy of a single service, fully one-third of those responding to the question cited the problem of teenage crime.

Teen crime was identified with public gambling, vandalism, alcoholic consumption, burglary and robbery. The general opinion of the respondents is that teen crimes could be reduced if the community had its own police substation. Since Richmond Heights is an unincorporated place, it does not have its own police department and is thus dependent upon the county government to provide such services. Because of the nature of the problem and the lack of local police services, the respondents feel that they are being inundated by acts that offend their sensibilities or that result in property loss. The residents give the impression of being helpless to alter this situation without acquiring access to improved police services. It appears that local concern is basically related to property crime rather than personal crime, for more than 75 percent of the residents viewed the community as a moderately safe environment. Only 14 percent thought of it as being unsafe.

Other services with which residents in this community expressed dissatisfaction and thought were problem provoking were fire protection, ambulance service, inadequate sewerage system, and improper drainage, in that order. These must be ranked as secondary problems, as the number reporting these problems was very much smaller than those who saw teenage crime as the principal problem. Paradoxically, when the respondents were asked what one condition they would recommend to make their neighborhood more desirable in terms of their families' needs, the largest single response was improved shopping facilities within the community. The next three items in terms of importance were larger homes, expanded police protection, and improved and supervised recreational resources for youth. No attempt has been made here to determine from which segment of the population these recommendations flow.

One issue that emerges in this context is the possible conflict in cultural orientation between the generations. The Richmond Heights population was previously identified as being found at the adaptive-suppressive point along the black cultural continuum, but it appears that the youth might possibly be maladaptive-expressive in terms of the set of norms which govern their conduct. If this is the case, the question might be what type of intervention strategy would be most appropriate in attempting to protect the long term investment of adults and, at the same time, insure more secure futures for youth, lest the dreams of one generation be shattered by those of another.

The Glenarden Response

Glenarden, a middle income community, experienced its most rapid growth during the decade of the sixties. It was the site of the development of an upper middle income housing tract and several large moderate income apartment complexes during this period. By 1970 only a minority of the population had resided in the community for more than ten years. Glenarden is a small incorporated place of less than 5,000 people, located only a few miles northeast of the District of Columbia.

This community, in evaluating its access to basic services, expressed the greatest concern with the lack of adequate fire protection. More than two-thirds of the respondents rated fire protection as unsatisfactory. Only two other services were identified as inadequate—police services and recreational services—and the level of expressed dissatisfaction was only about one-third that associated with the former service. When respondents were asked what service would make their neighborhood a better place in terms of their families' needs, the principal response was the provision of more recreational resources for the community's children. This was followed by an equal number of responses citing the need for improved fire protection and a number of general physical improvements, which included street paving, off-street parking, traffic lights, and so forth. A third but minor response was directed at the housing type mix. Several respondents expressed negative reaction to the development of apartment complexes in the community, and some even suggested the removal of some of the existing units.

The two concerns most often reflected in this set of responses are the possibilities that their homes might be destroyed or damaged by fire, and that their property might be stolen as a result of the inadequacy of the local police. The community presently must secure its fire protection from the nearby community of Kentland. There is a local police department, but this small unit is not thought by residents to be adequate to provide the quality of protection sought. The second concern reflects the group's interest in channeling youthful energies in an appropriate direction by providing a supervised recreational program. Unlike Richmond Heights, residents here did not indicate that youth were actually engaged in negative behavior, although there seems to exist a fear that if additional recreational outlets are not provided, negative behavior could be anticipated. At this point, however, the community response with respect to youth is geared towards a system of rewards (recreation), rather than penalties (police), as was the case in Richmond Heights.

The importance of demographic differences in explaining the varying attitudes toward youth in these two communities is an issue that should not be ignored (see Fig. 6–1). Both communities are youthful, but Richmond Heights shows a higher percentage of its population in the fifteen to nineteen category than does Glenarden. To what extent does this difference prompt a different kind of concern among parents? On the other hand, are these differences an outgrowth of class and/or culture related factors? It is assumed that the modal style in Glenarden is adaptive-assertive, but it is unknown how this identity expresses itself intergenerationally. However, it is clear that the respondents in the two communities view the behavior of youth in different ways—at least in terms of the recommended services that were thought would make the community a better place to live.

Wyandanch and East Palo Alto: An Example
of the Northern Model of Suburban Development

Wyandanch, New York and East Palo Alto, California are outlying ring communities which did not originate as predominantly black communities, as did the previous two communities described. There exist in both of these a black residential zone and a white residential zone. In East Palo Alto the two are effectively separated by the Bay Shore Freeway. Both these communities are enclaves surrounded by predominantly white communities, although the black community of Menlo Park is a physical extension of the black residential zone in East

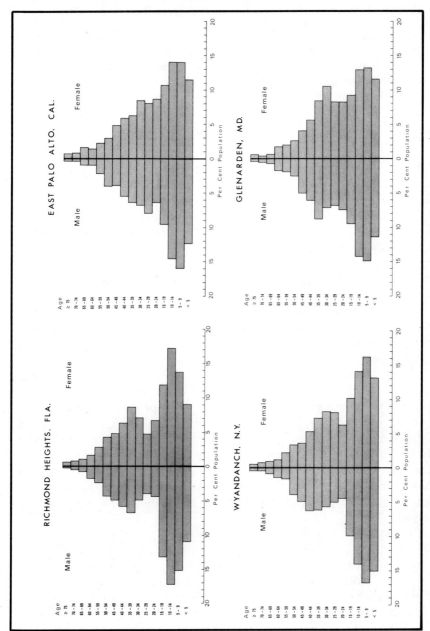

Figure 6–1.   The Age Structure of Selected All-Black Towns

Palo Alto. The emergence of East Palo Alto led a Standord University professor of creative writing to comment that East Palo Alto:

> . . . is one of the instant ghettos that have sprung up in the North and West since World War II. In the mid-fifties, it was a sprawl of lower-middle class homes among truck farms and flower fields in the flats beside the bay. Its black population, swollen by escapees from the ghettos of Oakland and Richmond, enlarged by block busting tactics of certain realtors, and increased still further by agencies that have used the area as a dumping ground for families displaced by freeways and slum clearance elsewhere, has now reached 24,000.[7]

If Wallace Stegner is correct, he has provided insight into how such communities evolve. However, his comment on population size does not conform to those of official estimates.

The residents of Wyandanch express intense dissatisfaction with the lack of adequate police protection. Only inadequate public transportation was viewed as a problem by a larger number of people. Fully two-fifths of the respondents rated police services as poor, while another one-third thought of them as being fair or better. On probing the matter of inadequate police services, one finds that a rise in crime is thought to be the result of inadequate police services. The activities that are most disturbing to the respondents are their perception of increased drug trafficking leading to juvenile delinquency, burglary, and robbery.

The residents in this community responded quite similarly to those in Richmond Heights, Florida in terms of their perception of the problem and their categorization of it as a police problem. Concern with teen crime looms large in both communities, although in Richmond Heights alcohol, public gambling, and vandalism are mentioned more often as dimensions of crime. The latter activities represent the more traditional and least severe aspects of deviance, whereas the activities that seem to be a part of the behavioral repertoire of the teen population of Wyandanch signal the presence of problems of a more serious nature.

Paradoxically, when Wyandanch residents were asked what services would make the community a better place for their families to live, they cited an improved sewer system and sidewalk paving. Following this recommendation was the need for a supervised recreational program for youth. Thus, in their attempt to alleviate the problem of teen crime, the residents of Wyandanch, like those of Glenarden, look to an effective recreation program to defuse what they see as a rising tendency toward juvenile criminal behavior.

The focal concern of the residents of East Palo Alto is quite similar to that of the Wyandanch sample—safety. More than 50 percent of the respondents viewed the effectiveness of the police in handling the problem as poor. As was previously noted, East Palo Alto is an unincorporated community and must depend on the county to provide protection. There is a local police substation within the community, but it is generally felt to be inadequately manned. The crimes most often mentioned as constituting part of the problem are drug use and burglary. From the comments made by the respondents, one would assume that a youthful drug culture is evolving in the community which has led to a burglary epidemic as means of securing valuables to support the habit. Unlike the residents of Wyandanch, those in East Palo Alto thought the best way to make their community more desirable was to reduce the level of drug dependency and burglaries; secondary attention was focused upon physical improvements. A third item, which was identified almost as many times as the need for physical improvements, was the need for unity within the community.

An examination of respondent satisfaction with public services in the growth communities shows that safety and recreation are the services that elicit the most intense responses. They are sometimes viewed as representing a combined vehicle needed to combat local criminal activity, although, in both Richmond Heights and East Palo Alto the need for a more effective police system transcends interest in making available improved recreational facilities.

In three of the four instances it appears that youth in these communities, like youth in the central city, are prone to conduct that is detrimental to community welfare. To what extent such conduct is related to heterogeneous community norms, the strength of the peer group in molding alternative norms, lack of adequate employment and recreational opportunity for youth, or the transfer of inner city life styles to alternative environments is unknown. Nevertheless, it is evident that the respondents feel that public services required to ameliorate the situation are inadequate.

Social Disorganization—a Recurring Theme

The indicators emerging out of this analysis as being more troublesome are those that Michael Flax has identified as public order and social disintegration. The variable employed by Flax to measure public order was the robbery rate. In these communities burglary was viewed as the most serious criminal offense in terms of frequency of occurrence, but it is also a measure of public order. The narcotics arrest rate was employed by Flax as an indicator of social disintegration. While a ratio index such as that developed by Flax is not possible in this instance, the prevalence of an emerging drug problem in two of the larger of these communities illustrates a decline in the quality of life in some suburban ring communities.

Mark Abrahamson, in a factor analytic study of the social structure of a sample of American cities, identifies burglary as one of the half-dozen variables that rank high on the social structural dimension that he labels disorganization-deviance.[8] The other variables are murder, assault, rape, crowded dwellings, and percent black. While Abrahamson labels their factor disorganization-deviance, he states: "Perhaps this factor could now as easily be called 'ghetto development.' "[9] It is a bit ironic that those engaged in moves which take them physically the farthest from the central city ghetto end up in environments that are beginning to take on some of the quality of life features of those environments they left behind. Dieter Zschock, viewing the situation of black youth in suburbia, feels that the resources to assist with the problems encountered in these environments are seldom available. In addressing himself to the dissatisfaction expressed by youth in this environment he states:

> Black youths complain that political leaders and other public officials either do not know or do not care about their views. The youths are equally critical of adults in their communities, including candid references to the attitudes of their own parents. Few adult leaders, even from the same minority group, have won the respect of these young people. Lack of commitment to community interests summarize the youths' negative view of the adult world.[10]

The latter writer's sample comes from Suffolk County in New York, the county in which the community of Wyandanch is located. From the survey responses in the case of Wyandanch, one could not concur in the opinion that residents are not interested in the welfare of the community. To what extent their interests are in agreement with those of youth cannot be answered from the information available.

Those communities which appear to be undergoing the greatest amount of disorganization—East Palo Alto and Wyandanch—were previously described as only marginally secure. The question now arising is whether it is possible to deter deviance and disorganization in marginally secure communities, even though a working class designation has been assigned them. This general issue was recently investigated by Vincent and Homel, in their attempt to identify high risk or vulnerable neighborhoods in which delinquency was likely to create a problem in a number of suburban communities in a medium-sized

Australian city.[11] Some variables they identify as characterizing high risk neighborhoods are also those that were employed in this study to identify marginally secure communities.

THE GENERAL RESPONSE OF THE UNIVERSE OF ALL-BLACK TOWNS

Looking once again at the universe of all-black towns it is obvious that the respondents view their communities differently in terms of their perceived safety. In no instance did the majority of the respondents view their communities as unsafe. In seven instances more than a fifth of the residents believed that they were living in unsafe communities. These include Robbins, Wyandanch, East Palo Alto, Kinloch, Lincoln Heights, Cooper Road, and East Chicago Heights. In the first two communities almost two-fifths of the residents believed their communities to be unsafe. None of the communities were better off than marginally secure, with the remainder being identified as insecure. Among those insecure communities which did not report high level fears of the lack of safety were those whose age structure show a paucity of youth and a disproportionate share of older persons, or secondarily, those that are more rural than suburban; these include Urbancrest, Roosevelt City, and North Fontana. The other communities which indicated that safety was not a major issue were the higher status communities, which were previously described as economically secure, or were found on the upper end of the marginally secure ladder.

Quality of Services and Political Status
The lack of resources to provide some of the services with which the respondents expressed limited satisfaction or even dissatisfaction may be a function of their political status. In those communities where the issue of safety is viewed as critical, there is an absence of political independence. These are communities which generally possess an unincorporated status, with the exception of Robbins. In both Wyandanch and East Palo Alto, residents expressed a preference for a change of political status. In the former community 2 percent of the respondents indicated a desire to become legally incorporated, while in the latter community 65 percent of the respondents expressed the same wish. Not all the unincorporated communities expressed this heightened desire to become politically independent: both Cooper Road and North Fontana, while seeking a change in status, wished to be annexed to their nearest neighbor community, Shreveport and Fontana respec-

tively. Of the remaining unincorporated communities the majority of respondents in Richmond Heights and Hollydale wish to retain their existing status.

The economically insecure of the incorporated places exhibit a mixed reaction to their current status, with only Robbins showing a clear preference for an alternative status. In the latter instance, almost 30 percent of the respondents thought they would be better off if they were annexed by a larger suburb. It appears unlikely, however, that the adjacent white communities of either Alsip or Midlothian would be inclined to assume the burden of upgrading the service package of Robbins. Some years earlier the city of Fontana rejected the notion that they annex North Fontana, a community only one-fifth as large as Robbins.

The Robbins case highlights the point that political independence alone does not bring about an improvement in the quality of life. Unless a higher modicum of economic and psychological security is available to the residents of these enclaves, it is unlikely that their public service package will be able to satisfy their needs. Under conditions of marginal security and worse, intergenerational conflict tends to show itself in the form of increased deviance and disorganization. The maladaptive-expressive mode of the black cultural continuum becomes pronounced among youth even though parents may express another subcultural mode. The complexity of the adult population's adaptation to the external world seems to bear directly on the quality of life available to them in their environmental microcosm. Before we turn to selected services in the private sector, a brief statement will be made regarding the critical issue of safety in selected black suburbanizing communities.

THE ISSUE OF A SAFE ENVIRONMENT IN BLACK SUBURBANIZING COMMUNITIES

The issue of the availability of auxiliary public services in black suburbanizing communities will not be broached here because of the lack of appropriate information. It is possible, however, to consider indirectly and obliquely the issue of safety in those communities for which the FBI secures annual uniform crime reports. Crime data are available for fifteen communities whose populations surpassed 25,000 in 1970, although crime rates are not reported for individual places within the 25,000–100,000 population range.

The absence of crime rates, both aggregate and for specific offenses, makes it difficult to discuss variations in the risk of victimization in these communities. The communities for which this information is

A

B

Figure 6–2. Contrasts in the Physical Design of Units Providing Political Services in Middle Income Glenarden, Maryland (A) and Low Income Roosevelt City, Alabama (B)

available are Carson, Daly City, Pomona, Richmond, and Hayward, California; East Orange, New Jersey; and Pontiac, Michigan in the 50,000–100,000 size class. In the 25,000–50,000 size class, information is available for East Cleveland and Shaker Heights, Ohio; Freeport and Hempstead, New York; Harvey and Maywood, Illinois; Plainfield, New Jersey; and University City, Missouri. Since dissatisfaction with the local police was most often expressed by residents of all-black towns in whose communities burglary was identified as the principal index of criminal behavior, the extent to which burglary was reported as a percentage of all type 1 or index crimes is employed as a measure of potential service satisfaction.

Burglary as an Index of the Quality of Safety

In 1965 burglary constituted approximately 42 percent of all index crimes in the nation. Since 1965 the national victimization rate for burglary has increased approximately 100 percent. Thus the protection of one's investment in property items has become an issue of some concern. Nationally the victimization rate for blacks exceeds that for whites. Whether or not the risk of property loss was a variable influencing persons to settle in any of the fifteen communities identified above is unknown, with the exception of University City, which was described in an earlier chapter.

The FBI's Uniform Crime Report in 1971 showed that burglary constitutes more than 42 percent of all crime in seven of the fifteen communities identified above (see Table 6-1). Burglary constituted almost half of the type 1 crime in Plainfield, New Jersey and 53 percent of crimes in this category in University City, Missouri. Burglary was at a low level in terms of the prevailing distribution of criminal activity in Shaker Heights and East Cleveland, Ohio and Hayward, California. The unusually low contribution of burglary to

Table 6–1.   The Incidence of Burglary and Violent Crime in Selected Black Suburbanizing Communities, 1971

Class I Communities (≥50,000 <100,000)	Burglary %	Violent Crime %
Carson	46.5	58.3
Daly City	36.2	43.7
E. Orange	43.3	62.9
Pomona	45.2	56.9
Pontiac	47.3	74.0
Richmond	47.5	62.6
Hayward	32.1	40.5
Class II Communities (≥20,000 <50,000)	Burglary %	Violent Crime %
E. Cleveland	32.0	50.4
Freeport	38.8	45.6
Harvey	35.4	58.2
Hempstead	34.6	41.4
Maywood	39.7	62.2
Plainfield	48.5	61.3
Shaker Hts.	22.8	32.8
University City	53.6	62.2

Source: Crime in the U.S., Uniform Crime Reports, U.S. Federal Bureau of Investigation, U.S. Government Printing Office, Washington, D.C., 1972.

the crime mix in Shaker Heights is probably associated with both the social rank and the stage in the life cycle of that community.

While these data describe the ratio of burglary to all crime at the community scale, it is safe to conjecture that blacks here, as in the central city, are relatively more often victims of these acts. To what extent these acts are disturbing and provoke fear among blacks who have recently selected these communities as places of residence is unknown. It is possible that superior police protection is available in these communities, as they constitute incorporated political entities with larger and better equipped police departments than was true of the all-black towns possessing the same political status.

Violent Crime and Safety

It is generally assumed that crimes of violence create the greatest anxiety among those residents in which fear for personal safety is believed to exist. The rate of violent crime in the nation's cities has been characterized by a sharp increase since 1965. Violent crimes are those acts directed at the individual, and causing physical and/or emotional harm. They include murder, rape, robbery, and assault. In 1965 crimes of this genre constituted 13 percent of all index crimes.

Robbery and assault are characterized by the higher incidence of occurrence among the group. These are the crimes that are often labeled street crimes. Thus persons who express fears for their personal safety are often expressing fear that they might possibly be robbed, raped, assaulted, or even killed while using the communities' streets, generally at night. Street crimes are sometimes viewed as a measure of public order, and the national citizenry tends to be in general agreement that public order is on the decline. In a 1965 survey, people were asked to what extent they felt unsafe walking alone at night; 35 percent answered in the affirmative. Seven years later, 42 percent responded in this way.[12] Blacks in this sample showed even greater fear than whites in terms of their personal safety.

To establish the relative rank of environments in the selected suburbanizing communities in minimizing fears for personal safety, the proportion of violent crime to all crime was determined. It is possible, however, to come away with an erroneous impression about crime levels when simply treating the problem in terms of the crime mix. In 1967 approximately 13 percent of all reported crime was violent crime. In this instance a plus and minus 5 percent variation around the mean was employed to identify those communities in which violent crime was relatively more or less severe than the average level. The communities in which violent crime was in excess of 17 percent of all crime include Maywood and Harvey, Illinois; East Cleveland, Ohio; and Pontiac, Michigan. The problem was most severe in Pontiac where 26 percent of all crime was violent crime.

The communities which fell on the low side of the mean, and thus can generally be viewed as safe communities, are Daly City and Hayward, California and Freeport and Hempstead, New York. The other communities in this group fell within the average range in terms of the crime mix. The two caveats that stand out here are (1) the difficulty of generalizing to the black population on the basis of total community data, and (2) the use of the crime mix rather than crime rates as an index of safety. The absence of more precise information leads one to employ these crude measures.

It appears that large low status communities situated beyond the margins of the central city possess some safety characteristics similar to those of central cities. A guarantee of a safe environment seems to represent a highly complex situation, which includes components of economic security and psychological security and how they interact to establish the potential for physical security. It is not shown that by simply moving beyond the central city one enhances the possibility of living in an environment where public order prevails.

PRIVATE SECTOR SERVICES

Not all the services that residents value or that might be employed in assuring the quality of life are associated with public delivery systems. Retail services and health care delivery represent two services most often provided by segments of the private sector of the economy, although the structure of the health industry is so interwined that a categorical identity is somewhat difficult to make. Seldom is the former item employed in evaluating environmental quality, since it is thought by some to simply represent a convenience. On the other hand, some measure of the latter dimension is almost always included among social indicators and/or quality of life variables. The presence or absence of such services among the survey communities tends to be related to the community size and locational advantage. The latter condition seems to be particularly important with respect to the availability of retail services.

Access to Health Resources

Access to good quality health care has only recently come to be thought of as a right of all Americans. Even though there has been some change in the thinking in this area, we are still a long way away from equal access to the nation's health care resources. In this instance one is simply attempting to determine if basic health resources are physically accessible to community users. It is apparent, though, that physical accessibility is not the same as individual accessibility. Thus, in attempting to evaluate individual access, analysts are often inclined to utilize a measure of mortality and/or morbidity as an expression of access.

Flax employed infant mortality rates as a health indicator and suicide rates as a mental health indicator in his attempt to evaluate the quality of life in eighteen metropolitan areas.[13] The former measure is often thought to be a good indicator of the effectiveness of health delivery systems. As was true earlier, information of this sort is generally unavailable for the communities of our sample. Others interested in access to medical care have sometimes polled individuals to determine if they think they have access to care, and how good they perceive that care to be.[14] Following this lead, the respondents in the all-black towns were asked about access to health care and to what extent they were satisfied with the care available.

Perceptions of the availability of quality health care among community respondents shows much variation. Likewise, the pattern of community satisfaction on the other items is not congruent with responses on the availability of health services. Only two communities provide care at the local level for most of their residents. These include Wyandanch and Lawnside. It should be noted, though, that approximately one-third of the respondents from Glenarden find primary health care available within the community. All the remaining communities are dependent on nonlocal providers for health care.

The response of the sample population on the quality of care item was that most persons perceive the care they receive to be adequate or at least moderately satisfactory. This we take to equate to a fair amount of confidence that they can obtain good care. Forty-four percent of Negroes and other races recently registered this attitude.[15] All the communities in our universe exceeded this level of faith in the available quality of care, yet several communities indicated only marginal confidence in the available quality of care. The communities falling in the latter category were East Chicago Heights, Robbins, Brooklyn, Lawnside, and Roosevelt City. Most of these are communities which were previously identified as economically insecure, with the exception of Lawnside. Oddly enough, Lawnside is the source of primary care for most of its residents.

Communities possessing a high level of confidence in the availability of quality care include North Fontana, Urbancrest, East Palo Alto, Lincoln Heights, and Wyandanch. East Palo Alto and Wyandanch, which often expressed dissatisfaction with aspects of their service delivery package, seem to show greater faith in the availability of health resources. In this instance there is no measure available to us that would permit a similar assessment of the health care resources in the suburbanizing communities.

The Availability of Retail Services

The availability of retail services is seldom employed in attempts to evaluate the quality of life. More than anything else this probably reflects the scale at which such studies are conducted. Within a given metropolitan area, retail outlets are so numerous that a measure of their presence would add little to our understanding of access at the local community or neighborhood scale. Even David Smith, whose analysis of social indicators also included an intraurban emphasis, failed to include retail access among his indicators of social well-being.[16] It might be that lack of access to such outlets simply constitutes an inconvenience and does not threaten what Edward Banfield has described as the "essential welfare."[17] Yet poverty zones are frequently characterized by an absence of retail outlets which provide goods and services at prices as favorable as those prevailing in zones of more intense competition.

Needless to say, the extent to which goods and services are found in close proximity to one's place of residence, in terms of its problem aspect, is conditioned by the extent that one is able to overcome the friction of distance and the extent to which one is not severely affected by the absence of price competition in local markets. Thus, while this variable is seldom employed as a social indicator, it seems that it is one of immense importance to blacks residing in selected outlying communities. Dissatisfaction with retail services represents the single most frequent response of dissatisfaction with all services among the respondents of the all-black towns.

Retail services are generally dichotomized into the convenience group category and the shopping group category. The former group generally includes nondurable goods and items that must be purchased frequently. Convenience items or low order goods are generally available at the neighborhood scale. Higher order goods are generally more centrally located to minimize the travel distance for the maximum number of potential customers. Because of the size of most of the all-black towns, one would not expect shopping goods generally to be available within the individual communities. On the other hand, the size of individual communities should dictate the range of convenience outlets that one might expect to locate in these communities. It is the availability and quality of convenience goods which is thought to be more critical in this instance, for they represent items required for daily sustenance.

A

B

Figure 6–3. A Record Shop Designed to Attract Black Clientele in East Cleveland, Ohio (A), and An Educational Service Facility for Low Income Children in North Fontana, California (B)

Among the fifteen all-black towns, only three provide low order goods and services of such a range that most respondents indicated that they shopped within the local community. The extent to which food purchases were made within these communities was thought to represent a good indicator of the availability of consumer items. Lawnside (93 percent), Wyandanch (79 percent), and East Palo Alto (79 percent) were the three communities in which residents seldom traveled beyond the community to purchase food. The only other communities in which as many as one-third of the residents purchased food within their home communities were Richmond Heights (44 percent) and Cooper Road (35 percent). Fewer than 20 percent of the residents in the remaining communities chose to purchase food in their home communities because of a lack of food outlets or a limited range of items. The use made of local outlets is most often a reflection of the size of the individual place.

But there are exceptions to this rule. For example, Lawnside, New Jersey, with fewer than 3,000 residents, embraces a community level shopping center within its realm. The community's ability to secure groups that were interested in developing a shopping center on community owned land must be considered a real coup. Most all-black towns have encountered great difficulty in attracting outside entrepreneurs who were willing to develop local sites either for commercial or industrial purposes. The location of this shopping center on a major traffic arterial provided it with the necessary advantage of serving a large population within a radius of several miles. Robbins, Illinois, one of the larger all-black towns, was one in which fewer than 20 percent of the residents reported that they made food purchases within the community (see Fig. 6-4).

Those purchasers who traveled beyond the community to secure food traveled on an average of about four miles. The shortest distances were traveled by the residents of Lincoln Heights, Ohio and Roosevelt City, Alabama (2.5 miles), while the longest distances were traveled by the residents of Hollydale, Ohio (7.7 miles). It seems that the traveled distance that is generally characteristic of persons seeking convenience goods is often exceeded by the residents of most of these communities. However, in some instances it appears that the journey-to-work pattern bears some resemblance to the journey-to-shop pattern.

Almost all the residents of these communities must purchase their shopping goods in alternate locations. Eleven of the fifteen communities indicated that they were without shopping goods outlets. Most often shopping goods are purchased in the larger nearby communities or regional shopping centers. In a few instances the central city serves as the location of durable goods purchased, but more often residents tend to be attracted to the medium sized communities which are located within easy proximity. Since most of the black suburbanizing communities are in the larger size categories (>20,000) it would appear that their retail access at all levels would be better than that of residents of the all-black towns.

The level of dissatisfaction with retail services runs the gamut from no dissatisfaction to more than 90 percent of the respondents complain-

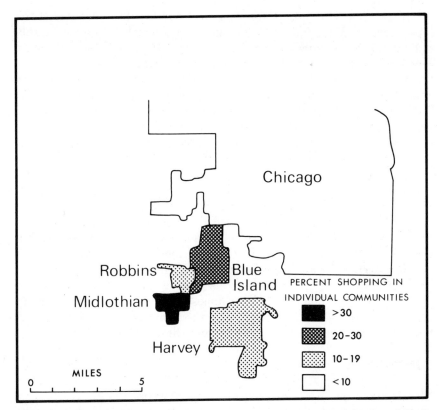

Figure 6-4. The Source of Food Purchases by Residents of Robbins, Illinois

ing of poor service. In four communities more than 60 percent complained that retail services were inadequate. These include Cooper Road (92 percent), Kinloch (81 percent), East Palo Alto (72 percent), and Brooklyn (100 percent). Given East Palo Alto's capability of providing most convenience goods, it is somewhat surprising to find such high level dissatisfaction. The communities which tend to be most pleased with the services to which they have access are Lawnside, North Fontana, and Hollydale. Lawnside, like East Palo Alto, basically provides a full range of convenience items, but they represent the two polarities in terms of consumer satisfaction.

The private sector does not appear any more proficient than the public sector in generating consumer satisfaction, if the response of the survey population is an accurate appraisal of the way residents in these communities view the services available to them. Less dissatisfaction was expressed with the availability of health care than with retail services. This might simply reflect the less frequent use of the latter service. East Palo Alto, a community which was often highly critical of other services, viewed health services as satisfactory, and a sizeable percentage in this community viewed the availability of health care as excellent. Unfortunately our responses do not indicate what level of care the respondent is expressing satisfaction with.

It does appear that in most instances dissatisfaction with retail services is related to physical access. When respondents were asked what retail service they would like to have in their community, it was generally one that was missing. In those communities where convenience goods were available, a desire was expressed for the presence of some shopping goods outlet (e.g., a department store). When convenience goods were limited, the wish to have a food market was frequently expressed. It is not clear that the retail mix within these communities does indeed represent a measure of the quality of life, but it is true that residents desire easier access to convenience goods. This situation might represent a condition that is somewhat unique to the character of all-black towns, and one that has to do with their small size and physical location. One would not suppose that the level of dissatisfaction with retail services would be of the same order in black suburbanizing communities as is true among these small enclaves.

SUMMARY

This chapter has been devoted almost totally to service availability within the context of the all-black towns. It was not possible to compare the suburbanizing communities on most of these same measures, although there was a crude attempt to indirectly assess the quality of safety. Since economic security seems to be the most important dimension of service satisfaction, there is little question that the quality of life in the suburbanizing communities is of a higher order than the former. But in those communities which show signs of marginal security and less, we would anticipate responses similar to those described here.

�֍ *Chapter 7*

Black Suburbanization: Retrospect and Prospect

Black suburbanization represents a new and emerging settlement form among a population that is essentially in the third stage of the settlement process in the United States. The first stage was marked by rural dominance in the South, followed by movement from a rural setting to a small town setting. At present, most blacks are clustered in large central cities, and most whites are dispersed throughout the metropolitan ring, often in the same metropolitan areas where blacks show or are approaching numerical dominance in the central cities.

PREFERRED LIVING ENVIRONMENT

In 1971 the largest percentage (54 percent) of the white population polled indicated a preference for a rural or small town environment.[1] The expressed black preference for such environments was substantially less (33 percent), and the percentage selecting small urban environments was slightly greater (34 percent) than for either the rural/small town or large urban environments.[2] Recent reports substantiate the fact that a growing number of whites are acting on their preferences by establishing residence outside of metropolitan areas but within easy access to them.[3] This is in keeping with the findings of the Zuiches-Fuguitt study, as reported in Mazie and Rawlings, which indicated that most Wisconsin residents prefer a small town environment, but wish to have this environment within a 30-mile radius of a large city.[4] This latter movement pattern, we assume, represents the emergence of exurbia as a distinct settlement form. Thus as blacks begin to participate in the modal settlement form, a new settlement form has already begun to emerge. However, the issues here are whether blacks have access to alternate settlement forms in keeping with their expressed preferences on the one hand, and on the other hand, what quality of life dimensions are available to them in these alternate environments.

THE PLACE OF ORIGIN OF BLACK AND WHITE SUBURBAN MOVERS

It has required more than a generation for blacks to become a noticeable factor in the suburban environment. The scale of the black presence in this environment increased most rapidly during the decade of the sixties, and yet the number of new residents from elsewhere was less than a half-million. No doubt the reasons that black persons in the suburban ring went essentially unnoticed were as follows: (1) they were confined to a series of dispersed communities where they resided in the unofficial black quarters; (2) their places of residence were such that they seldom coincided with the myth of suburbia; (3) they constituted essentially a limited skill work force whose services were required by an upper income population; (4) their presence was obscured by the rapid rate of black settlement in the central city; and finally (5) because their presence did not spur neighborhood transition. Similarly, one might conclude that the zone of origin of suburban blacks, for the first time (the decade of the sixties), was dominated by the direct movement of people from the central city.

White movement to individual suburban communities during both the fifties and sixties was dominated by movers from elsewhere in the SMSA or outside the SMSA.[5] While the relative contribution of the central city to white suburbanization is less than from the two alternate sources, it should not be permitted to obscure the volume of white movement from the central city. Joseph Zikmund also has ignored the class composition of white movers vis-à-vis their mover origins. Since it is the middle class white population that has resided in the suburban ring for the longest period of time, it is only logical to assume that their adult children will establish residence elsewhere in the ring.

Likewise, since it is that segment of the population that is most mobile, it is also logical to assume that it will most often be involved in intermetropolitan migration that fosters suburban residential choice. Thus the largest category of potential white movers left in the central city is the white working class. Since this group of potential suburban movers constitutes a smaller percentage of the total white population than the middle class, and this is reflected in current place of residence, then white movers from the central city should be expected to represent the smaller share of all movers to suburban locations. The black moving pattern, on the other hand, is the reverse of this.

Black suburban ring movers resided most recently in the central city of their respective metropolitan areas. These movers represent a growing middle class and an expanding working class who have grown dissatisfied with the housing package available to them in the central city. We contend that most of these movers are attempting to upgrade their housing package rather than acquire improved access to employment. That this pattern is emerging in those central cities whose ghettos have expanded to the city's edge further supports the idea that the territory beyond the ghetto edge is more likely to be included in one's awareness space than environments associated with more remote housing sectors.

The earlier moves to outlying black colonies are likely to have been associated more often with employment opportunity than the merits of the housing package. If this is the case the black colonies would more often serve as the place of residence of lower status and working class black populations than the type of movers previously described. Likewise a larger share of these movers no doubt originated in locations other than the central city. Colonization, then, with its specific requirements in terms of work force orientation and skills was attractive only to that segment of the black population which could adapt to its requirements. It appears evident that some of the children of the original settlers have chosen to reside in contiguous or nearby communities on reaching adulthood. This second or later generation pattern of movement might be predicated on the same motivating forces that prompt central city black movers to seek suburban residence.

The pattern just described cannot be verified in terms of direct observation, as the larger and older black colonies imbedded in white middle status communities have been largely ignored by researchers. Nevertheless, this pattern of black suburban bifurcation makes sense in terms of the two described sets of motivating factors. It appears somewhat paradoxical that the initial movers to the suburban ring often resided in outlying black colonies near the places of residence of the white upper classes. The more recent pattern seems to be directly linked to the process of central city ghettoization. In either case, the objective and subjective status of the black population determined which of the two processes a given individual or household would participate in. Until only recently, colonization seems to have represented the only road open to blacks that permitted access to a suburban location.

THE ROLE OF RACE ON THE IDENTITY
OF COMMUNITIES OF BLACK ENTRY

The scale of black suburbanization was accelerated during the middle sixties. Thus many of the communities in which blacks have settled during the post-1965 period were new to that population. We are unaware how the new residents perceive their environment, but one thing is obvious, and that is the extent to which the new population has or has not acquired access to alternative environments free of racial identity. Most suburbanizing blacks have found themselves members of an ethnic community at the neighborhood scale. For those who assumed that black suburbanization would be associated with black dispersion at the micro scale, this simply has not been the case.

Francine Rabinovitz recently examined the extent to which dispersion characterized (at the community level) black suburbanization in the Los Angeles ring and concluded that "blacks are present in only three suburbs in concentrations that approximate their income distributions."[6] She cautions the reader, however, that other variables beyond income could lead to a nonrandom distribution.[7] This is a very significant point and one that should guide researchers and policy makers in their attempts to determine the kinds of racial mixes sought by individuals possessing a given set of characteristics. To date, advocates of black suburbanization seem to be motivated by the plight, writ large, of central city populations, as opposed to cautionaries, who see middle class white suburban residence as a device for maintaining their values uncontaminated, or pluralists, whose conscious or unconscious motivations reflect fear that government will unwisely intervene and thereby threaten the pluralist position.

Anthony Downs, an advocate of opening up the suburbs to black occupancy, tends to represent the first of the intellectual positions described above.[8] He is of the opinion that segments of the mainstream poor should be assisted in their escape from the ghetto to the sanctuaries of suburbia. This, he believes, would prove beneficial to the mover population in that they would acquire access to middle class values, and at the same time the larger society would benefit. Nathan Glazer, a noted sociologist, represents the second intellectual position described above. In his cautionary wisdom he was led to state, "To my mind, the suburbanization of blacks proceeds at a pace related to their occupational and economic rise, and the benefits to be gained from attempting a massive hastening of this pace seem doubtful."[9] The latter scholar contends that Downs is advocating economic rather than racial integration and that the two should not be confused. He indicates that there is little support for the Downs position and that public intervention in favor of such a position is unwarranted.

When reviewing the position of scholars as it relates to the issue of black suburbanization the results are mixed, but this is to be expected since the positions taken by social scientists often reflect their own experiences in the social world. While this is true, it should not preclude the development of policy positions and their evaluation on their merits. If one accepts the cautionary position of Glazer, then one might assume that the forces which have been described here will continue at work, and the outcome of the operation of these forces will likewise continue. On the other hand, is the kind of intervention being advocated by Downs likely to make a significant difference?

BLACK RESIDENTIAL PATTERNS
AND THE NEED FOR EFFECTIVE POLICY

In attempting to assess the future settlement pattern of blacks in urban America, the above two intellectual positions provide an appropriate starting point. They constitute the interventionist/noninterventionist dichotomy in terms of the public sector response to patterns of population distribution. There already exists an interest in the development of a national urban growth policy that fosters growth in selected regional centers and thus reduces the pressure associated with the piling up of migrants from distressed areas in the nation's larger central cities. Lowdon Wingo, in a recent assessment of a series of statements on national urban growth policy, indicates that three themes emerge.[10] These basic themes are: (1) the race–internal migration theme, (2) the quality of life theme, and (3) the welfare effects of political fragmentation.[11] Two of these themes have been emphasized in this work, but in a nonpolicy context. Another economist, addressing himself to this issue from the perspective of policy development, states that what is described as a national growth policy is in fact a national territorial distribution policy.[12] William Alonzo, in viewing this issue at the micro scale, states the following:

> Overall metropolitan levels of population and employment are set largely by economic and demographic forces at national and international levels. Local policy affects primarily the intrametropolitan form and distribution of that development, and if it is set by the selfish interest of the component municipalities, it does so inefficiently and unjustly. A suburb may be able to keep population or industry out, but it can do so only by directing it to other suburbs or by keeping it cooped up in the central city.[13]

SOCIAL SCIENTISTS AND THE
POLICY DILEMMA

The problems focused on here can hardly be considered nonpolicy issues, and the above positions detail the policy implications at a variety of levels. Thus, on the issue of black suburbanization—which simply constitutes one facet of adjustment to national and local economic and social forces—we find ourselves lining up with Downs on the need for an interventionist strategy, while at the same time rejecting his specific recommendations. The position of noninterference, which we interpret to represent the Glazer position, is rejected out of hand as a status quo position that does not have the built-in, self-correcting mechanism that he implies exists. Rabinovitz, in responding to the second intellectual position (represented by Glazer), states:

> I believe the analysts who do so, really mean that the market system is producing a relatively stabilizing pattern in the political, social, and spatial relations of blacks and whites, that there is now some black migration and little pressure for further "opening" the suburbs and therefore policy makers no longer need to respond. They cannot mean, given the nature of existing evidence, that the market response is sufficient or equitable for blacks, only that it has successfully produced a pattern which currently dampens intense demand for change.[14]

It is true that previous policies designed to alter the status quo have not produced the change anticipated, but this may simply reflect the fact that these policies dealt with the problem of residential dispersion at the symbolic level rather than at the material level. No doubt the ineffectiveness of national policy to correct the situation is rooted in conflict between policies at different levels on the one hand, and a traditional deference to consensus on the other. Thus piecemeal intervention of the sort that is motivated by symbolic pressures is unlikely to have any meaningful effect.

A hands-off attitude provides the intellectual community the luxury of simply explaining the status quo without endangering its reputation by delving into the arena of prescription. Prescription, then, is left to those who are willing to assume the risks associated with unpopular recommendations. In a country as large and diverse as the United States, any policy that threatens to reward one group at the expense of another is likely to be unpopular. On the other hand, to deny the outcome of a set of unregulated forces under the guise that all groups are being treated fairly is to fail to assume responsibility for changes that penalize a larger segment of the population than they reward. The manner in which blacks have acquired housing in the suburban ring is a case in point. A few blacks are advantaged by the process, but by and large the process touches only a small segment of the population. Even so, there is enough change associated with the process to permit those so inclined to justify the status quo.

In retrospect, it is apparent that the settlement process that has led to the concentration of larger numbers of blacks in the suburban ring has insured that many of the problems that confronted individuals and families in previous environments will continue to confront them in the new ones. Unless these conditions are to be considered normative, new intervention policies need to be formulated and subsequently evaluated in terms of their impact on both the life changes of blacks, and on the larger society.

A SUGGESTED STRATEGY FOR INTERVENING IN THE HOUSING ALLOCATION PROCESS

Among the forces that shape the pattern of black residential distribution in metropolitan areas, none is as pervasive as the operation of the housing market. The complex of interacting forces that undergird the structure of the housing industry, and the manner in which housing is allocated in terms of its cumulative effect, makes it almost impossible for alternative distribution patterns to emerge. The actions of real estate agents, financial institutions, and public policy tend to support the existing pattern. True, larger numbers of individual blacks have exercised greater options in terms of residential choice during the recent period, but the number who are able to exercise meaningful options is so small that the modal process of allocating housing to blacks remains unaltered. The current practice of maintaining a high level of economic homogeneity at the neighborhood or small community scale makes it unusually difficult to alter the distribution pattern. The apparent desire to maintain economic homogeneity in newer residential areas resulted in voiding the impact of housing legislation passed in the late sixties to provide minorities and lower income populations a greater range of choice in selecting a residential environment. This attitude is manifest in the highest chambers of the nation.

In 1971 President Nixon indicated that he was opposed to forced economic integration.[15] Some are of the opinion that this public pronouncement might have affected the Black Jack decision, which was then still pending before the courts. The Black Jack decision essentially upheld the right of communities to determine their economic character by banning housing that might alter that character. Thus

235 and 236 housing was largely developed inside the central city or built in predominantly black communities in the metropolitan ring. Some mayors of the all-black towns found themselves in a double bind with regard to this housing package. When they wished to exclude housing associated with this legislation, they found themselves in the position of being viewed as black racists by other blacks and as non-cooperative by federal and local officials who were interested in placing these units in environments of least resistance. Thus black communities were not accorded the option of choosing the economic character of their communities. While the operation of the housing market is not the sole determinant of the present pattern of residential distribution, it is the principal operating force that has led to this outcome.

The manner in which the housing market operates is responsible for the spatial patterns of black suburbanization. In our previous discussion of the dual and segmented markets, an attempt was made to relate these to the emergence of specific black distributional patterns within the suburban ring. Thus, given the economic status of most blacks, the acquisition of a suburban plot can take place only within the framework of the trickle-down process, at least in those environments where housing segmentation is the dominant process. In those environments where the dual market operates, it is possible to secure housing outside of the trickle-down context. During boom periods it is possible for blacks to substantially upgrade their housing environment under conditions of filtration, but during periods of economic downturn the housing industry is among the hardest hit. Thus those dependent upon the filtering process as a means of improving their housing package are severely disadvantaged.

What seems to be needed to minimize the disadvantages of the segmentation process is a substitute allocation mechanism based on some of the qualities of the dual market. Instead of a duality that is predicated on race, a new allocation mechanism is needed that would be based on the development of life style communities. Thus life style would substitute for race in the development of housing on individual sites. Such practices already exist in an informal way, as is evidenced by the creation of housing developments designed to cater to the tastes of individuals either in life style or stage in the life cycle. But these normally represent developments which are part of the segmented market, or housing developed by the public sector for the poor and/or elderly.

In order to successfully alter the way the current market operates, life style communities would have to be identified and formalized throughout the metropolitan area. Thus, starting with existing housing developments within a given metropolitan area, subcommunities would be identified on the basis of the modal life style of their residents. Each life style community would then be called upon to develop for itself norms of conduct that would be deemed appropriate for persons or households seeking membership. Persons aspiring to reside within a specific housing environment, as identified in life style terms, must be willing to conform to the rules of conduct established by that community. Each subcommunity, in conjunction with a larger central agency, would necessarily monitor itself to insure that its life style would not be altered by those whose values are in conflict with those of the community. The monitoring process would have to make certain that individuals were not excluded from a given community on the basis of race, lest we simply legitimate the status quo. While this might appear to represent a simplistic notion on the one hand—and one that requires excessive intervention in the operation of the free market on the other—it is justified on the grounds that only in stable communities are all citizens likely to achieve the quality of life that they find satisfying.

Support for the development of formal life style communities is not likely to be high. Yet if we are to have communities in which the individual has options in terms of residential choice—options not totally based on race or economic status—some modification of the existing housing allocation mechanism will be required. If some communities turn out to be basically white and others basically black it will simply reflect, at least ideally, life style choices based on cultural manifestations that assume importance in the life of the individual or family. If such a program was encouraged to develop, the issue of racial integration as we know it, at least in the area of housing allocation, would be without meaning.

A structure of this sort would make unnecessary the kind of tactics recommended by Downs to open up the suburbs. Such tactics tend to be demeaning to blacks, and in order to succeed, at least in terms of the goals established by Downs, they must be approved by the white majority on its terms. There is little question that the Downs position is a well meaning one, but it is unlikely to be acceptable to either whites or blacks. Most of all, it would not alter the basic housing allocation process. The life style community schema would insure the maintenance of a pluralist society, and thus the fears of Glazer, at least on this dimension, should be abated. Needless to say, such a scheme would require a major modification of the housing development and allocation process. For those who contend that the problem will work itself out—that by some magical year the concerns of today will have evaporated, and thus we need only await these changes—we would indicate that there is little evidence in support of that position.

It is clear that this schema, in terms of its rough outline, will not resolve many of the basic problems confronting urban America, and that this simply represents a starting point. Given that the principal emphasis in this study has been on the residential environment, we feel that an attempt to model satisfying residential environments must begin by altering the way the housing market operates. The current allocation procedure results in the development of black residential environments, whether in the cities or in the suburbs, that are threatening, and hardly conducive to the maintenance of life styles that might be thought of as productive.

The suggested schema has not been fully developed and to be feasible would require the attention of the intellectual community to see that it is properly developed and made workable. We are suggesting at this point a conceptual format which, if found workable, could serve as the basis for allocating housing in a metropolitan context. If made operational, such a schema would lead to a major reordering of the residential development process and ideally to the elimination of the need to discuss the process of suburbanization in traditional racial terms.

THE FUTURE OF BLACK METROPOLITAN SETTLEMENT PATTERNS AND OTHER QUALITY OF LIFE MEASURES

Throughout this book the persistent emphasis, directly or indirectly, has been on the quality of life for blacks in metropolitan America. A number of attributes were chosen that would provide crude measures of how blacks who have settled in the metropolitan rings of the nation's largest SMSAs are faring on these selected dimensions. It was assumed that the residential environment to which one gained access was critical in influencing the total quality of life performance. Thus, in gauging the future life chances of this population, we have come to the conclusion that the housing allocation process is in need of major revision, lest the gains that have apparently accrued to selected black movers prove ephemeral. While housing is obviously an important measure of the quality of life, equal attention was devoted to the nature of the educational environment to which blacks were acquiring access. This factor is thought by some to undergird the life chances of future generations. If economic and psychological security are the ultimate influences on the quality of life of given individuals or households, then it is essential that the kind of education be provided wherein both basic skills and a sense of positive identity are transmitted and inculcated at an early age. The educational environment, at least for participating families, is an important part of the residential environment. Thus it is difficult to separate the two, and there is evidence that educational systems influence residential choice.

THE ISSUE OF THE EDUCATIONAL ENVIRONMENT

Because of the assumed influence of educational systems on residential choice, emphasis in this paper centered around two focal concerns. These concerns were the quality or climate of the school environment, and cognitive achievement. Admittedly, the measures employed in attempting to evaluate these components were crude, and the data available on which performance could be evaluated were incomplete. Nevertheless this approach to the problem is viewed here as valid, although the outcome of this specific analysis does not permit the development of a definitive position. The whole question of the role of the school environment as it relates to the nature of social interaction between pupils and between pupils and teachers on cognitive development does not seem to be well understood.

Nancy St. John, in her recent assessment of the outcomes of a number of school desegregation efforts, sheds almost no light on pupil-teacher relationships as a dimension of school climate.[15] It is obvious, though, that she considers it important, as the following statement attests: "A school staff committed to the promotion of favorable race relations is probably a key factor to many happily desegregated schools in addition to the preschools studied by Crooks."[16] In her concluding chapter she again emphasizes the importance of school climate when she states, "The selection and training of school staff for biracial schools appears all-important. The principal and the faculty have the responsibility for structuring the interracial climate of the school."[17]

Much research will be required before we will be able to specify precisely the roles played by school climate or tone on pupil behavior and cognitive achievement. It is sometimes demonstrated that black entry into a previously all-white school environment creates anxiety on the part of some participants in that environment. It has also been found that teachers are often less receptive to changes in the racial composition of the schools than are students. Both are generally more receptive, however, than are parents. Since suburbanizing blacks are most often working class people who have established a foothold in neighborhoods which were previously predominantly white, we anticipate that some anxiety will show itself in the school environment and thus promote a school tone that could work against black achievement, unless some direct efforts are made to alter the tone in a positive direction.

The extent to which the tone is rewarding or penalizing is likely to vary from one school setting to another depending on the cultural characteristics of the entering blacks, those of the resident white children, and of the staff. Black teachers almost always follow black children into suburban school systems undergoing racial change, but there is usually a variable time lag until some perceived critical level of black children in the school population is reached. Some suburban school systems feel no obligation to hire black teachers unless there is a sizeable black school population in the local school system. These various social and cultural dislocations are thought to be related to school climate, but they tend for the moment to defy explanation in terms of how they influence learning.

Another issue we confronted in our analysis was that of racial isolation in the schools. Since the issue of racial school desegregation has commanded so much attention during the last two decades, and since it has traditionally represented an outcome that was sought more by blacks than by whites, it was only fitting to attempt to ascertain if this goal was being attained as a result of black movement to the suburban ring. If the limited data available to us are representative of the situation emerging in most suburban zones of recent black entry, the prospects of goal attainment are small indeed. The schools, like the residential environments in which they are found, are usually in the process of racial transition. Generally the speed with which schools go through the transition surpasses that which characterizes neighborhood change. In some high status communities meaningful efforts are made to support racially balanced schools; in other communities attempts at racial balance are seldom voluntary.

Racially isolated or imbalanced schools are unlikely to disappear as long as the mechanism employed to reduce the imbalance is simply to place a certain ratio of white and black children in a common school environment. Unfortunately, blacks can seek redress of grievances related to educational opportunity only through the courts. The legal outcomes designed to redress those grievances have frequently failed, particularly at the elementary school level, in terms of the expected set of educational outcomes. These failures, however, can often be attributed to the methods of implementing the decisions and need not represent goals for which solutions were sought.

Our legalistic interpretation of race in the United States is partially responsible for the outcome. We previously suggested that blacks have encountered a wide variety of experiences in the United States that influence how they relate to one another and to members of other races. If school integration as it is currently conceived is to prove workable, then persons to be placed in a given school environment, both black and white, must be selected on the basis of individual traits that will minimize damage to all members and heighten the possibility of benefits, beyond mere cognitive achievement. While this is a much more difficult task than that of achieving an established racial range within individual schools, it is an imperative task if this issue is ever to be acted upon forthrightly.

It seems that the current desegregation schemes have been programmed to fail. This has led to attempts to invalidate claims of educational merit thought to be associated with school desegregation. The general issue of school desegregation does not appear to find any greater support in suburbia than it does in central cities, particularly in the context of neighborhood change. If blacks continue to gain access to residential environments in the ways previously described, then school desegregation will have to be imposed on a nonvoluntary basis. The attitudes of elected school officials in a number of suburban school districts tend to cause them not to support busing and other techniques designed to promote racial mixing for what they interpret as social rather than educational purposes. The continuing opposition to school desegregation in the North threatens to weaken all attempts at school desegregation in the nation if it does not evolve voluntarily. Thus the legal mechanism designed to redress a grievance is often unable to deliver the desired solution because it cannot free itself from its own legalistic yoke—that is, its narrow interpretation of race as a nominal category and subsequent attempts to attain some preordained racial balance.

The housing environment and the educational environment have been assigned critical roles in this assessment of the quality of life prevailing in those suburban ring communities in which blacks have established residence. These elements are thought to be critical because they relate to current gains and are variables that will play a major role in shaping the life chances of the children of these mover households. The various other internal attributes which were examined by us are often viewed as less consequential, yet these issues should not be relegated to a position of unimportance. It is frequently difficult to separate the neighborhood effect from the residents' perception of their housing package, for the residential package employed to evaluate aspects of the quality of life is not easily partitioned.

ECONOMIC AND PSYCHOLOGICAL
SECURITY AS QUALITY OF LIFE MEASURES

Equally important in any assessment of quality of life are measures of economic security. It is these measures that often determine access to a specific residential environment, and thus serve as the base around which other quality of life measures revolve. However, it must be remembered that locational access varies as a function of both timing and the operation of social constraints that may not be directly related to economic security, although the two are likely to be highly correlated. This point is raised here so the reader will not overlook the forces that led to the creation of the all-black towns on the one hand, and the processes that support current black entry into suburban ring communities on the other. The temporal dimension as well as the regional effect have played pervasive roles in the patterns that have evolved. These patterns, however, have been undergirded by the economic security factor.

It was shown that a number of the black towns are residual communities in which aging populations are spending the waning years of their lives in both physical isolation and economic marginality. But we have likewise shown that all such communities are not relics of past historical settlement preferences. Some of the all-black towns are characterized by population growth based not solely on natural increase but on migration from the outside. The growth communities generally show signs of greater economic security. The manner in which economic security interacts with the norms and cultural position of individual blacks is likely to influence their choices of residential environment, and thus the external world continues to play the most active role in establishing the potential for economic security. The settlement patterns that evolve—and consequently the emergent life styles that define the character of these settlements—are indirectly invoked by those decision makers who influence the state of the larger economy.

Economic security is the single most important variable influencing access to alternative environments, yet economic security is not always matched by the presence of psychological security. The lag effect between the two frequently threatens the loss of the former. In order to acquire the ultimate dimension of the quality of life—happiness—there must be a closing of the gap between economic security and psychological security. Our assessment of the latter attribute is no doubt the weakest, both from a methodological perspective and in the choice of variables selected. This is an area still uncharted, and our excursion into this realm is preliminary at best.

To better understand the condition of blacks in urban America, not only must we attempt to delve into aspects of critical variables operating in the external environment, but we must secure a greater understanding of how these factors affect the inner world of the individual. Psychological security strongly influences which cultural modality (as defined earlier) will be assumed by individual blacks. It is these modalities that determine how the individual presents himself on herself to the larger society.

In our view, the conditions of extreme economic marginality that prevailed in the South for a lengthy period, coupled with the maintenance of a social caste system, resulted in the development of the adaptive-suppressive cultural mode. The tendency for aspects of this mode to be practiced in environments where there is no perceived need seems to intensify the conflict between generations. Thus a precarious condition often characterizes the relationship between economic and psychological security. A more complete understanding of this relationship is required, both within and between generations, if we are to develop greater insight into black response to various behavioral settings.

A BRIEF REVIEW OF THE PROCESS OF BLACK SUBURBANIZATION

Emphasis throughout this work has centered on environmental access and environmental character. The evidence that blacks were acquiring access to environments with which they previously had only limited experience, prompted investigation of the character of these environments to ascertain how they might have contributed to individual and group well-being. Ideally, one would have proceeded to select a set of sample communities which represented new environments of blacks residence, and to collect data to satisfy this goal. Instead, the primary data for this study were secured from a variety of communities possessing a suburban ring location in which the majority of the residents were black. The latter decision made the task of the previously stated goal more difficult, while at the same time making it easier to evaluate the process by which blacks acquired access to suburban residential environments. Thus we have satisfied less well the initial goal, but insight acquired into what might be thought of as the secondary goal will hopefully minimize the weaknesses associated with primary goal accomplishment.

The environments that have served as our principal units of observation were communities which were identified as all-black towns. Because of the historical role of some of these communities it has been much easier to place the concept of black suburbanization in both a spatial and temporal context. The writer's long standing interest in these communities likewise made the task of moving to the larger problem easier than would ordinarily have been the case. While we have attempted to address the larger issue of black suburbanization, we have done so from a territorial base that focused on the presence of a set of often isolated black communities that evolved some distance from the city, even before the process of suburbanization got underway.

Some of the all-black towns, even today, possess little in the way of environmental attributes that are frequently associated with suburbia, and appear not to have been influenced by what is going on around them. Others, because of their proximity to the major axes of suburbanization, have been transformed from once rural communities composed of a parochial population, to emerging bedroom communities whose populations are cosmopolitan. In balance, too many of these communities continue to resemble the former condition rather than the latter. Still, it should not be overlooked that it was this group of communities which provided segments of the black population their first opportunity to live in a protected environment and yet have access to some of the resources of the city.

Since many of these communities are small and without political power, they are seldom the focus of public attention. Their needs are frequently enormous but, overlooked as they are by the appropriate centers of power, are seldom addressed. It is true that some communities qualified for a measure of federal assistance during the height of the war on poverty, but years of denial have often left them in a state where more than nominal support will be required to provide their residents with amenities to qualify them even minimally as suburban. The plight of these communities has on occasion prompted them to respond that they wished to be annexed to the larger adjoining suburban community. Though most are politically independent, this is not enough to promote satisfaction with the environment of occupance. In short, most of these communities are in serious need of assistance if they are ever to be transformed into living environments of opportunity rather than despair.

Moving from the essentially static all-black towns to the dynamic growing black populations in a selected set of target communities identified as suburbanizing, we shifted from one temporal setting to another. In some metropolitan ring communities black entry is occurring at a rapid rate, but the process of black suburbanization is most often associated with spatial extension of the ghettoization process, with all that that implies regarding the quality of life dimensions for its residents. The most active suburban growth communities are spatial extensions of central city ghettos. Thus, the principal pattern of black acquisition of residential environments remains intact even though the process is now occurring beyond the margins of the central city.

The argument made previously for intervention in the way the housing market operates, and support for the development of life style communities, was aimed at improving black access to stable residential environments. It is true that a small segment of the black population with annual earnings well above the national median has various options in the residential selection process, but the evolving community patterns are hardly modified by this action. Unless we intervene, in well thought out ways, no amount of pious proclamations will suffice to alter the status quo. Black suburbanization as it is now occurring simply represents another settlement phase, and not a major reordering of the way blacks acquire residential access and subsequently access to the preferred quality of life package that is available to others possessing the same objective status.

※

Notes

CHAPTER ONE

1. Reynolds Farley, "The Changing Distribution of Negroes within Metropolitan Areas: The Emergence of Black Suburbs," *American Journal of Sociology*, January 1970, pp. 512–529. ∨

2. Harold X. Connolly, "Black Movement into the Suburbs," *Urban Affairs Quarterly*, September 1973, pp. 91–111, and William W. Pendleton, "Blacks in Suburbs," *The Urbanization of the Suburbs*, edited by Massotti and Hadden, Beverly Hills, Calif.: Sage Publications, 1973, pp. 171–184.

3. Anthony Downs, *Opening Up the Suburbs*, New Haven: Yale University Press, 1973.

4. Angus Campbell, *White Attitudes Toward Blacks*, Ann Arbor, Mich.: The Institute for Social Research, 1971.

5. Russell B. Adams, "Metropolitan Area and Central City Population, 1966–1970—1970," *Annales de Geographie*, Mars-Avril 1972, p. 178.

6. Alan Kirschenbaum, "City-Suburban Destination Choices Among Migrants to Metropolitan Areas," *Demography*, May 1972, p. 329.

7. *Ibid.*

8. Lenora Berson, "A Closer Look—Philadelphia," *City*, January/February 1971, p. 42.

9. Robert C. Weaver, "Class, Race and Urban Renewal," *Land Economics*, August 1960.

10. Robert C. Weaver, *The Urban Complex*, Garden City, N.Y.: Doubleday, 1964, p. 227.

11. Irene B. Taeuber, "Migration, Mobility, and the Assimilation of the Negro," *Population Bulletin*, November 1958, pp. 137–138.

12. Harold M. Rose, "The All-Negro Town: Its Evolution and Function," *The Geographic Review*, July 1965, pp. 362–381.

13. Carter G. Woodson, *The Rural Negro,* Association of Negro Life and History, Washington, D.C., 1930, pp. 110–119.

14. *Ibid.*, pp. 121–122.

15. In the description of the all-black towns in the following chapters data has been collected for only fifteen communities, instead of the seventeen which make up the universe. The decision not to interview in Scotlandville, Louisiana and Fairmount Heights, Maryland was based on the nature of those communities and cost considerations. Scotlandville has a population that is twice the size of the largest community in which the field survey was conducted (East Palo Alto, California) and probably represents the greatest extremes in a black community in its size class (20,000). This results from the presence of a sizeable university community, which is associated with the presence of Southern University, that gives it the appearance of similar suburban developments elsewhere. On the other extreme is the housing environment that is more nearly typical of that developed for low income blacks in the ring of other southern SMSAs. Fairmount Heights, Maryland was not included in the field survey, largely because of its limited potential for developing additional residential accomodations for black households, growing out of the absence of vacant land.

16. Harold M. Rose, "All-Black Town: Suburban Prototype or Rural Slum," *People and Politics in Urban Society,* edited by Harlan Hahn, Sage Publications, Beverly Hills, California, 1972, pp. 399–406.

17. Brian J. L. Berry, *The Human Consequences of Urbanization,* London: Macmillan 1973, p. 53.

18. Harold M. Rose, *Social Processes in the City: Race and Urban Residential Choice,* Commission on College Geography Resource Paper No. 6, Association of American Geographers, Washington, D.C., 1969, pp. 3–5.

19. These estimates were arrived at by multiplying the national black growth rate during the decade by the black population present in 1960 and subtracting from the 1970 black population. While this constitutes a crude measure, it does provide a reasonable estimate of the volume of movement in these communities over time.

20. Albert I. Hermalin and Reynolds Farley, "The Potential for Residential Integration in Cities and Suburbs: Implications for the Busing Controversy," *American Sociological Review,* October 1973, p. 605.

21. *Ibid.*, p. 606.

22. George Sternlieb and W. Patrick Beaton, *The Zone of Emergence,* New Brunswick, N.J.: TransAction Books, 1972, p. 1.

23. The absence of such communities might in part be related to the manner in which they were originally defined in terms of minimum population. But more importantly it might have reflected the orientation of a small group of blacks at the time they settled in the North. The implication here is that a larger segment of the movers to the North prior to the "Great Migration" possessed a rural outlook and exhibited greater interest in creating settlements in what was then the rural countryside.

24. Connolly, *op. cit.,* p. 92.

25. Joseph S. Himes, "Some Characteristics of the Migration of Blacks in the United States," *Social Biology* 18 (4) (December 1971), pp. 360–362.

26. Farley, *op. cit.*

27. This observation was made during the field investigation in Lawnside, New Jersey. New residents were located in new housing subdivision in a segment of Lawnside that was somewhat physically isolated from the older community. Thus they viewed themselves, and were viewed by others as a distinct group.

28. Downs, *op. cit.*, p. 31.

29. Robert C. Weaver, "Housing and Associate Problems of Minorities," *Modernizing Urban Land Policy*, Marion Clawson, editor, Baltimore: The Johns Hopkins University Press, 1973, p. 73.

30. *Ibid.*, p. 77.

31. Solomon Sutker, "New Settings for Racial Transition," *Racial Transition in the Inner Suburb*, Edited by Soloman and Sara G. Sutker, New York: Praeger Publishers, 1974, pp. 1–5.

32. Brian J. L. Berry, "Short Term Housing Cycles in a Dualistic Metropolis," *The Social Economy of Cities,* edited by Gary Gappert and Harold M. Rose, Beverly Hills, Calif.: Sage Publications, 1975, p. 170.

33. Hermalin and Farley, *op. cit.*, p. 605.

34. Phoebe H. Cottingham, "Black Income and Metropolitan Residential Dispersion, *Urban Affairs Quarterly* 10, No. (3) (March 1975), p. 287.

35. Donald I. Warren, "Suburban Isolation and Race Tension: The Detroit Case," *Social Problems*, Winter 1970, pp. 330–335.

36. *Ibid.*, p. 334.

37. Long Beach which received approximately 7,500 black residents was only 8.2 per cent black by the end of the decade. But its population of more than 300,000 should technically eliminate it from the suburban category. Cottingham (*op. cit.*) identifies such places as suburban cities and did not identify them as legitimate suburban entities in his analysis of racial differences in suburban selection rates among the residents of Philadelphia.

38. Mahlon R. Straszheim, "Housing Market Discrimination and Black Housing Consumption," *Quarterly Journal of Economics,* February, 1974, p. 21.

39. Reeve D. Vanneman and Thomas A. Pettigrew, "Race and Relative Deprivation in the Urban United States," *Race*, 13 (4) (1972), p. 478 (see Table 9).

40. *Ibid.*, p. 475.

41. Peter C. Labovitz, "Racial Change Comes to the Suburbs," *Planning 1970*, p. 146.

CHAPTER TWO

1. *One Year Later,* Frederick A. Praeger Publishers, New York, 1969.

2. Angus Campbell, *White Attitudes Toward Black People,* Ann Arbor, Mich.: The Institute for Social Research, 1971.

3. *Ibid.*, p. 96.

4. *Ibid.*, p. 124.

5. Thomas F. Pettigrew, "Attitudes on Race and Housing: A Social

Psychological View," *Segregation in Residential Areas,* p. 43. National Academy of Sciences, Washington, D.C., 1973.

6. *Ibid.,* p. 52.

7. Harold M. Rose, "The All-Negro Town: Its Evolution and Function," *The Geographical Review*, July 1965, p. 374.

8. Frederick M. Wirt and others, *On the City's Rim, Politics and Policy in Suburbia,* Lexington, Mass.: D. C. Heath, 1972.

9. Harold M. Rose, "The All-Black Town: Suburban Prototype or Rural Slum?" *People and Politics in Urban Society,* edited by Harlan Hahn, pp. 397–433.

10. Rose, *op. cit.,* pp. 373–375. Fairmount Heights, Maryland, which was included in the initial analysis, was dropped from the field survey because it possessed only limited possibility for additional development resulting from the scarcity of available residential sites. This community was, however, included in the larger group of communities on which a variety of statistical analyses were performed. An additional group of six communities has been added to the original nine which were not previously investigated.

11. *Ibid.,* p. 375.

12. Glen H. Beyer, *Housing and Society,* New York: Macmillan, 1965, p. 488.

13. Bernard J. Frieden, "Blacks in Suburbia: The Myth of Better Opportunities," *Minority Perspectives*, Lowdon Wingo, editor, Washington, D.C.: Resources for the Future, Inc., 1972.

14. Bernard J. Frieden, "Housing and National Urban Goals: Old Policies and New Realities," *The Metropolitan Enigma,* edited by James Q. Wilson, Cambridge, Mass.: Harvard University Press, 1968, p. 161.

15. Frieden, *op. cit.,* p. 42.

16. *Building the American City, Report of the National Commission on Urban Problems,* p. 67.

17. John F. Kain and John M. Quigley, "Measuring the Value of Housing Quality," *Journal of the American Statistical Association*, June 1970, p. 533.

18. The term substandardness as it is used in Table 2–4 includes housing that is defined as dilapidated plus that which the Census Bureau describes as deteriorating. In some instances the term substandard is used only to describe housing which is dilapidated. The use of the term substandard to encompass both housing categories has on occasion brought a negative reaction from local public officials.

19. John B. Lansing and Robert W. Marans, "Evaluation of Neighborhood Quality," *Journal of the American Institute of Planners,* May 1969, pp. 195–199.

20. *Ibid.,* p. 197.

21. Peter Marcuse, "Social Indicators and Housing Policy," *Urban Affairs Quarterly,* December 1971, p. 199.

22. *Ibid.,* p. 210.

23. Leland S. Burns and Frank G. Mittelback, "A House Is a House Is a House," *Industrial Relations,* October 1972, p. 421.

24. Oscar Newman, *Defensible Space,* New York: Macmillan 1972, pp. 106–107.

25. Daniel Stokols, "A Social-Pscychological Model of Human Crowding Phenomena," *Journal of the American Institute of Planners,* March 1972, p. 75.

26. Bruno Bettelheim, "Mental Health in the Slums," *The Social Impact of Urban Design,* p. 31.

27. George W. Carey, "Density, Crowding, Stress, and the Ghetto," *American Behavioral Scientist,* March/April, 1972, p. 505.

28. Stokols, *op. cit.,* p. 78.

29. Leonard Blumberg and Michael Lalli, "Little Ghettos: A Study of Negroes in the Suburbs," *Phylon,* Summer 1966, pp. 117–131.

30. Reynolds Farley, "The Changing Distribution of Negroes Within Metropolitan Areas: The Emergence of Black Suburbs," *American Journal of Sociology,* January 1970, p. 523.

31. *Ibid.,* p. 524.

32. Rose, *op. cit.,* pp. 408–409.

33. *Jobs and Housing,* A Study of Employment Opportunities for Racial Minorities in Suburban Areas of The New York Metropolitan Region National Committee Against Discrimination, New York, 1970.

34. Dieter K. Zachock, "Poverty Amid Affluence in Suburbia," *Economic Aspects of Suburban Growth,* p. 78.

35. George S. Sternlieb and W. Patrick Beaton, *The Zone of Emergence,* New Brunswick, N.J.: TransAction Books, 1972, p. 47.

36. John F. Kain and John M. Quigley, "Market Discrimination, Home Ownership and Savings Behavior," *American Economic Review,* June 1972, p. 272.

37. Peter C. Labovitz, "Racial Change Comes to the Suburbs," *Planning 1970,* p. 148.

38. John B. Lansing, Charles W. Clifton, and James N. Mortan, *New Homes and Poor People,* Ann Arbor, Mich.: Institute for Social Research, 1969, pp. 48–49.

39. J. Tait Davies, "Middle Class Housing in the Central City," *Economic Geography,* July 1965, pp. 239–242.

40. Hugh O. Nourse and Donald Phares, "Socio-economic Transition and Housing Values: A Comparative Analysis of Urban Neighborhoods," *The Social Economy of Cities,* edited by Gary Gappert and Harold M. Rose, Beverly Hills, Calif.: Sage Publishers, 1975, p. 206.

41. James T. Little, *Housing Market Behavior and Household Mobility Patterns in a Transition Neighborhood,* Working Paper HMSI, Institute for Urban and Regional Studies, Washington University, St. Louis, 1973.

42. *Ibid.,* pp. 5–6.

43. Nourse and Phares, *op. cit.,* p. 201.

44. Mahlon R. Straszheim, "Housing Market Discrimination and Black Housing Consumption," *Quarterly Journal of Economics,* February 1974, p. 40.

45. Brian J. L. Berry, "Short-term Housing Cycles in a Dualistic Metropolis," *The Social Economy of the Cities,* edited by Gary Gappert, and Harold M. Rose, Beverly Hills, Calif.: Sage Publications, 1975, p. 169.

46. Little, *op. cit.,* p. 15.

47. George Sternlieb and W. Patrick Beaton, *The Zone of Emergence,* New Brunswick, N.J.: TransAction Books, 1972, p. 49.

48. Little, *op. cit.,* p. 22.

49. The author was granted permission to utilize the raw data from a 1974 survey of black University City movers by Project Director, Professor Charles Leven, Institute for Urban and Regional Studies, Washington University, St. Louis, Missouri.

50. Constance A. Nathason, "Moving Preferences and Plans Among Urban Black Families," *Journal of the American Institute of Planners* 40 (5) (September 1974), p. 357.

51. John F. Kain, "Racial Discrimination in Urban Housing Markets and Goals for Public Policy," Paper prepared for W. E. B. Du Bois Institute Conference, Atlanta, Georgia, October 3–5, 1974, p. 31.

52. George and Eunice Grier, "Obstacles to Desegregation in America's Urban Areas," *Race,* July 1964, p. 17.

CHAPTER THREE

1. Robert C. Weaver, "Class, Race and Urban Renewal," *Land Economics,* August 1960, pp. 356–359.

2. Bernard J. Frieden, "Blacks in Suburbia: The Myth of Better Opportunities," *Minority Perspectives,* p. 39.

3. Weaver, *op. cit.,* p. 357.

4. In two instances the respondents included the description *fair*—a description which did not appear on the questionnaire. If the respondents who reported fair are distinguished from those reporting good, then more than 50 percent of the respondents in Wyandanch and in Lawnside consider their children to be receiving less than a good education.

5. James S. Coleman and Others, *Equality of Educational Opportunity,* Washington, D. C.: U.S. Government Printing Office, 1966.

6. In the Fall of 1973 a Federal District Court Judge ruled that the Kinloch School District was racially segregated and was ordered to desegregate, by having the children of Kinloch assigned to schools in larger contiguous predominantly white school district of Florrisant-Ferguson.

7. James W. Guthrie, George B. Kleindorfer, Henry M. Levin, and Robert T. Stout, *Schools and Inequality,* The MIT Press, Cambridge, Massachusetts, 1971, p. 89.

8. *Ibid.*

9. Robert Coles, *The South Goes North,* Boston: Little, Brown, 1972, p. 449.

10. Jack Slater, "Learning Is an All-Black Thing," *Ebony,* September 1971, pp. 88–92.

11. Thomasyne L. Wilson, "Notes Toward a Process of Afro-American Education," *Harvard Educational Review,* August 1972, p. 378.

12. *Ibid.*

13. Robert L. Crain and Carol S. Weisman, *Discrimination, Personality, and Achievement,* Seminar Press, New York, 1972, pp. 161–171.

14. *Ibid.,* p. 155.

15. David J. Armour, "The Evidence on Busing," *The Public Interest,* Summer 1972, pp. 99–102.

16. *Ibid.,* pp. 115–116.

17. Thomas F. Pettigrew and others, "Busing: A Review of the Evidence," *The Public Interest,* Winter 1973, pp. 88–118.

18. Gordon Foster, "Desegregating Urban Schools: A Review of Techniques," *Harvard Educational Review*, February 1973, p. 30.

19. *Ibid.,* p. 31.

20. Lillian B. Rubin, *Busing and Backlash, White against White in an Urban School District*, University of California Press, Berkeley, 1972, p. 53.

21. The above statement was drawn from personal correspondence with principal.

22. *Ibid.*

23. Leo F. Schnore, "The Social and Economic Characteristics of American Suburbs," *North American Suburbs*, The Glendessary Press, Berkeley, California, 1972. John Kramer, editor, pp. 102–105.

24. *Ibid.,* p. 106.

25. William M. Dobriner, *Class in Suburbia,* Prentice-Hall, Englewood Cliffs, N.J., 1963, p. 96.

26. Robert E. Jennings and Mike M. Milstein, "Citizen's Attitudes in School Tax Voting," *Education and Urban Society,* May 1973, pp. 299–300.

27. *Ibid.,* p. 303.

28. James S. Coleman and Others, *Equality of Educational Opportunity,* Washington, D.C.: U.S Government Printing Office, 1966, p. 325.

29. Herbert Gintis, "Education, Technology, and the Characteristics of Worker Productivity," *The American Economic Review,* May 1971, p. 274.

30. Coleman, *op. cit.,* pp. 316–319.

31. *Ibid.,* p. 317.

32. *Ibid.,* p. 316.

33. Marshal S. Smith, "Equality of Educational Opportunity: The Basic Findings Reconsidered," *On Equality of Educational Opportunity,* edited by Frederick Mosteller and Daniel P. Moynihan, New York: Vintage Books, 1972, pp. 277–279.

34. *Ibid.,* p. 278.

35. *Ibid.,* pp. 307–310.

36. Eric A. Hanushek, *Education and Race,* Lexington, Mass.: Lexington Books, 1972, p. 70.

37. Ray C. Rist, *The Urban School: A Factory for Failure,* Cambridge, Mass.: MIT Press, 1973, pp. 48–63.

38. Robert Coles, *op. cit.,* p. 451.

39. Robert R. Mayer and Others, *The Impact of School Desegregation in a Southern City,* Lexington, Mass.: Lexington Books, 1974, p. 59.

40. *Ibid.*

41. Reynolds Farley and Alma F. Taeuber, "Racial Segregation in the Public Schools," *American Journal of Sociology,* January 1974, pp. 901–903.

42. Eric A. Hanushek, *op. cit.,* pp. 45–46.

43. Mayer, *op. cit.,* pp. 54–55.

44. *Ibid.*

45. Coles, *op. cit.,* p. 474.

46. *Ibid.*

47. Personal correspondence with principal.

48. *Ibid.*

49. Harold X. Connolly, "Black Movement into The Suburbs," *Urban Affairs Quarterly,* September 1973.

50. Robert R. Mayer, *op. cit.*

51. Edna Bonacich and Robert F. Goodman, *Deadlock in School Desegregation, A Case Study of Inglewood, California,* New York: Praeger, 1972, pp. 34–35.

52. *Ibid.*

53. *Ibid.*

54. Robert J. Havighurst, *The Public Schools of Chicago,* The Board of Education of the City of Chicago, Chicago, 1964, p. 145.

55. Harvey Molotch, "Racial Integration in a Transition Community," *American Sociological Review,* December 1969, p. 880.

56. Gloria Powell, *Black Monday's Children,* New York: Appleton-Century-Crofts, pp. 252–254.

57. *Ibid.*

58. Reginald L. Jones, "Racism, Mental Health, and the Schools," *Racism and Mental Health,* edited by Charles V. Willie and others, Pittsburgh: University of Pittsburgh Press, 1973, p. 344.

59. Gloria J. Powell, "Self-Concept in White and Black Children," *Racism and Mental Health,* edited by Charles V. Willie and others, Pittsburgh: University of Pittsburgh Press, 1973, pp. 305–306.

60. Alan B. Wilson, *The Consequences of Segregation: Academic Achievement in a Northern Community,* Berkeley, Calif.: The Glendary Press, 1969, p. 35.

61. *Ibid.*

62. *Ibid.*

63. *Ibid.*

64. Lillian B. Rubin, *Busing and Backlash,* Berkeley, Calif.: University of California Press, 1972, p. 35.

65. *Ibid.,* p. 29.

66. Pomona Unified School District Group Testing Program, *Statistical Report for School Year 1972–1973,* School and Community Services Report.

67. Ted Sell, "Pomona Gropes for Stability in Storm of Ethnic Change," *Los Angeles Times,* January 24, 1971.

68. *Ibid.*

69. Thomas Sowell, "Black Excellence—The Case of Dunbar High School," *The Public Interest,* Spring 1974, p. 18.

70. *Ibid.,* p. 19.

71. Christine Rossell, "Measuring School Desegregation," *Political Strategies in Northern School Desegregation,* David J. Kirby and others Lexington, Mass.: Lexington Books, 1973, p. 171.

72. Iver Peterson, "Newark and New York Look Beyond Busing," *The Sunday New York Times,* August 11, 1974.

73. *The Fleischman Report* (on the Quality, Cost, and Financing Elementary and Secondary Education in New York State), Vol. 1, New York: Viking Press, 1973, p. 242.

74. George S. and W. Patrick Beaton, *The Zone of Emergence,* Transaction Books, New Brunswick, New Jersey, 1972. Sternlieb, *op. cit.,* p. 136.

75. Ronald D. Henderson, "School Climate in White and Black Elementary Schools," *Urban Education,* January 1975, p. 382.

76. *The Third Evaluation Report of the Shaker Schools Plan,* Shaker Heights City School District, Shaker Heights, Ohio, 1974.

77. *Analysis of Student Achievement Test Scores in the Pasadena Unified School District Between 1969 and 1973,* Vol. II, Research Report No. 73/74–12, Pasadena Unified School District, Pasadena California, May 1974.

CHAPTER FOUR

1. Sidney Goldstein and Kurt B. Mayer, "The Impact of Migration in the Socio-Economic Structure of Cities and Suburbs," *Sociology and Social Research,* October 1965.

2. Harold M. Rose, "The All-Negro Town: Its Evolution and Function," *The Geographical Review,* July 1965, pp. 362–381.

3. E. Franklin Frazier, *The Negro In the United States,* revised edition, 1957, pp. 279–290.

4. Jessie Bernard, *Marriage and the Family Among Negroes,* Englewood Cliffs, N.J.: Prentice-Hall, 1966, pp. 28–30.

5. Herbert J. Gans, *The Urban Villagers,* New York: The Free Press, 1962 (paper), pp. 242–243.

6. *Ibid.,* pp. 244–260.

7. St. Clair Drake and Horace R. Cayton, *Black Metropolis,* New York: Harcourt, Brace, 1945, pp. 495–525.

8. Edward C. Banfield, *The Unheavenly City,* Boston: Little, Brown, 1970, pp. 46–48.

9. Joseph D. Mooney, "Urban Poverty and Labor Force Participation," *The American Economic Review,* March 1967, p. 107.

10. *Ibid.*

11. Harold M. Rose, "The Spatial Development of Black Residential Subsystems," *Economic Geography,* January 1972, pp. 50–51.

12. Drake and Cayton, *op. cit.,* pp. 521–525.

13. Bernard, *op. cit.,* pp. 32–34.

14. L. Allan Eyre, "The Shantytowns of Montego Bay, Jamaica," *Geographical Review,* July 1972, p. 397.

15. *Ibid.,* pp. 398–399.

16. Andrew Brimmer, "Economic Situation of Blacks in the United States," *The Review of Black Political Economy,* Summer 1972, p. 44.

17. Daniel M. Fusfeld, "Transfer Payments and the Ghetto Economy," *Transfers In An Urbanized Economy,* editors, K.E. Boulding, Martin Pfaff, and Anita Pfaff, Belmont, Cal.: Wadsworth Publishing, 1973, p. 79.

18. Morton S. Baratz and William G. Grigsby, "Thoughts on Poverty and its Elimination," *Journal of Social Policy* 1 (2) (1972), p. 121.

19. Dieter Zschock, "Poverty Amid in Affluence in Suburbia," *Economic Aspects of Suburban Growth,* Dieter K. Zschock, editor, State University of New York, Stony Brook, N.Y., 1969, p. 87.

20. Daniel P. Moynihan, *The Politics of a Guaranteed Income,* New York: Random House, 1973, p. 40.

21. Daniel P. Moynihan, "The Schism In Black America," *The Public Interest,* Spring 1972, p. 7.

22. Frances F. Piven and Richard A. Cloward, *Regulating the Poor: The Functions of Public Welfare,* New York: Pantheon Books, 1971, pp. 240–246.

23. Bradley R. Schiller, "Empirical Studies of Welfare Dependency: A Survey," *Journal of Human Resources,* Vol. VIII (supplement), 1973, p. 27.

24. Gordon F. DeJong and William L. Donnelly, "Public Welfare and Migration," *Social Science Quarterly,* September 1973, p. 341.

25. *Ibid.,* p. 343.

26. Sav A. Levitan, Martin Rein and David Marwick, *Work and Welfare Go Together,* Baltimore: Johns Hopkins University Press, 1972, pp. 16–17.

27. *Ibid.,* p. 17.

28. Neal Walker and Luther Tweeten, "Determination of Participation Rates in Major Federally Subsidized Public Assistance Programs," *The Rocky Mountain Social Science Journal,* October 1973, p. 32.

29. *Ibid.,* p. 33.

30. Elizabeth Durbin, "Work and Welfare: The Case of Aid to Families With Dependent Children," *The Journal of Human Resources,* Vol. VIII (Supplement), 1973, p. 112.

32. It should be noted the two major entry zones were not included in this detailed analysis of well-being; they include Mt. Vernon, New York and Inglewood, California.

32. Rose, *op. cit.,* "The All-Negro Town," pp. 364–365.

33. Brian J.L. Berry and Frank E. Horton, *Geographic Perspectives on Urban Systems,* Englewood Cliffs, N.J.: Prentice-Hall, 1970, p. 329.

34. David R. Meyer, "Classification of U.S. Metropolitan Areas by Characteristics of their Non-white Populations," *City Classification Handbook: Methods and Applications,* edited by Brian J.L. Berry, New York: John Wiley & Sons, 1972, p. 64.

35. Reynolds Farley, *Growth of the Black Population,* Chicago: Markham Publishing, 1970, p. 112.

36. *Ibid.*

37. Charles V. Willie, "Perspectives From the Black Community," *Population Reference Bureau Selection No. 37,* June 1971, p. 1.

38. Eleanor Holmes Norton, "Population Growth and the Future of Black Folk, *Population Reference Bureau Selection No. 43,* October 1973, p. 2.

39. *Ibid.,* p. 3.

40. William W. Pendelton, "Blacks in Suburbs," *The Urbanization of the Suburbs,* edited by Louis H. Masotti and Jeffrey K. Hadden, Beverly Hills, Calif.: Sage Publications, 1973, p. 177.

41. *Ibid.,* p. 178.

42. *Population and the American Future,* p. 97.

43. Charles F. Westoff and Norman B. Ryder, "Contraceptive Practice Among Urban Blacks in the United States, 1965" *The Milbank Memorial Fund Quarterly,* April 1970, part 2, discussion, p. 236.

44. *Ibid.,* p. 237.

45. *Ibid.,* p. 230.

46. Eleanor Holmes Norton, *op. cit.,* p. 2.

47. Karl E. Bauman and J. Richard Udry, "The Difference in Unwanted Births Between Blacks and Whites," *Demography,* August 1973, p. 320.

48. Westoff and Ryder, *op. cit.,* p. 217.

49. The derived derivation scores are based on the difference between the deflated fertility for each community and the established hypothesized norm.

50. P. Neal Ritchey, "The Fertility of Negroes Without Southern Rural Experience: A Re-examination of the 1960 GAF Study Findings with 1967 SEO Data," *Population Studies,* March 1973, p. 128.

51. Westoff and Ryder, *op. cit.,* p. 223.

52. Bauman and Udry, *op. cit.,* p. 325.

53. *Ibid.,* p. 327.

54. Paul C. Glick, "Marriage and Martial Stability Among Blacks," *The Milbank Memorial Fund Quarterly,* XLVII (2) (April 1970), Part 2, p. 112.

55. Hugh Carter and Paul C. Glick, "Trends and Current Patterns of Marital Status Among Non-white Persons," *Demography* 3 (1) (1966), pp. 280–281.

56. *Ibid.,* p. 280.

57. Ira L. Reiss, *The Family System in America,* New York: Holt, Rinehart, and Winston, 1971, p. 294.

58. Robert O. Blood, Jr., *The Family,* New York: The Free Press, 1972, p. 294.

59. "What to Do When You Are Under Stress," *U.S. News & World Report,* September 24, 1973, p. 51.

60. Wilbur Zelinsky, *The Cultural Geography of the United States,* Englewood Cliffs, N.J.: Prentice-Hall, 1973, pp. 77–78.

61. Ray Simon Bryce-La Porte, "The Slave Plantation: Background to Present Condition of Urban Blacks," Beverly Hills, Calif.: Sage Publications, 1971, p. 258.

62. Robert Coles, *The South Goes North,* Little, Brown and Company, Boston, 1971, pp. 53–209.

63. *Ibid.,* p. 63.

64. Robert Coles, "It's the Same, but It's Different," *Daedalus,* Fall 1965.

65. William H. Grier and Price M. Cobbs, *The Jesus Bag,* New York: McGraw-Hill, 1971, p. 22.

66. Lee Rainwater, *Behind Ghetto Walls,* Chicago: Aldine, 1970, p. 377.

67. Gunnar Myrdal, *An American Dilemma,* Harper, New York 1944, p. 958.

68. Marc Fried, *The World of the Urban Working Class,* Cambridge, Mass.: Harvard University Press, 1973, p. 229.

69. *Ibid.*

70. Samuel D. Proctor, "Survival Techniques and the Black Middle Class," *Black Life and Culture in the United States,* Rhoda L. Goldstein, ed. New York: Thomas Crowell, 1971.

71. Kenneth B. Clark, *Dark Ghetto,* New York: Harper & Row 1965, p. 13.

72. Max Lerner, "The Negro American and His City: Person in Place in Culture," *Daedalus,* Fall 1968, p. 1403.

73. David Sopher, "Place and Location: Notes on the Spatial Patterning of Culture," *Social Science Quarterly,* Sept., 1972, p. 324.

74. G. M. Lewis, "The Distribution of the Negro in the Conterminous United States," *Geography,* November 1969, pp. 410–418.

75. Donald W. Meinig, "The Mormon Culture Region: Strategies and Patterns in the Geography of the American West, 1847–1964." *Annals of the Association of American Geographers,* June 1965, pp. 191–220.

76. Lewis, *op. cit.*

77. Lee Rainwater, *op. cit.,* p. 369.

78. Donald W. Meinig, *op. cit.,* p. 217.

79. Wilbur Zelinsky, *op. cit.,* p. 73.

80. Sidney Kronus, *The Black Middle Class,* Columbus, Ohio: Charles E. Merrill, 1971, pp. 28–29.

CHAPTER FIVE

1. Neil N. Gold, "The Mismatch of Jobs and Low-Income People in Metropolitan Areas and its Implications for the Central-City Poor," *Population, Distribution, and Policy,* U.S. Commission on Population Growth and the American Population, Vol. 5, Sara Mills Mazie, editor, Washington, D.C.: U.S. Government Printing Office, 1972, p. 461.

2. Ben J. Wattenberg and Richard M. Scammon, "Black Progress and Liberal Rhetoric," *Commentary,* April 1973, p. 37.

3. Andrew Brimmer, "Economic Situation of Blacks in the United States," *The Review of Black Political Economy,* Summer 1972, p. 35.

4. *Ibid.,* p. 36.

5. Jack E. Nelson, "The Changing Economic Position of Black Urban Workers," *The Review of Black Political Economy,* Winter 1974, pp. 36–40.

6. The eight communities which had been initially included in this group were those that conformed to our definition of the all-black town, but were not included among the group in which the field investigation was undertaken in the summer of 1972 and that group of communities which conform to what we previously identified as pseudo towns. These include Scotlandville, Louisiana; North Amityville, New York; and Fairmont Heights, Maryland under the first category and Willowbrook, Florence-Graham, and Westmont, California; and Brownsville and Browardale, Florida under the second. Information on the magnitude and character of socioeconomic change is not available for the pseudo communities as they were not formally identified by the Census Bureau in 1960.

7. Harold X. Connolly, "Black Movement into the Suburbs," *Urban Affairs Quarterly,* September 1973, p. 92.

8. *Ibid.,* p. 103.

9. Nelson, *op. cit.,* p. 41.

10. *United States Summary, General Social and Economic Characteristics,* 1970 Census of Population, Table 91.

11. Daniel O. Price, *Changing Characteristics of the Negro Population,* U.S. Department of Commerce, Washington, D.C., 1969, p. 156.

12. Bennett Harrison, *Education, Training, and the Urban Ghetto,* Baltimore: The Johns Hopkins University Press, 1972, pp. 130–140.

13. Philip M. Hauser, "Demographic Factors in the Integration of the Negro," *Daedalus,* Fall 1965, p. 854.

14. Harold X. Connolly, "Black Movement into the Suburbs," *Urban Affairs Quarterly,* September 1973, p. 103.

15. *Ibid.,* p. 105.

16. Jan E. Dizard, "Black Identity, Social Class and Black Power," *Psychiatry,* May 1970, pp. 196–203.

17. *Ibid.,* p. 201.

18. *Ibid.,* p. 202.

19. *Ibid.,* p. 203.

20. William Brink and Louis Harris, *The Negro Revolution in America,* New York: Simon and Schuster, 1964, p. 109.

21. Charles Keil, *Urban Blues,* Chicago: University of Chicago Press, 1966, p. 187.

22. William McCord, John Howard, Bernard Friedberg and Edwin Harwood, *Life Styles in the Black Ghetto,* New York: W. W. Norton, 1969, p. 111.

23. *Ibid.,* pp. 111–112.

24. Charles S. Johnson, *Growing Up in The Black Belt,* Schocken Books, New York, 1967, p. 156.

25. Gold, *op. cit.*

26. Charles M. Christian, "Emerging Patterns of Industrial Activity Within Large Metropolitan Areas and Their Impact on the Central City Work Force," *The Social Economy of Cities,* Gary Gappert and Harold M. Rose, editors, Beverly Hills, Calif.: Sage Publications, 1975, pp. 238–242.

CHAPTER SIX

1. Michael J. Flax, *A Study in Comparative Urban Indicators: Conditions in 18 Large Metropolitan Areas,* The Urban Institute, Washington, D.C., 1972.

2. Ben Chieh-Liu, "Variations in the Quality of Life in the United States By State, 1970," *Review of Social Economy,* Vol. 32, No. 2, October, 1974, p. 132.

3. Lowdon Wingo, "The Quality of Life: Toward A Microeconomic Definitions," *Urban Studies* 10 (3) (February 1973), p. 7.

4. *Ibid.,* p. 14.

5. Joel D. Aberbach and Jack L. Walker, "The Attitudes of Blacks and Whites Toward City Services: Implications for Public Policy," *Financing the Metropolis,* John P. Crecine, editor, Beverly Hills, Calif.: Sage Publications, 1970, p. 522.

6. Kristin Hunter, "Soul City North," *Philadelphia Magazine,* May 1972, p. 100.

7. Wallace Stegner, "East Palo Alto," *Saturday Review,* August 1, 1970, p. 12.

8. Mark Abrahamson, "The Social Dimensions of Urbanism," *Social Forces,* March 1974, p. 378.

9. *Ibid.*

10. Dieter K. Zschock, "Black Youth in Suburbia," *Urban Affairs Quarterly,* September 1971, p. 68.

11. T. Vinson and R. Homel, "Crime and Disadvantage," *British Journal of Criminology,* January 1975, pp. 21–31.

12. *Social Indicators, 1973,* Washington, D.C.: U.S. Government Printing Office, 1973, p. 73.

13. Flax, *op. cit.*

14. *Social Indicators, op. cit.*

15. *Social Indicators, op. cit.*

16. David M. Smith, *The Geography of Social Well-Being,* New York: McGraw-Hill, 1973, pp. 120–133.

17. Edward C. Banfield, *The Unheavenly City Revisited,* Boston: Little, Brown, pp. 4–9.

CHAPTER SEVEN

1. Sarah M. Mazie and Steve Rawlings, "Public Attitude Towards Population Distribution Issues," Population Distribution and Policy, Commission on Population Growth and the American Future, Vol. 5, editor, Sarah Mills Mazie, Washington, D.C.: U.S. Government Printing Office, 1973, p. 605.

2. *Ibid.*

3. *Sunday New York Times,* May 18, 1975, p. 44.

4. Mazie and Rawlings, *op. cit.,* p. 604.

5. Joseph Zikmund II, "Sources of the Suburban Population: 1955–1960 and 1965–1970," *Publius,* Winter 1975, p. 16.

6. Francine F. Rabinovitz, *Minorities in Suburbs: The Los Angeles Experience,* Working Paper No. 31, Joint Center for Urban Studies, Cambridge, Massachusetts, 1975, p. 16.

7. *Ibid.*

8. Anthony Downs, *Opening Up the Suburbs,* New Haven: Yale University Press, 1973.

9. Nathan Glazer, "Opening Up the Suburbs," *The Public Interest,* Fall 1974, p. 106.

10. Lowdon Wingo, "Issues in a National Urban Development Strategy for the United States," *Urban Studies,* February 1972, p. 15.

11. *Ibid.*

12. William Alonzo, "Urban Zero Population Growth," *Daedalus,* Fall 1973, p. 205.

13. *Ibid.,* p. 196.

14. Rabinovitz, *op. cit.,* pp. 54–55.

15. Charles M. Haar and Demetrius S. Iatridis, *Housing the Poor in Suburbia,* Ballinger Publishing Co., 1974, p. 323.

16. Nancy St. John, *School Desegregation, Outcomes for Children,* John Wiley & Sons, New York, 1975.
17. *Ibid.,* p. 76.
18. *Ibid.,* p. 125.

Index

About the Author

Harold M. Rose is Professor of Geography and Urban Affairs at the University of Wisconsin-Milwaukee. He has served as chairman of the Graduate Program in Urban Affairs since 1970. His major research interests have focussed on spatial aspects of black migration and mobility. Professor Rose's work has appeared in all of the major American Journals of Geography. In 1974 he was the recipient of the American Geographical Society's Van Cleef Memorial medal. He will serve as the President of the Association of American Geographers in 1976–77.